Savor
the
Flavor
of
OREGON

**A Cookbook Compiled
by The Junior League of Eugene**

ISBN 0-9607976-1-0

Book design: John Crocker
Typesetter: Koke Printing Company
Edited by: JLE Cookbook Committee & Baden & Company
Printed in the United States of America
Koke Printing Company, Eugene, Oregon

First printing August 1990   30,000
Second printing March 1991   40,000

The Junior League of Eugene
Cookbook Committee Chairpersons:
Suzi Creech   1990-91
Eddie McKinnon   1989-90
Carol McCornack   1988-89
Jeanie Snyder   1987-88

A Tasty Tale . . .

Start with generous portions of the freshest and purest ingredients you can find.

Get a line on a wild salmon or a beautiful rainbow trout from rushing white water rivers. Treat yourself to mountain huckleberries or cultured valley strawberries. Domestic beef and sheep graze amid the peaceful greens of the Willamette Valley. Pick fruits, nuts, and vegetables that have a dash of sun and a sprinkle of rain.

Add the spice of a life not quite tame and the zest of a challenge to make every moment creative.

Mix and season to suit your own style with just a pinch of homegrown humor. And you'll have a taste for life that is rich and rewarding; hearty and healthy. You'll have a true taste of Oregon.

The Junior League of Eugene gratefully acknowledges
Weyerhaeuser Company
for its financial contribution and support of this book.

Volunteers Trained for Community Service

The Junior League of Eugene is an organization of women
committed to promoting volunteerism and to improving
the community through the effective action
and leadership of trained volunteers.
Its purpose is exclusively educational and charitable.

Table of Contents

Savor
the
Flavor
of
APPETIZERS

❦ ❦ ❦

Old English Cheese Ball
Serves: 20

1 pound Old English cheese
2 tablespoons chopped onion
3 tablespoons chopped green
  pepper
4 stuffed green olives, chopped
1 small dill pickle, chopped
1 hard boiled egg, chopped
12 soda crackers, crushed
4 tablespoons mayonnaise
1/4 cup chopped pecans
1 teaspoon parsley
1/4 teaspoon paprika

In a large bowl or mixer, blend together cheese, onion, green pepper, olives, dill pickle, egg, crackers and mayonnaise. Form into a ball, wrap in plastic and chill for 24 hours. Mix chopped pecans, parsley and paprika together on a sheet of waxed paper. Roll cheese ball in this mixture. Serve with assorted crackers or fresh vegetables.

NOTE: If Old English cheese is not available you may substitute softened cheddar cheese.

Dill Dip
Yield: 1⅓ cups

2/3 cup mayonnaise
  (may use light)
2/3 cup sour cream
  (may use plain yogurt)
1 teaspoon dill weed
1 teaspoon beau monde seasoning
1 teaspoon dried parsley
  or
1 tablespoon fresh minced parsley
1 teaspoon minced green onion

Mix all together; chill 2 to 3 hours.

NOTE: This is great served with raw vegetables, chips or as a salad dressing.

Pacific Seafood Spread

Serves: 20

1/2 pound shrimp or crab meat
1/4 cup lemon juice
3 ounces cream cheese, softened
1/3 cup mayonnaise
1/2 teaspoon garlic salt
1 tablespoon chopped green onion

Soak shrimp or crab meat in lemon juice in a small bowl for 15 minutes. Mash together the cream cheese and mayonnaise. Add garlic salt and green onion to the cheese mixture; mix well. Add shrimp or crab; mix well. Chill for at least one hour. Serve with crackers.

Spicy Cheese Ball

Serves: 10

1 (8-ounce) package cream cheese, softened
1 tablespoon steak sauce
1/4 teaspoon garlic powder
4 to 6 shakes Tabasco
Chopped walnuts
Chopped parsley

Mix first four ingredients well with fork. Chill for 2 to 4 hours. Shape into a ball and roll in walnut and parsley mixture. Serve with crackers.

Artichoke Dip

Yield: 2½ cups

1 (14-ounce) jar marinated artichoke hearts, drained and chopped
1 cup grated parmesan cheese
1 cup mayonnaise
1 (4-ounce) can diced green chiles
1 tablespoon chopped pimiento (optional)

Combine all ingredients; bake uncovered at 350 degrees for 30 minutes. Serve hot with corn chips.

Olé Bean Dip

Serves: 8

1 (7-ounce) can bean dip
1/2 pint sour cream
8 ounces cream cheese, softened
10 drops Tabasco sauce
2 tablespoons dry taco seasoning
  mix
1/4 cup chopped green onions
1/2 teaspoon salt
1 cup grated cheddar cheese

Mix first seven ingredients together, pour into pie plate or quiche dish and top with cheddar cheese. Bake at 350 degrees for 15 minutes.

Nacho Bean Dip

Serves: 20

1 (30-ounce) can refried beans
1/2 cup Mexican relish sauce
  or salsa
1 teaspoon garlic salt (not
  powder)
1 small onion, chopped
3 avocados, peeled and mashed
1 tablespoon lemon juice
1/3 cup mayonnaise
1 pint sour cream
1 pound shredded cheddar cheese
1 pound shredded Monterey Jack
  cheese
1 (4-ounce) can chopped black
  olives
2 to 3 medium size tomatoes,
  seeded and coarsely chopped

First, mix together refried beans, Mexican relish sauce or salsa, garlic salt and onion; spread in a layer on a very large platter. Second, mix together avocados and lemon juice; spread over first layer. Third, mix together mayonnaise and sour cream; spread over second layer. Fourth, sprinkle cheddar cheese over third layer. Fifth, sprinkle Monterey Jack cheese over fourth layer. Top with chopped olives and tomatoes. Serve with tortilla chips.

Fresh Tomato Salsa

Serves: 8

3 fresh green jalapeno or
  serrano chiles, stems
  removed and finely chopped
1 to 2 tablespoons chopped
  fresh cilantro
12 green onions, chopped
1/3 cup salad oil
1/3 cup red wine vinegar
3 to 4 large tomatoes, peeled,
  seeded and chopped

Gently combine all ingredients in a medium-size bowl. Serve with Mexican foods (i.e., nachos), over avocado halves, or with chips as a dip.

NOTE: If you make this sauce ahead, cover tightly and chill for no more than 24 hours. This is a very spicy sauce.

Dilled Shrimp Dip

Yield: 1½ cups

1 (8-ounce) package cream cheese,
  softened
1/4 cup milk
1/4 cup mayonnaise
1/2 teaspoon dill weed
1 tablespoon chopped onion
1 teaspoon Accent
  or
1 teaspoon seasoned salt
1/8 teaspoon salt
1/4 to 1/2 teaspoon Tabasco sauce
6½ ounces fresh salad shrimp

Mix all ingredients; refrigerate until well chilled.

NOTE: Great with raw vegetables or chips

Hot Crab Dip
Serves: 20

1 (8-ounce) package cream cheese, softened
8 ounces fresh crab meat
1 clove garlic, minced
1/4 cup mayonnaise
1 teaspoon onion juice
1 teaspoon prepared mustard
1 teaspoon powdered sugar
2 tablespoons white wine
Salt to taste

Mix all ingredients and heat over medium temperature on top of stove, or place in moderate oven until heated through. If this mixture gets too hot it may separate. Serve with crackers.

Salmon Spread
Serves: 8

6 to 8-ounces cooked salmon
1 (8-ounce) package cream cheese
2 tablespoons minced onion
1 tablespoon fresh dill
  or
1 tablespoon fresh tarragon
1/2 cup sour cream
Salt to taste
Freshly ground pepper to taste
2 tablespoons lemon juice
Fresh dill (garnish)
Fresh tarragon (garnish)

Put all ingredients in food processor and process until well blended; approximately 1 minute. Mound into attractive glass bowl and refrigerate until ready to use. Garnish with fresh herbs. Serve with crackers and a small knife for spreading.

Mock Boursin Cheese Spread

Yield: 1½ cups

2 teaspoons toasted sesame seeds
2 tablespoons chopped fresh
  parsley
1 teaspoon fine herbs
1 large clove garlic, crushed
1 (8-ounce) package cream cheese,
  softened
1 cup ricotta cheese
1 teaspoon red wine vinegar

24 hours before serving, mix all ingredients well. (Use a steel blade of food processor, electric mixer, or stir vigorously by hand). Chill 24 hours. Serve with crackers or raw vegetables.

NOTE: This can be shaped into a ball and rolled in chopped parsley or nuts, if desired.

Avocado Crab Dip

Serves: 8

1 large avocado, peeled, seeded
  and cut in cubes
1 tablespoon lemon juice
1 tablespoon grated onion
1 teaspoon Worcestershire sauce
1 (8-ounce) package cream cheese
1/4 cup sour cream
1/4 teaspoon salt
7 to 8-ounces crab meat

Place first seven ingredients into food processor and blend well. Add crab, mix by hand. Serve with chips or crackers.

Mustard Vegetable Dip

Yield: 1 cup

1/2 cup mayonnaise
1/4 cup mustard, (stone ground
  or Dijon)
3 tablespoons sugar
1/2 teaspoon garlic salt
1 tablespoon oil

Mix all ingredients and chill. Serve as a dip with your favorite vegetables.

Chutney

Yield: 5 pints

1 quart vinegar
1 cup finely chopped onion
1 cup chopped ginger root
5 cloves garlic, chopped
3 small jalapeno peppers,
  seeded
7 cups sugar
2 tablespoons salt or to taste
1 cup chopped raisins
1 cup chopped currants
1 cup chopped nuts
8 cups coarsely chopped apples
  (Golden Delicious)

Combine vinegar, onions, ginger, garlic, peppers, sugar and salt. Boil, uncovered, for 1 hour, until ingredients cook down and reach the consistency of syrup.

Add raisins, currants, nuts and apples. Cover and cook for 1 to 2 hours, until thick. Pour into jam jars and seal.

NOTE: This can be served over cream cheese on crackers. It is also good with turkey, ham and pork.

Mexican Hot Bean Dip

Serves: 40 to 50

1 (8-ounce) package cream cheese
1 pint sour cream
1 (30-ounce) can refried beans
1 envelope Lipton onion soup mix
20 drops Tabasco sauce
1/2 cup chunky salsa
Shredded Monterey Jack cheese
Shredded cheddar cheese

Mix first six ingredients and place in a 9 x 13-inch casserole dish. Top with Monterey Jack and cheddar cheese to about ½-inch thickness. Bake at 350 degrees for 15 to 20 minutes, until bubbly. Serve hot with tortilla chips.

Tangy Shrimp Spread
Serves: 6

7 ounces salad shrimp
1/2 small onion, minced
3 tablespoons lemon juice
1 (8-ounce) package cream cheese,
  softened

Blend all ingredients. Cover and refrigerate for a few hours or overnight. Let stand at room temperature before serving with crackers.

NOTE: It is better refrigerated overnight and be sure it is tangy with lemon juice.

Bermuda Onion Dip
Serves: 6

2 cups sliced red onions
1/2 cup vegetable oil
2 tablespoons lemon juice
1 tablespoon salt, or to taste
1/2 tablespoon sugar
1/4 cup bleu cheese

Pour boiling water over onions and let stand for 2 to 3 minutes. Drain. Add remaining ingredients and refrigerate for 2 days. Drain before serving.

NOTE: Serve with dipping style chips.

Quick Chile Fondue Dip
Serves: 10

1 cup shredded Monterey Jack
  cheese
1 cup shredded mozzarella cheese
1 (8-ounce) package cream cheese,
  cubed
1/2 cup mayonnaise
1 (4-ounce) can chopped chiles
1/2 teaspoon onion powder

Combine all ingredients in a 2-quart saucepan. Cook over medium heat until cheese has melted. Transfer to a fondue pot to keep warm.

NOTE: Dip sliced vegetables, french bread cubes, or corn chips in the mixture.

Shrimp-Cheese Spread
Serves: 12

3 tablespoons water
1 envelope gelatin
1 (10¾-ounce) can cream of
   mushroom soup
1 (8-ounce) package cream cheese,
   softened
1 cup chopped celery
1 cup chopped green onion
1 cup mayonnaise
1 cup baby shrimp or crab

Soften gelatin in water. In saucepan, combine soup and gelatin and heat through. Add cream cheese and blend. Add rest of ingredients. Pour into a 2-quart mold; chill until set. Serve with bread or crackers.

Layered Crab Spread
Serves: 12

Layer #1
1 (12-ounce) package cream
   cheese, softened
2 tablespoons Worcestershire
   sauce
1 tablespoon lemon juice
2 tablespoons mayonnaise
1 small onion, grated fine
Garlic salt to taste

Layer #2
1 (6-ounce) jar chili sauce

Layer #3
1 cup crab meat

Layer #4
½ cup shredded mozzarella,
   Monterey Jack or cheddar
   cheese

Chopped black olives

Blend ingredients for first layer and spread in a 9-inch pie plate with a lip. Add next 3 layers. Top with black olives, if desired. Serve with cocktail bread or crackers.

Savory Stuffed Mushrooms
Serves: 6 to 8

1/4 pound pork sausage
12 to 16 fresh mushrooms
(medium to large)
1/4 cup butter
3 tablespoons minced green
pepper
3 tablespoons minced onion
1½ cups fresh bread cubes
1/4 teaspoon salt
1/8 teaspoon pepper
1/8 teaspoon cayenne pepper

Fry sausage, drain and crumble; set aside. Wash mushrooms, remove stems and chop fine; set aside. Heat 2 tablespoons butter in frying pan and sauté mushroom caps on bottomside only for 2 to 3 minutes. Remove from pan and arrange rounded side down in shallow baking pan. Heat remaining butter in same skillet. Sauté chopped stems, green pepper and onions until tender. Remove from heat. Mix all ingredients, except mushrooms caps, in a bowl. Mound filling high in mushroom caps and press in firmly. Bake at 350 degrees for 15 minutes.

NOTE: This is a nice appetizer, it can also be used as a side dish to accompany a lightly flavored main course.

Crab-Avocado Boats
Serves: 6

3 tablespoons butter, divided
2 tablespoons flour
1/2 teaspoon salt
2/3 cup milk
1 tablespoon lemon juice
1/2 pound fresh crab meat
(can substitute shrimp meat)
3 large avocados, halved and
seeded
1/4 cup fine dry bread crumbs
1/4 teaspoon dried marjoram,
crushed

In saucepan, melt 2 tablespoons butter and blend in flour and salt. Add milk all at once. Cook and stir until thick and bubbly. Add lemon juice; fold in crab. Arrange unpeeled avocado halves in shallow baking dish. Spoon crab mixture atop. Melt remaining butter; toss with bread crumbs and marjoram; sprinkle over filled avocados. Bake at 350 degrees for 10 minutes.

Shrimp stuffed Mushrooms
Crab in Avocado Boats

Artichoke Dip with Bread Sticks
Yield: 4 cups

1 (14-ounce) can artichoke hearts
  or bottoms, drained
1 cup freshly grated parmesan
  cheese
1 (8-ounce) package cream cheese,
  softened
1/2 cup mayonnaise
1/2 teaspoon dried dill
1 clove garlic, minced
Bread sticks

Coarsely chop artichokes; set aside. In food processor or blender, mix parmesan cheese, cream cheese, mayonnaise, dill and garlic; blend until smooth. Add chopped artichokes and mix. Spread mixture into a 10-inch pie plate. Smooth the surface. Bake at 400 degrees for 15 minutes until hot and bubbly. Serve immediately with bread sticks.

Hot and Spicy Artichoke Dip
Serves: 25

1½ cups grated parmesan cheese
1 cup mayonnaise
1 can water packed artichoke
  hearts, drained and chopped
2 cloves garlic, minced
4 green onions, thinly sliced
1 (7-ounce) can diced green chiles
1 tablespoon Tabasco, or to taste

Combine all ingredients. Place in a shallow, greased 7 x 12-inch baking dish. Bake at 350 degrees for about 30 minutes or until lightly browned. Serve with sturdy crackers or french bread.

Seafood Dip
Serves: 10

1 pound seafood (shrimp or crab)
1/2 pound sharp cheddar cheese,
  grated
1 bunch green onions, chopped
1 small jar diced pimiento
4 tablespoons mayonnaise

Mix seafood with cheese, onions and pimiento. Mix in mayonnaise and blend.

NOTE: Serve on a lettuce leaf with wheat crackers.

Asparagus Ham Roll-Ups
Serves: 20

20 stalks fresh asparagus
1 (8-ounce) package cream cheese, softened
1 teaspoon dill weed
1 teaspoon fresh or dried chives
1/4 to 1/2 teaspoon garlic powder
1/2 teaspoon lemon pepper
10 full slices of Black Forest Ham or Proscuitto

Cook asparagus stalks about 3 minutes in boiling water or steam, just until tender-crisp. Drain and plunge into ice water. Drain again and dry carefully with paper towels; set aside. Combine cream cheese, dill weed, chives, garlic and lemon pepper. Cut ham slices in half, crosswise. Spread with cream cheese mixture. Roll around each asparagus spear. Chill well for several hours.

Herb Chicken Nuggets
Serves: 4 to 6

4 chicken breast halves, skinned and boned
3/4 cup margarine
2 cups dry bread crumbs
1 cup grated parmesan cheese
1 teaspoon salt
2 teaspoons dried thyme
2 teaspoons dried basil

Cut chicken into 1-inch pieces. Melt margarine; remove from heat. Combine remaining ingredients; mix well. Dip chicken pieces first in margarine, then in bread crumb mixture; coat well. Spread on cookie sheet that has been covered with foil and greased. (A non-stick spray may be used). Bake at 400 degrees for 15 to 20 minutes. Serve on a platter or pack for a picnic!

NOTE: Children love these and so do adults! They do not taste like the ones from fast-food restaurants.

Tiropetes
Yield: 2½ dozen

1 (3-ounce) package cream cheese
1/3 pound feta cheese
3 ounces gruyere cheese, grated
1 egg
2 tablespoon chopped parsley
5 sheets phyllo dough (14" x 20")
1/2 cup butter, melted

Beat cream cheese and feta cheese until light. Mix in gruyere. Add egg; beat until blended. Add parsley. Lay out 1 sheet of phyllo, brush lightly with butter; cut into 3-inch wide strips about 14-inches long. Place one heaping teaspoon cheese filling in one corner. Fold over making a triangle, continue folding (as if folding a flag) to make a triangle. Place on an ungreased baking sheet. Bake at 375 degrees, about 10 minutes, until puffed and golden. These may be cooled and frozen. To re-heat, place frozen pastries on baking sheet in a 375 degree oven for 10 minutes.

Oriental Chicken Wings
Serves: 6

12 chicken wings
1/4 cup soy sauce
1/4 cup pineapple juice
2 tablespoons sugar
1/2 teaspoon ground ginger
1 tablespoon lemon juice
5 drops Tabasco sauce
1 clove garlic, crushed

Cut tips off chicken wings and discard. Break or cut wings in half at the joint. Place wings on a cookie sheet lined with foil. Mix remaining ingredients. Bake at 350 degrees for 1½ hours, basting with sauce every 15 minutes.

NOTE: This dish is good hot or cold. It can be served as an appetizer or as a main dish.

Grilled Shrimp and Sausage Appetizers
Serves: 12

Dipping Sauce:
1/4 cup orange marmalade
1 teaspoon brown mustard
1/2 teaspoon horseradish

1 pound Italian style link sausage
1 pound fresh medium-size shrimp
1 cup beer
1 tablespoon Rex crab boil (spice mix available at seafood markets)

For dipping sauce: Mix marmalade, mustard and horseradish; chill 1 to 2 hours.

Cut sausage into 1/2-inch thick slices (peel first if necessary). Brown sausage for 5 to 10 minutes until nicely colored; drain and set aside. Clean shrimp and marinate in mixture of beer and crab boil spice mix for 1 to 2 hours. Alternately skewer sausage and shrimp on small bamboo skewers. Barbecue for 5 to 10 minutes, turning frequently until shrimp and sausage are fully cooked.

Stuffed Mushrooms
Serves: 4

12 large mushrooms
1/4 cup butter or margarine
1 teaspoon basil
1/4 teaspoon salt
1 clove garlic, minced
1/2 cup whipping cream
1/4 cup fresh grated parmesan cheese
1/2 cup Italian seasoned bread crumbs
1/2 teaspoon basil
1 tablespoon butter, melted

Wash mushrooms, remove and chop stems; set aside. Sauté mushroom caps in butter for 30 seconds; remove. Add chopped stems to skillet and sauté for 2 minutes. Add basil, salt, garlic and whipping cream. Heat to boiling, cook and stir until reduced by 1/2. Add parmesan. Spoon mixture into mushroom caps. In a small bowl, mix bread crumbs, basil and melted butter. Sprinkle the crumb mixture on top of the stuffed mushrooms. Broil until browned.

23

Cheesey Bacon Broils

Serves: 24

6 English muffins
8 thin slices bacon, finely
   chopped, uncooked
2¼ cups shredded sharp
   cheddar cheese
Catsup to bind together bacon
   and cheese (¼ to ½ cup)

Spread mixture on split English muffins and broil on low in the oven. Cook until bacon is cooked. Watch so it doesn't burn. Cut in quarters and serve.

NOTE: This can double as a simple luncheon dish. Also, they are a favorite with the kids!

Sticky Wings

Serves: 4

1 cup soy sauce
1/2 cup sugar
1/2 teaspoon ginger
1 teaspoon garlic powder
2 pounds chicken wings
1/4 cup margarine, melted

Mix soy sauce, sugar, ginger and garlic. Place wings in glass dish. Pour marinade over wings and refrigerate for 4 hours or overnight. Remove wings from marinade and place in a large glass baking dish. Brush with margarine. Bake at 325 degrees for 2 hours, turning once. Serve warm or refrigerate and serve later cold.

Crab Mousse

Serves: 12

1 (8-ounce) package cream cheese
1½ cups mayonnaise
1 (10¾-ounce) can cream of
   celery soup
6 ounces crab meat
1½ cups finely chopped celery
1 medium onion, chopped fine
1 envelope gelatin
1/4 cup hot water

Put cream cheese in saucepan and melt on low temperature. Add mayonnaise and soup; stir well. Add crab, celery and onion; stir. Dissolve gelatin in hot water and mix with other ingredients. Put into a mold or fancy bowl and refrigerate 2 to 3 hours before serving.

Filbert Stuffed Mushrooms

Serves: 8

16 large mushrooms, stems removed and saved
2 tablespoons margarine
1/2 cup dry bread crumbs
1/2 cup roasted, finely chopped
filberts
1 clove garlic, finely minced
1 tablespoon finely chopped green
onion
1/2 teaspoon basil
2 tablespoons sour cream
1/4 cup grated parmesan cheese
1/8 teaspoon paprika
8 filberts, halved
1/2 cup white wine

Clean and dry mushrooms. Scoop out with melon ball scoop. Finely chop stems in food processor or by hand. Sauté stems in margarine for 2 to 3 minutes. Remove from heat and combine with crumbs, filberts, garlic, onion, basil and sour cream. Mix well. Mound filling into cavity of each mushroom. Mix cheese and paprika. Spread small amount on each mushroom. Place a half filbert in center of each mushroom. Place mushrooms in shallow baking dish and pour wine around base of mushrooms. Bake at 350 degrees for 10 to 15 minutes and serve.

Pickled Bean Roll Up

Serves: 20

8 ounces cream cheese, softened
4 green onions, chopped
3/4 teaspoon seasoned
black pepper
Thinly sliced salami
Pickled beans

Mix the cream cheese, onions and pepper. Cover and refrigerate several hours or a day ahead to allow flavors to blend. Before preparing, remove from refrigerator and allow cheese to sit at room temperature to soften. To assemble: spread each slice of salami with a thin layer of cheese mixture. Place a pickled bean on each slice and roll up. Cut in bite-size pieces.

NOTE: These are good served with bread sticks.

Shrimp Puffs
Serves: 4 to 6

Puffs:
1/4 cup butter
1/2 cup water
1/2 cup sifted flour
2 eggs
Salt to taste

Filling:
12 ounces tiny shrimp
1 cup chopped celery
2 tablespoons chopped green
onions
3 hard boiled eggs, chopped
2/3 cup mayonnaise
2 tablespoons lemon juice
Salt to taste

To make puffs: Combine butter and water in saucepan; heat to boiling. Stir in flour and salt. With wooden spoon, stir until batter forms a thick, smooth ball that follows the spoon around the pan. Remove from heat; cool slightly. Beat in eggs, one at a time, until mixture is thick and shiny-smooth. Drop by teaspoonfuls 1-inch apart on greased cookie sheets. Bake at 400 degrees for 20 minutes or until puffed and golden. Cool.

To make filling: In a medium bowl, combine shrimp, celery, green onions and eggs; mix well. In a separate bowl, blend mayonnaise, salt and lemon juice. Fold into shrimp mixture and chill. To asssemble puffs: Pull or cut the top off the puffs, stuff with filling and serve.

Greek Appetizer
Serves: 8

2 tablespoons chopped fresh basil
3 tablespoons chopped sun dried
tomatoes
2 tablespoons crumbled feta
cheese
1 (8-ounce) package cream cheese,
softened
1 loaf french bread

Wash basil, pat dry and chop coarsely. Blot oil from sun-dried tomatoes and chop coarsely. Combine first four ingredients. Slice bread in thin slices. If using a large loaf, cut each slice in half. Spread with cheese mixture. Each slice may be decorated with a small basil leaf or a strip of tomato.

Smoked Salmon Mousse

Serves: 12

12 ounces smoked salmon
1/2 cup butter, melted
1 cup sour cream
1 tablespoon lemon juice
1 tablespoon finely chopped onion
1 teaspoon dill weed

In blender or food processor, purée salmon. Drizzle in butter until well combined. Continue to blend, adding sour cream gradually, then lemon juice, onion and dill. It will be thin. Refrigerate several hours, or overnight, until set.

Tortilla Wedgies

Serves: 16

5 to 6 teaspoons salsa
5 to 6 flour burrito size tortillas
   Butter
1 pound Monterey Jack cheese,
   grated
1 pound cheddar cheese, grated
1 (8-ounce) can diced green chiles
1 (15-ounce) can black olives,
   chopped
1 bunch green onions, diced

Spread butter around edge of tortilla to prevent burning. Spread 1 teaspoon salsa over tortilla. Layer with ¼ of the Monterey Jack cheese, cheddar cheese, chiles, olives and green onions. Repeat layers, starting with salsa, using ¼ of the filling until 4 or 5 tortillas high, ending with a tortilla on top. Wrap in foil. Bake at 350 degrees on a cookie sheet for 20 minutes or until cheese is melted in center. (Open foil for a few minutes at the end of cooking so top is browned.) Cool before cutting into wedges.

27

Tortilla Roll-Ups
Yield: 120 pieces

3 (8-ounce) packages cream
   cheese, softened
1 cup sour cream
1 (4-ounce) can chopped chiles
4 green onions, thinly sliced
1 dozen extra large flour tortillas
Salsa

Mix cream cheese and sour cream with electric mixer. Add chiles and sliced green onions. Trim tortillas to make a square. Spread sour cream mixture on tortilla. Roll up and wrap in plastic wrap. Refrigerate at least 1 to 2 days. Cut into 1-inch lengths. Serve with salsa.

Caviar Pie
Serves: 12 to 16

6 hard boiled eggs, chopped
3 tablespoons mayonnaise
1½ cups minced green onion
1 (8-ounce) package cream cheese,
   softened
2/3 cup sour cream
4 ounces caviar
Lemon wedges
Parsley sprigs

Prepare at least 4 hours before serving or the day before. Grease an 8-inch spring form pan. Combine chopped eggs with mayonnaise and spread evenly over bottom of pan. Sprinkle green onion over egg mixture. Blend cream cheese and sour cream until smooth. Using a wet spatula, spread cream cheese mixture over onion layer. Cover pan and chill for 3 hours or overnight. Before serving, top with caviar and spread to pan edges. To serve: run knife around sides of pan, loosen spring form and lift off. Garnish with lemon wedges and parsley sprigs. Serve with plain unsalted crackers or wafer crackers.

Addiction
Serves: 12 to 16

1 (16-ounce) box oyster crackers
1 cup corn oil
1¼ teaspoon dill weed
1 teaspoon lemon-pepper
1 teaspoon garlic powder

Place crackers in large bowl. Add oil and spices; mix well. Leave out on counter and stir often over a 3 hour period. Place in a tin or air tight container for storage. Note: This is a quick and easy finger appetizer.

Shrimp Stuffed Mushrooms
Serves: 6

1/4 cup minced green onions
1/4 cup minced celery
1/4 cup butter
Salt to taste
1/8 teaspoon cayenne pepper
1/2 pound raw shrimp, de-veined and chopped
1 egg
1/4 cup mayonnaise
5 slices bread, crusts removed
1/4 pound fresh mushrooms, washed and stems removed and discarded
Shredded cheddar cheese

Sauté onion and celery in butter until soft. Add salt, cayenne pepper and chopped shrimp; sauté until pink. Remove from heat. In a bowl, whip the egg and mayonnaise together. Cut bread into small pieces. Combine all the ingredients and fill mushrooms. Top with shredded cheddar cheese. Bake at 400 degrees for 10 minutes.

Savor
the
Flavor
of
BEVERAGES

Raspberry Liquor
Yield: 2 quarts

2 cups sugar
1 quart vodka
2 pints fresh raspberries

Mix the sugar and vodka. Pour into a 3-quart glass jar with a lid. Stir in the raspberries and cover. Store in a cool dark place. Once a week for 8 weeks, open the container and stir. Strain through a cheese cloth after 8 weeks and bottle.

NOTE: This is wonderful to sip or serve over ice cream or fruit.

Eggnog Boozie
Yield: ½ gallon

6 eggs, separated
1/2 cup sugar
1 cup bourbon
1/2 cup brandy
1 cup whipping cream
2 cups milk
1 quart vanilla ice cream
Nutmeg

Beat egg yolks until lemon yellow and creamy. Add sugar; mix well. Slowly add bourbon and brandy. (If added too quickly, it will cook the egg yolks.) Add whipping cream and milk. Using a knife, break ice cream in small pieces, and mix with egg, liquor and milk mixture. In another bowl, beat egg whites until very stiff. Fold into milk mixture very slowly. Refrigerate for 2 to 3 hours before serving. Sprinkle each serving with a bit of nutmeg.

NOTE: If you have a party of 10 or more people, you need to double the recipe to make 1 gallon of eggnog. Great for any holiday party.

Kahlua

Yield: 2 fifths

1 quart water
3 cups granulated sugar
3 tablespoons instant coffee
  granules
2 tablespoons imitation vanilla
1 fifth vodka

In a large pan, combine water, sugar and instant coffee. Boil very gently for one hour. Let cool. Add imitation vanilla and vodka; mix well. Pour into bottles and store in cupboard.

NOTE: This is delicious in coffee or over ice cream.

Limeade Punch

Yield: 3 quarts

1 (12-ounce) can orange juice
  concentrate
2 cans water
1 (12-ounce) can limeade concentrate
1 (½ to 1-quart) bottle 7-up, soda,
  ginger ale or champagne
Ice cubes
Lime slices

In a large pitcher, mix orange juice concentrate and 2 cans water. Mix in limeade concentrate and ½ the amount of water called for on the can. Mix in 7-up or other sparkling beverage. Chill or serve with ice. Garnish with lime slices.

Gin Punch

Serves: 24

1 cup grenadine syrup
1 (46 to 48-ounce) can unsweetened grapefruit juice
1 (46 to 48-ounce) can unsweetened orange juice
2 cups gin
1 quart 7-up (diet or regular)
Ice cubes

Mix grenadine, grapefruit juice, orange juice and gin. Chill. Before serving, add 7-up and ice cubes.

Berry Patch Lemonade

Serves: 10 to 12

1 pound berries, (i.e., strawberries, raspberries, blackberries), fresh or frozen, unsweetened
1 (12-ounce) can lemonade concentrate
4 (12-ounce) cans cold water
Ice cubes
Mint leaves or whole berries

Purée fruit in a blender, pour through a fine strainer to remove the seeds. Mix lemonade with 4 cans cold water in a 2-quart pitcher. Add puréed berries, blend and chill completely. Pour over ice in tall glasses and garnish with mint sprigs or whole berries.

Pink Party Punch

Serves: 32

4 (6-ounce) cans pink lemonade, partially thawed
1½ quarts club soda, chilled
2 (1 pint, 8-ounce) bottles Rosé wine, chilled
1 cup cognac
1 lemon, thinly sliced
Ice cubes

Combine first four ingredients in a large punch bowl. Add ice. Float lemon slices on top.

Tangy Fruit Punch

Yield: 3 quarts

1 (12-ounce) can frozen apple juice concentrate
1 (12-ounce) can frozen lemonade concentrate
1 (12-ounce) can frozen orange juice concentrate
2 (1-quart) bottles ginger ale
Ice cubes

Mix together apple, lemonade and orange juice concentrates. Add ginger ale, pour over ice cubes.

NOTE: You may want to double this recipe for a large crowd.

Fruit Cooler Punch
Serves: 32

1 (6-ounce) can frozen lemonade
  concentrate
1 (8-ounce) can crushed pineapple
1 (10-ounce) package frozen
  strawberries, thawed
3 (1-quart) bottles ginger ale,
  chilled
Crushed ice

In a blender, combine lemonade, pineapple and straw-berries; blend on high speed until completely smooth. Add ginger ale; mix. Pour over crushed ice in a punch bowl. Serve.

Acapulco Apple Punch
Yield: 2 quarts

2 lemons
2 oranges
1/4 cup granulated sugar
1/4 teaspoon cinnamon
1 (6-ounce) can apple juice
  concentrate, thawed
1 (25.4-ounce) bottle sparkling
  cider, chilled
2 cups soda water, chilled

Slice 1 lemon and 1 orange into thin slices. Using a sharp knife, peel the other orange in a spiral, resulting in ½-inch wide strip of peel. Squeeze juice from orange and reserve. Squeeze juice from the other lemon and mix with the reserved orange juice. Put the orange and lemon slices in a 2 to 2½-quart pitcher. Add sugar and cinnamon to pitcher and crush the ingredients together using a long handled spoon or potato masher. Stir the reserved orange-lemon juice mixture and apple juice concentrate into the crushed fruit in pitcher. Chill no more than 2 hours. When ready to serve, stir in spar-kling cider and soda water. Taste, add more soda if necessary. Pour into 8 wine glasses and garnish each with a piece of orange peel.

Rum Punchkin
Yield: 2 quarts

1/2 cup lemon juice
3/4 cup sugar
1 cup cranberry juice
1 cup orange juice
1 cup strong tea
1 fifth rum
12 whole cloves
   Ice cubes or dry ice
1 pumpkin, hollowed out

Mix all ingredients together. Serve the punch in a pumpkin with dry ice.

NOTE: This makes a great punch for a Halloween party.

Fruity Rum Punch
Yield: 3 quarts

2 quarts pineapple juice
2 cups light rum
2 cups orange juice
1/2 cup limeade (can be made
   from frozen concentrate)
1/3 cup lemon juice
Ice cubes

In a glass or plastic container, blend all ingredients; chill. Serve over ice cubes in glasses or make an ice ring and serve in a punch bowl.

NOTE: Garnish with fresh pineapple wedges, orange or lime slices, or maraschino cherries.

Sangria
Serves: 4 to 6

1 (1-quart) bottle dry red wine
4 to 6 tablespoons sugar
1 stick cinnamon
Juice of 1 lemon
1/2 cup brandy
1 (6-ounce) bottle soda water
Ice cubes

Several hours before serving, pour wine into a pitcher. Add sugar, cinnamon and lemon juice. Stir occasionally. Before serving, add brandy, soda and ice cubes.

NOTE: This is a great cold beverage to serve before a Spanish or Mexican dinner party.

Peachy Champagne

Serves: 10 to 12

4 medium size ripe peaches
1/4 cup sugar
2 tablespoons lemon juice
3/4 cup water
1 bottle inexpensive dry
   champagne
Mint leaves (optional)

Peel, halve, pit and coarsely chop peaches. Place fruit in a blender or food processor with sugar, lemon juice and water. Blend until smoothly puréed. Cover and refrigerate for up to 3 hours. To make drinks, pour about ¼ cup peach purée into glass; slowly add champagne to top of glass. Stir to blend and garnish with mint leaves.

Party Punch

Serves: 20

1 orange, thinly sliced and halved
1½-quarts cranberry juice
1 (6-ounce) can frozen orange
   juice concentrate
1/4 cup fresh lemon juice
1/2 cup grenadine syrup
2 to 3 cups vodka (optional)
1 quart ginger ale, chilled
2 cups club soda, chilled

Fill a 1-quart ring mold about ½ full with water; freeze. Overlap halved orange slices on top of ice. Add just enough water to freeze oranges into mold. Freeze. Combine juices, grenadine syrup and vodka in a punch bowl; chill until ready to serve. Unmold ice ring and float, decorative side up, in the bowl. Gently stir in ginger ale and club soda.

Chocolate Nog

Serves: 12

1 quart eggnog
1 (5½-ounce) can chocolate
   syrup
1/4 cup Creme de Cacao
1 cup whipping cream
Chocolate curls (optional)

Combine eggnog, chocolate syrup and Creme de Cacao; cover and chill. Before serving, beat whipping cream to soft peaks. Reserve ½ cup of the whipped cream for garnish. Fold the remaining whipped cream into the eggnog mixture. Pour into serving glasses. Dollop with reserved whipped cream. Garnish with chocolate curls, if desired.

Homemade Irish Cream Liqueur
Yield: 5 cups

1¾ cups Irish whiskey, brandy, rum, bourbon, or Scotch whiskey
1 (14-ounce) can Eagle brand sweetened condensed milk
1 cup whipping cream
4 eggs
2 tablespoons chocolate flavored syrup
2 teaspoons instant coffee granules
1 teaspoon vanilla extract
1/2 teaspoon almond extract

In blender container, combine all ingredients; blend until smooth. Store in a tightly covered container in refrigerator up to one month. Stir before serving, over ice if desired.

Open House Punch
Yield: 5 quarts

2 quarts iced tea
2 (6-ounce) cans frozen lemonade concentrate
2 (6-ounce) cans frozen limeade concentrate
2 cups cranberry juice
2 (28-ounce) bottles ginger ale
2 fresh limes
2 fresh lemons

Pour iced tea into a punch bowl. Stir in lemonade, limeade, and cranberry juice. Just before serving, add ginger ale and ice. Garnish with lime and lemon slices.

Orange Breakfast Drink
Serves: 4

1 (12-ounce) can frozen orange juice
3 cans water
2 bananas
2 cups whole frozen strawberries

Place ingredients in a blender and mix. Fruit should remain slightly chunky. Pour into glasses.

NOTE: Great with muffins or bagels for a quick breakfast.

Frosted Bourbon

Serves: 16

1 (6-ounce) can orange juice
  concentrate
1 (6-ounce) can lemonade
  concentrate
Water
1 cup very strong tea
1 cup bourbon
1 to 2 quarts 7-up or ginger ale

1 or 2 days ahead of serving: Mix orange and lemonade concentrates with water (as directed on cans). Add tea and bourbon. Pour into a large bowl or other freezer container and freeze. To serve, remove container from freezer. Scrape frozen mixture into cocktail glasses (½ full). Fill to the top with 7-up or ginger ale.

NOTE: You may garnish with mint springs, maraschino cherries or fresh fruit. You may want to try this with rum for a change.

Brandy Ice

Serves: 4 to 6

1 quart vanilla ice cream
4 to 5 jiggers of Brandy
3 to 4 jiggers of Creme de Cacao
1 to 2 jiggers of Kahlua
Nutmeg (optional)

Fill blender with ice cream. Add liqueurs and blend, (the amount of liqueur added will determine thickness of drink). Pour into snifters or crystal glasses, top with nutmeg, if desired.

Summer Slush

Serves: 4 to 6

1 (6-ounce) can lemonade
  concentrate, thawed
1 bottle red wine
6-ounces water
7-up

Combine lemonade concentrate, wine and water. Pour into an ice-cube tray and freeze. To serve, put 2 cubes in each glass and fill with 7-up.

NOTE: This is a great summer, low-alcohol drink.

40

Dr. Teton's Springtime Tonic

Serves: 6

6-ounces vodka
3-ounces Peachtree schnapps
1 (6-ounce) can frozen grapefruit
juice concentrate
8 mint sprigs

Fill blender ¾ full with ice cubes. Add vodka, schnapps and grapefruit juice concentrate. Blend until smooth. Serve in lo-ball glasses or white wine goblets. Garnish with mint sprigs.

Uncle Dick's Tom & Jerry's

Serves: 20 to 25

1 dozen eggs, separated
3/4 pound sugar, (ground
extra fine in blender)
1 teaspoon cream of tartar
1 cup whipping cream (optional)
1 pint dark rum
1 pint brandy
Hot water

Beat yolks until smooth and lemon in color, gradually add 1 cup sugar, continue beating until thick and creamy and sugar is completely dissolved. In a large bowl, beat egg whites, add cream of tartar and remaining sugar (gradually); beat thoroughly, but not until dry. Add egg yolk mixture to egg white mixture and beat thoroughly. If desired, add cream, which will make batter a little thinner. Stir rum and brandy together. Using Tom and Jerry cups, pour in 1-ounce of liquor mixture; add egg mixture, until cup is ⅔ cup full. Fill to the top with hot water (not boiling) and sprinkle with nutmeg.

Cranberry Tea

Serves: 16

2 quarts cranberry juice cocktail
2 to 3 cinnamon sticks
1 cup sugar
2/3 cup lemon juice
1½ cups orange juice
   Water

Put cranberry juice and cinnamon sticks into a gallon-size pot and boil for 10 minutes. Add sugar and return to a boil. Add lemon and orange juices. Pour into a gallon size container and add water to fill. Serve hot or cold.

NOTE: You may serve this hot in a large coffee pot.

Hot Wine Cranberry Cup

Yield: 10 cups

1 quart cranberry juice cocktail
2 cups water
1 cup sugar
1 (4-inch) stick cinnamon
12 whole cloves
Rind of 1/2 lemon
1 bottle Rosé wine
1/4 cup lemon juice

Combine all ingredients except wine and lemon juice. Boil, stirring, until sugar is dissolved. Simmer for 15 minutes, then strain. (Can be stored in refrigerator at this point). When ready to serve, add wine and lemon juice to the cranberry syrup. Heat, but do not boil. Keep warm on "simmer" or in a crockpot set on "high".

NOTE: This is a great punch to serve at Christmas parties.

Hot Cider Punch

Serves: 30

2 quarts apple cider
6 (3-inch) sticks cinnamon
12 whole cloves
1 (36-ounce) can pineapple juice
6 cups orange juice
2 cups lemon juice
1 quart ginger ale (if punch
   is served cold)

In a large pot, simmer cider, cinnamon sticks and cloves together for 15 minutes. Remove spices from cider. Add pineapple, orange and lemon juices and heat thoroughly. Serve hot, or if desired, chill mixture, add ginger ale and serve over ice or in large punchbowl.

NOTE: For cold punch, garnish with slices of pineapple, oranges or maraschino cherries. Float in punch or freeze in a block of ice.

Hot Holiday Drink
Yield: 2 gallons

1 gallon cider
1 quart cranberry juice
1 quart orange juice
2 quarts instant tea
2 sticks cinnamon
Cloves

Mix all ingredients and simmer for 10 minutes. Remove cloves and serve warm.

Hot Cranberry Citrus Punch
Yield: 2½ quarts

1 (32-ounce) bottle cranberry
  juice cocktail
2 cups orange juice
1/2 cup reconstituted lemon
  juice
1/2 cup honey
1/4 cup reconstituted lime
  juice
3 whole cloves
2 cinnamon sticks
1 (32-ounce) bottle ginger ale
  Cinnamon sticks (optional)

In a large kettle, combine first seven ingredients and simmer over medium heat for 15 minutes. Remove spices. Just before serving, add ginger ale and heat through. Serve hot. If desired, garnish with a cinnamon stick in each cup.

Cafe de Mejico
Serves: 1

3/4-ounce Kahlua
1/2-ounce Tequila
6 to 8 ounces hot coffee
Whipped cream

Measure Kahlua and Tequila into a coffee mug. Fill the mug with hot coffee. Top with whipped cream and serve.

French Hot Chocolate
Serves: 16 to 18

3/4 cup semi-sweet chocolate
  bits
1/2 cup light corn syrup
1/3 cup water
1 teaspoon vanilla
1 pint whipping cream
2 quarts milk

In a saucepan, combine chocolate, corn syrup and water. Heat over low heat, stirring constantly until chocolate is melted. (This can also be done in a double boiler or the microwave). Remove from heat, stir in vanilla. Cover and refrigerate until mixture is cool. In a large mixing bowl, beat whipping cream at medium speed, gradually add the cooled chocolate. Continue beating until mixture mounds when dropped from a spoon. Chill. Just before serving, heat milk to scalding. Pour into heated coffee pot or carafe. Fill serving cups half full of chocolate-cream mixture and add hot milk to the top. Stir gently.

Savor
the
Flavor
of
SOUPS

Market Day Bean Soup
Serves: 12

1/4 cup kidney beans
1/4 cup black beans
1/4 cup mung beans
1/4 cup navy beans
1/4 cup pinto beans
1/4 cup lentils
1/4 cup blackeyed peas
1/4 cup yellow split peas
1/4 cup green split peas
Barley (optional)
1 bay leaf
1 teaspoon thyme
1 tablespoon parsley
1 smoked hamhock
1 (28-ounce) can tomatoes
 undrained and broken up
2 medium onions, chopped
6 stalks celery, chopped
2 cloves garlic, minced
Salt and pepper to taste
1 pound link sausage, uncooked,
 cut into bite-size pieces
2 boneless chicken breasts,
 uncooked
1/2 cup chopped parsley
1/2 cup red wine (optional)

In a soup pot, combine beans, peas, spices and ham-hock with 3-quarts water. Simmer, covered, for 2½ to 3 hours. Add tomatoes, onions, celery, garlic, salt and pepper. Simmer, uncovered, 1½ hours, until creamy, stirring occasionally. Remove rind from ham. Slice ham and chicken. Add ham, chicken and sausage to pot. Simmer for 30 to 45 minutes. Add parsley and wine.

NOTE: This is best made a day before serving as the flavor improves with age.

Christmas Eve Fish Stew
Serves: 6

1 pound white fish (cod or
   snapper)
1 onion, chopped
1 clove garlic, minced
2 tablespoons butter
1/3 cup white wine
1½ cups chicken broth
2 potatoes, chopped
1 carrot, sliced
1 celery stalk, sliced
3/4 teaspoon salt
1/2 teaspoon marjoram
2 bay leaves
2 tablespoons parsley
2 tomatoes, chopped
6 to 8 mushrooms, quartered
2 tablespoons cornstarch
1/4 cup cold water

Cut fish into large bite-size pieces. Remove any bones; set aside. Sauté onions and garlic in butter until clear and tender. Add wine, broth, potatoes, carrots, celery and dry seasonings. Simmer for 15 to 20 minutes. Add parsley, tomatoes, mushrooms and fish. Simmer for 5 to 10 minutes. Fish should look flaky. Combine cornstarch and water then add to soup. Simmer for 5 more minutes.

Mt. Bachelor Steak Soup
Serves: 6 to 8

1 pound steak, cut up and
   browned
1/2 pound butter or margarine
2 cups flour
8 cups water
1 carrot, chopped
1 onion, chopped
1 celery stalk, chopped
1 (12-ounce) package frozen
   mixed vegetables
1 (14½-ounce) can tomatoes,
   chopped
4 tablespoons instant beef
   bouillon or au jus mix
Pepper to taste

Cut up steak, brown and set aside. Make a roux, using butter, flour and 2 cups of water. Place roux in a stock pot. Add remaining ingredients. Simmer for 1½ to 2 hours.

NOTE: This is very easy. It is an excellent winter supper soup. This is very thick.

Mushroom Bisque
Serves: 4 to 6

1/4 cup margarine
1 pound mushrooms, chopped
2 onions, sliced
1/3 cup chopped parsley
2 cloves garlic, minced
1/4 teaspoon thyme
1 teaspoon lemon pepper
7 beef bouillon cubes
1/3 cup flour
3 cups milk
Salt to taste

In a large kettle, melt margarine over medium heat. Add mushrooms, onions, parsley, garlic, thyme, lemon pepper and bouillon cubes. Cook, stirring occasionally, until vegetables are very limp. Stir in flour. Transfer about ½ of the mixture to a blender and mix while adding enough milk to allow blender to run easily until mixture is puréed. Return blended mixture to kettle and add remaining milk. Cook over medium heat, stirring often, until hot and thickened. Salt to taste.

NOTE: Serve with condiments of your choice; parmesan, croutons, green onions, more fresh mushrooms, dash nutmeg, or oyster crackers.

Moen's Meaty Minestrone
Serves: 8

3/4 cup dry kidney beans
7 cups water
1 (16-ounce) can tomatoes, cut up
1½ pounds beef stew meat, cut into 1-inch cubes
1/2 medium head cabbage, cut in pieces
1 large carrot, sliced
1 large onion, sliced
1 clove garlic, minced
1 tablespoon salt
2 teaspoons basil
1/4 teaspoon pepper
1/3 cup elbow macaroni
1 package frozen cut green beans
Grated parmesan cheese

Wash kidney beans and place in dutch oven or large kettle. Add water and bring to a boil. Cook for 2 minutes. Turn off heat, cover and let stand for 1 hour. Drain liquid from tomatoes into beans, reserving tomatoes. Add meat, cabbage, carrot, onion, garlic, salt, basil and pepper to beans. Cover and simmer over low heat for 1½ hours or until meat is tender. Add tomatoes, macaroni and green beans. Simmer for an additional 15 minutes. Serve with a sprinkle of grated parmesan cheese.

Chicken-Indian Soup
Serves: 6

1 whole chicken fryer (equalling
    2 cups diced)
1/2 medium onion, chopped
6 cups water
Chicken instant bouillon or
    bouillon cubes
Additional water, as needed
3 medium size carrots, chopped
3 stalks celery, chopped
1/2 cup uncooked rice
1/2 teaspoon garlic powder
1 teaspoon curry powder
1 cup frozen peas (optional)
1/2 cup raisins (optional)
Salt to taste
Cayenne pepper to taste

Boil whole chicken and onion in six cups water. Simmer for 40 minutes. Remove chicken and reserve broth. Add water and chicken bouillon to make 6 cups broth; set aside. Remove skin and bones from chicken and dice to make 2 cups; set aside. Simmer carrots, celery, rice, garlic powder and curry powder in broth for 30 minutes, or until rice is cooked. (If desired, add the frozen peas and raisins to the broth and cook along with the rice).

Mulligatawny Soup
Serves: 6

1 small chicken, cooked
3 tablespoons butter
3/4 cup rice
1 cup chopped onion
1 cup grated carrot
1/2 cup diced apple
2 teaspoons curry powder
1/2 teaspoon saffron
1/4 teaspoon pepper
2 quarts chicken stock
1/4 cup flour
1/2 cup milk
1 cup half and half

In a stock pot, cook chicken in water. Remove chicken and reserve stock. Skin, bone and dice chicken; set aside. Melt butter in a large saucepan and sauté rice, stirring frequently. Add onion and carrot; sauté until vegetables soften slightly. Add apple, curry powder, saffron, pepper and chicken stock. Cook until carrots are done. Blend flour with milk until smooth. Add to soup to thicken. Add chicken to soup. Stir in half and half and heat carefully without boiling.

50

Cacciucco
Serves: 6

1/2 cup olive oil
2 cloves garlic, minced
1 anjo chile (small red
   pepper) seeds removed
3 tablespoons tomato paste
1/2 cup white wine
2 cups water
1/2 teaspoon salt
1 pound white fish
1/2 pound medium-size shrimp,
   shelled
12 ounces fresh shelled clams

In a large saucepan, heat oil and sauté garlic, chile, and tomato paste. Turn heat to low, cover and simmer for 15 minutes, stirring occasionally. Add wine and simmer, uncovered, for an additional 15 minutes. Stir in water and salt, bring to boil and add white fish. Reduce heat to low and simmer until fish is opaque. Add shrimp and clams; heat. Remove chile and serve immediately.

NOTE: This can be served as an introduction to a large Italian dinner, or as a main dish for a light supper.

Cream of Spinach Soup
Serves: 6

1 (10-ounce) package frozen
   chopped spinach
1 small onion, chopped
2½ cups chicken broth
3 tablespoons butter
3 tablespoons flour
2 cups milk
1/2 cup whipping cream
1 cup sour cream
1/4 teaspoon grated nutmeg
Salt and pepper to taste

Cook spinach and onion in chicken broth for 10 to 15 minutes in a covered saucepan. In a soup pot, melt butter and stir in flour. Gradually stir in milk, cream and sour cream. Stir over low heat until mixture bubbles and thickens slightly. Add spinach mixture and nutmeg; stir well. Do not let soup come to a boil. Taste and add salt and pepper, if desired.

Rainy Day Soup
Serves: 10

2⅓ cups dry Great Northern
  beans
6 cups water
4 cups water
4 cups chicken broth
1 pound Kielbasa sausage,
  sliced
1¼ cups chopped onion
1/2 green pepper, chopped
2 cloves garlic, chopped
2 cups canned tomatoes,
  undrained and chopped
1 cup diced carrots
1/4 cup water
1 teaspoon salt
1 teaspoon dried oregano leaves
  or
1 tablespoon fresh chopped
  oregano
1/4 teaspoon freshly ground
  pepper
1 bay leaf

Wash and sort beans. In a 5-quart saucepan, combine beans and 6 cups of water. Bring to a boil, reduce heat; simmer, uncovered, for 2 minutes. Remove from heat and let stand for 1 hour; drain (reserving 1 cup liquid and 3 cups cooked beans). Combine 4 cups water and chicken broth; bring to a boil. Add drained beans (all but reserved 3 cups). Reduce heat, cover and simmer for 1½ hours or until beans are tender. In a large skillet, sauté sausage for 3 minutes. Add onions, green pepper and garlic; sauté until onions and green pepper are tender. Stir in remaining ingredients. Bring to a boil. Reduce heat, cover and simmer for 30 minutes. Remove bay leaf. In a food processor or blender, purée the reserved bean liquid and beans. Stir this into the sausage mixture. Simmer, uncovered, until thoroughly heated.

Super Chicken Gumbo

Serves: 6

2 tablespoons bacon or chicken fat
1 medium onion, diced
1/3 cup diced green pepper
1 quart chicken broth
1 (16-ounce) can tomatoes,
   undrained
2 teaspoons salt
1/8 teaspoon pepper
1/3 cup long grain rice,
   uncooked
2 tablespoons chopped parsley
1 bay leaf
2 to 3 cups cooked chicken or
   turkey
1 cup okra, frozen or canned,
   cut up

Put all ingredients except chicken and okra in a covered pot and simmer for 40 minutes. Add cut up chicken and okra and continue to simmer another 20 minutes. Remove bay leaf and serve.

Jambalaya

Serves: 4 to 6

1/2 cup chopped green onion
1/2 cup chopped white onion
1 large green pepper, cut in
   strips
1/2 cup chopped celery (with
   a few leaves)
1 teaspoon minced garlic
1/3 cup butter
1/2 to 1 pound raw shrimp,
   peeled and de-veined
24 raw oysters (may
   substitute 1 cup cubed ham)
1 (16-ounce) can tomatoes
1 cup chicken broth
1/2 teaspoon salt
1/4 teaspoon red cayenne pepper
1 cup raw rice
Tomato juice

In a large pan, sauté onions, green pepper, celery and garlic in butter until tender, but not browned. Add shrimp and oysters; cook for 5 minutes. (If ham is substituted, add the ham when the rice is added.) Add the tomatoes, broth, salt, cayenne and rice; stir and cover. Cook on low for 25 to 30 minutes, until rice is done. (If mixture becomes too dry, add tomato juice.)

Cioppino
Serves: 4

2 onions, diced
2 cloves garlic, minced
1 green pepper, chopped
2 cups tomato juice
1/2 cup burgundy wine
1 (28-ounce) can tomatoes
1 teaspoon dried oregano
1 teaspoon dried parsley
1/2 teaspoon dried basil
1/4 teaspoon ground pepper
1 pound halibut, cut in chunks
12 medium raw shrimp, shelled
1/4 pound sea scallops

Put onions, garlic, green pepper and tomato juice in a large saucepan; cook until vegetables are tender. Add wine, tomatoes and spices; cover and cook for 10 minutes. Add halibut, shrimp and scallops; cover and cook for 15 minutes. Uncover and cook an additional 5 minutes.

Refreshing Gazpacho
Serves: 6

1 large cucumber, peeled, cored
   and seeded
2 tomatoes
1 green pepper, halved and seeded
1 medium yellow onion, peeled
   and halved
3 cups tomato juice, divided
1/3 cup red wine vinegar
1 tablespoon olive oil
1/8 to 1/4 teaspoon tabasco
1/8 teaspoon ground pepper
3 to 4 cloves garlic, minced
Croutons (optional)

In a food processor, combine ½ the cucumber, 1 tomato, ½ the green pepper, ½ the onion and 1 cup tomato juice; puree. Chop up the remaining cucumber, tomato, green pepper and onion; place in individual serving bowls. Pour purée into a large bowl, add remaining tomato juice, vinegar, oil, tabasco, pepper and garlic; chill for 2 hours. To serve, pour into bowls and pass chopped vegetables and croutons.

NOTE: This is wonderful served on a hot summer night with crusty french bread and barbecued fish.

Hamburger-Rice Soup

Serves: 6 to 8

1½ pounds hamburger
1 cup chopped onion
1 cup cubed raw potatoes
1 cup diced carrots
1/2 cup diced celery
1/4 cup rice
1 (28-ounce) can stewed
  tomatoes
1 small bay leaf
1/2 teaspoon thyme
1/4 teaspoon basil
4½ teaspoons salt
1/8 teaspoon pepper
1½-quarts water

Sauté hamburger and onion until brown; drain. Add other ingredients. Reduce heat and simmer at least 1 hour.

NOTE: This is good served with cheese bread.

Italian Oven Chowder

Serves: 6 to 8

Non-stick vegetable oil spray
1 onion, chopped
1 (15½-ounce) can garbanzo
  beans, drained
1 (16-ounce) can stewed
  tomatoes, undrained
1/2 pound zucchini, sliced
1½ cups dry white wine
1/4 cup butter
1 teaspoon dried basil, crumbled
1 teaspoon minced garlic
1/4 teaspoon freshly ground
  pepper
1 teaspoon salt
1 bay leaf
1 cup grated Monterey Jack cheese
1 cup grated romano cheese
1 cup whipping cream

Preheat oven to 400 degrees. Spray a 4-quart baking dish with non-stick vegetable oil spray and add first 11 ingredients. Cover tightly and bake at 400 degrees for 1 hour, stirring every 20 minutes. Blend in cheeses and whipping cream. Cover and bake until cheeses melt, about 10 minutes. Serve immediately.

Tortellini and Sausage Soup
Serves: 8

1 pound Italian sausage, casings
   removed
1 cup coarsely chopped onions
2 cloves garlic, sliced
1/2 cup water
5 cups beef broth, homemade or
   canned
1/2 cup dry white wine
1 cup carrots, thinly sliced
2 cups tomatoes, peeled, seeded
   and chopped
1/2 teaspoon basil
1/2 teaspoon oregano leaves
1 (8-ounce) can tomato sauce
1½ cups sliced zucchini
8 ounces (2 cups) frozen meat or
   cheese tortellini
3 tablespoons chopped parsley
1 medium green pepper, cut in
   ½-inch pieces
Grated parmesan cheese

In a large 5-quart pan, brown sausage. Remove from pan, drain (reserving 1 tablespoon drippings); set aside. Sauté onions and garlic in reserved drippings until tender. Add water, broth, wine, carrots, tomatoes, basil, oregano, tomato sauce and sausage. Bring to a boil. Reduce the heat and simmer, uncovered, for 30 minutes. Skim off any fat that forms. Stir in zucchini, tortellini, parsley and green pepper. Simmer for an additional 35 to 40 minutes, until tortellini are tender. Garnish each serving with parmesan cheese.

Ma Blick's Chicken Soup
Serves: 6

3½ pounds chicken, cut up
8 cups water
2 medium onions, chopped
2 cups chopped celery
2 cups chopped carrots
3 chicken bouillon cubes
2 teaspoons salt
1 teaspoon curry powder
2 teaspoons Worcestershire sauce
1 to 2 cups noodles
   (i.e., corkscrew)

Put all ingredients except noodles into a large stock pot. Bring to a boil, reduce heat and simmer for 1 hour. Remove chicken, let broth simmer another hour or two. Take chicken off bones and return chicken to pot. Add noodles and cook until noodles are done.

Creamy Cauliflower Soup
Serves: 8

2 cups water
1 medium head cauliflower, broken into florets
1 medium onion, sliced
2 tablespoons butter or margarine
2 tablespoons flour
1 cup chicken broth
1/2 teaspoon celery salt
1/8 teaspoon pepper
1 cup half and half, at room temperature
Freshly ground nutmeg
Fresh parsley sprigs

Bring 2 cups water to a boil in a 3-quart saucepan. Add cauliflower and onion to boiling water. Return water to a boil; reduce heat, cover pan and simmer until cauliflower is tender (about 10 minutes). Do not drain. Pour entire contents of saucepan into a blender or food processor and blend on high until smooth; set aside. Melt butter in the same saucepan, stir in flour and slowly add chicken broth. Bring to a boil and stir constantly for 1 minute. Stir in cauliflower mixture, celery salt and pepper; heat just to boiling. Reduce heat, gradually add half and half. Cook until soup is heated through. Do not bring to a boil once the half and half has been added. Sprinkle each serving with nutmeg and add a sprig of parsley.

Curried Chicken Mushroom Soup
Serves: 8

3/4 cup butter or margarine
1 small onion, chopped
2 celery stalks, diced
1½ teaspoons curry powder
3/4 cup flour
6 cups chicken broth, homemade or canned
2 cups diced cooked chicken
2 cups sliced mushrooms, sautéed in butter
3 cups half and half, at room temperature

Melt butter in a large saucepan. Add onion and celery and cook until tender; stir in curry and flour. Gradually add in chicken broth, stirring constantly. Bring to a boil, then simmer for 30 minutes. Remove soup from heat and strain. Return soup to pan, gradually add half and half. Stir in chicken and mushrooms. Heat soup through, do not bring to a boil. Serve.

Meatball Soup
Serves: 10 to 12

4 (10½-ounce) cans beef broth,
  undiluted
1 onion, diced
4 carrots, chopped
4 celery stalks with leaves,
  chopped
2 cups water
1 (16-ounce) can tomato sauce
1 (16-ounce) can stewed tomatoes
1/4 teaspoon ground oregano
1/4 teaspoon chili powder
1/4 cup dried parsley flakes
1 cup shredded cabbage

Meatball mixture:
1 pound ground beef
1 egg
1/4 cup uncooked rice
1/2 teaspoon chili powder
1/4 teaspoon pepper

Empty beef broth into a 6-quart kettle, let simmer while preparing vegetables. Add onion, carrots and celery; bring to a boil. Stir occasionally, reduce to medium heat. Add water, tomato sauce, and stewed tomatoes. Add seasonings and parsley, cook for 30 minutes, then add shredded cabbage. Cook over medium heat until vegetables are tender, about 10 minutes, stirring occasionally.

For meatballs: Mix together ground beef, egg, rice and seasonings until well-blended. Form into ½-inch balls. Drop into soup mixture and let cook for 45 minutes.

Chinese Eggflower Soup
Serves: 6

6 cups low-sodium chicken broth
1 teaspoon soy sauce
1 tablespoon cornstarch
1/4 cup cold water
2 dozen chinese pea pods
1 egg, well-beaten
4 to 6 sliced radishes

Bring broth and soy sauce to a boil. Mix cornstarch and water; add to boiling soup and cook, stirring constantly for 1 minute. Add pea pods to soup. As soon as soup returns to a boil, drizzle egg into soup, stirring quickly. Serve immediately, garnished with radish slices.

NOTE: Kids love to make this. This makes a good first course for a Chinese dinner.

Oregon Coast Fish Chowder
Serves: 8

4 tablespoons butter
1 cup sliced onions
1 teaspoon thyme
3 cups diced potatoes
1 cup sliced celery
8 cups hot water
2 teaspoons salt
1/4 teaspoon pepper
2 pounds fresh tomatoes
1½ cups diced carrots
2 pounds white fish, cut in
  bite-size chunks

Melt the butter in a deep kettle and add the onions and thyme. Cook until onions are tender. Add potatoes, celery, hot water, salt and pepper. Cover and simmer for 5 minutes. Add tomatoes and carrots. Simmer, uncovered, for about 1 hour. Add fish chunks to the kettle. Cover and simmer for an additional 30 minutes.

Cream of Broccoli Soup
Serves: 6

2 cups water
1 (13¾-ounce) can chicken
  broth, fat removed
1/2 teaspoon salt
6 cups fresh broccoli, cut into
  1-inch pieces
1 cup sliced carrots
1 medium onion, peeled and
  quartered
3/4 cup skim milk
1 tablespoon butter or margarine
1/4 teaspoon ground black pepper

In a large saucepan, bring water, chicken broth and salt to a boil over high heat. Add broccoli, carrots and onion. When mixture boils, reduce heat to medium, cover and cook until broccoli is tender, about 15 to 20 minutes. Put 1 cup of vegetables and liquid into a blender or food processor, cover and blend for 40 to 50 seconds, until smooth. Pour into a bowl. Repeat with remaining vegetables and liquid. Stir in milk and butter until melted. Sprinkle with pepper.

French Vegetable Soup
Serves: 16

3 cups water
1 cup white navy beans
1/8 cup olive oil
2 onions, diced
1 (28 ounce) can Italian
  whole tomatoes
12 cups chicken stock
1½ cups diced carrots
1½ cups diced potatoes
1/2 cup chopped celery leaves
1 teaspoon salt
Black pepper to taste
1½ cups fresh green beans,
  cut into 1-inch pieces
1½ cups sliced zucchini
8 cloves garlic, minced
5 tablespoons dried basil
2 tablespoons tomato paste
1/2 cup freshly grated parmesan
  cheese
1/3 cup olive oil

Bring 3 cups water and beans to a boil. Remove from heat and soak, covered, for 1 hour. Return to heat and continue simmering, until tender, about 1½ hours; set aside. Heat oil in a large stock pot and sauté onions until soft and golden. Add tomatoes and chicken stock; bring to a boil. Add carrots, potatoes, celery leaves, salt and pepper; simmer uncovered for 15 minutes. Add white navy beans (with liquid), green beans and zucchini; simmer for 15 minutes. In a blender or food processor, purée garlic and basil together. Add tomato paste and cheese. Slowly pour in olive oil with processor running. Add this mixture to the soup and bring to a simmer.

Harvest Soup
Serves: 6

1 pound ground beef
1/2 cup chopped onion
1 (28-ounce) can whole tomatoes
2 cups hot water
3/4 cup sliced celery
3/4 cup cubed red potatoes
1 cup sliced carrots
3/4 cup sliced mushrooms
2 tablespoons barley (optional)
1 bay leaf
Salt to taste
1/2 teaspoon pepper
1/4 teaspoon basil
3 tablespoons honey
1/2 to 1 teaspoon herb
   seasoning (optional)

Brown hamburger with onions, drain off fat. Add tomatoes and break up with a spoon. Add hot water and remaining ingredients. Simmer until vegetables are tender, about 35 to 45 minutes.

Garden Gazpacho
Serves: 6

1 (46-ounce) can tomato juice
1/2 small onion
1 green pepper, seeded and
   chopped
1 large cucumber, peeled,
   seeded and chopped
2 medium tomatoes, seeded
   and chopped
1 (8-ounce) can whole green
   chiles
2 teaspoons Worcestershire
   sauce
1/2 teaspoon garlic powder
3/4 teaspoon seasoned salt
Tabasco to taste
1/4 teaspoon freshly ground
   pepper
2 tablespoons chopped green
   onions

Pour tomato juice in a large bowl. Using a food processor, coarsely mince the onion and green pepper together, and add to the tomato juice. Separately chop the cucumber, tomatoes and green chiles; add to the tomato juice mixture. Stir in Worcestershire sauce, garlic powder, seasoned salt, tabasco and pepper. Top with green onions. Chill.

Potato-Cheese Soup
Yield: 9 cups

4 cups sliced potatoes, peeled
2 cups water or vegetable stock
2 teaspoons salt
1 small onion, sliced
1 tablespoon oil
5 parsley sprigs
3 cups milk
1 cup grated cheddar cheese
2 tablespoons butter
1 teaspoon salt
1/4 teaspoon pepper
Garlic powder to taste

In a stock pot, cook the potatoes in water with salt until tender. Drain the potatoes, reserving the water. Transfer potatoes to a bowl and set aside. In the same pot, sauté onion in oil until it is soft. Place ½ of the potatoes, ½ of the potato water, onion and parsley in blender, (no more than ½ full), and purée until potatoes are smooth. Return the potato mixture to the pot, add reserved potatoes and milk, stirring continuously. Add the cheese, butter, salt, pepper and garlic powder. Cook over medium heat until the cheese is melted and the soup is hot, but do not boil.

NOTE: If you use new potatoes, there is no need to peel them.

Halibut Crab Chowder
Serves: 6

5 slices bacon, diced
3/4 cup chopped onion
1/3 cup chopped green pepper
2 cups peeled and diced
    potatoes
1½ cups water
1½ teaspoons salt
1/4 teaspoon white pepper
1½ pounds fresh halibut
1/2 pound crab meat
1 (8-ounce) can whole corn,
    drained
2 cups half and half
3 tablespoons flour
2 cups milk
1½ tablespoons butter
Fresh snipped parsley (garnish)

Sauté bacon, onion and green pepper in a large soup kettle. Add potatoes, water and seasonings. Cover and simmer 10 minutes, or until potatoes are nearly tender. Cut halibut into chunks and add to soup. Cover and simmer 7 to 8 minutes. Add crab, corn and half and half to soup. Place flour and milk in a pint jar; shake well. Add to soup mixture, stirring constantly over medium heat, until chowder has thickened slightly. Add butter. Sprinkle with parsley. Serve hot.

Tortilla Soup
Serves: 4 to 6

1 onion, chopped
1 fresh jalapeno pepper,
 seeded and chopped
2 cloves garlic, minced
2 large tomatoes, peeled
 and chopped
4 cups stock (chicken or beef)
1 can tomato soup
1 teaspoon cumin
1/2 teaspoon chili powder
 Salt and pepper to taste
1/2 teaspoon lemon pepper
2 teaspoons Worcestershire sauce
4 corn tortillas, sautéed lightly
 (may substitute crumbled corn
 chips)
1 avocado, peeled, seeded and
 cubed
Grated cheddar cheese
Grated Monterey Jack cheese
Sour cream

Sauté onion, jalapeno pepper, garlic and tomatoes in large kettle for several minutes. Add stock, soup and seasonings. Simmer for 1 hour. About 10 to 20 minutes before serving, tear tortillas into bite-size pieces and add to soup. Place cubed avocado and grated cheese in individual bowls and ladle hot soup on top. Garnish with sour cream, and crisp chips.

Cabbage Soup
Serves: 6 to 8

2 cups diced potatoes
2 cups sliced carrots
2 cups chopped onions
2 cups chopped celery
8 cups chicken stock
1 large head green cabbage,
 cored and chopped
1/2 teaspoon caraway seeds
Garlic powder to taste
Salt and pepper to taste
Sour cream (optional)

In a large soup kettle, combine potatoes, carrots, onions, celery and stock. Bring to a boil, reduce heat and simmer, covered, for 30 to 45 minutes, or until vegetables are tender. Add cabbage and sprinkle with caraway seeds. Do not stir. Cover and cook another 5 minutes. Stir and add seasonings. Cook for an additional 5 minutes. Serve, garnished with sour cream, if desired.

Won Ton Soup
Serves: 8

1 pound ground pork
1 egg
1/2 of an (8-ounce) can
   water chestnuts, minced
2 green onions, minced
2 teaspoons salt
2 teaspoons ground ginger
4 teaspoons soy sauce
1/2 teaspoon monosodium
   glutamate
1/4 teaspoon pepper
1 pound won ton skins

   Broth:
8 cups chicken broth
1 teaspoon soy sauce
2 green onions, chopped
1 or 2 celery stalks, chopped
2 dozen snow peas
6 mushrooms, sliced
1/2 of an (8-ounce) can
   water chestnuts

Mix together pork, egg, ½ can water chestnuts, green onions, salt, ginger, soy sauce, monosodium glutamate and pepper. Place 1 teaspoon of mixture in center of each won ton skin. Moisten edge with water and fold to form a triangle, press to seal edges. Overlap opposite corners, moisten with water and press firmly. Boil won tons in water for 8 minutes and drain. Heat chicken broth, adding soy sauce, green onions, celery, snow peas, mushrooms and water chesnuts. Add won tons; heat through. Serve.

Curried Carrot Soup
Serves: 6

2 tablespoons oil
1 large onion, chopped
1 clove garlic, minced
1 teaspoon curry powder
1 teaspoon flour
3 cups chicken broth
3 to 4 large carrots, peeled
   and sliced
1 cup plain yogurt, divided
1/4 teaspoon salt (or to taste)
1/4 teaspoon cayenne pepper (or
   to taste)
1/3 cup roasted peanuts,
   chopped

Cook onion and garlic in oil until limp. Add curry and flour, cook for 30 seconds. Add broth and carrots, cook for 15 to 20 minutes, until carrots are tender. Put ingredients in a blender or food processor and purée with ¾ cup yogurt. Add salt and cayenne pepper. Adjust to taste. Chill before serving. Serve with spoonful of reserved ¼ cup yogurt and top with peanuts.

NOTE: This soup may be served hot or cold.

Sausage Lentil Soup
Serves: 6

1¼ cups dry lentils, rinsed
5 cups water
1½ pounds Polish sausage,
  sliced
1 (6-ounce) can tomato paste
3 potatoes, peeled and cubed
1 medium onion, chopped
1 cup chopped carrot
1/2 cup chopped celery
1½ teaspoons beef bouillon
  granules
3/4 teaspoon dried thyme,
  crushed
1/8 teaspoon pepper

In a large pan, combine lentils and 5 cups water; bring to a boil. Reduce heat, cover and simmer for 30 minutes. Add remaining ingredients. Cover and cook on low for 2 hours. Skim off fat before serving.

Fisherman's Stew
Serves: 4

2 slices bacon
1 cup sliced mushrooms
1 large onion, chopped
2 cloves garlic, minced
1 tablespoon flour
1 teaspoon chicken bouillon
  granules
1/4 teaspoon thyme
1 (8-ounce) bottle clam juice
1 cup dry white wine
1 bay leaf
1/2 pound fresh white fish
  (halibut, sole or cod)
  or
1 pound frozen white fish,
  partially thawed
2 small zucchini, sliced

Cook bacon, reserving drippings; set aside. In a 2-quart saucepan, sauté mushrooms, onion and garlic in drippings. Blend in flour, bouillon and thyme. Add clam juice, wine and bay leaf. Bring to a boil, reduce heat and simmer for 15 minutes. Add fish and simmer for an additional 10 to 15 minutes. Add zucchini, cook on low heat until tender. Remove bay leaf; add crumbled bacon and serve.

Creamy Vegetable Soup
Serves: 6

1 medium onion, diced
1 medium carrot, diced
1 small stalk celery with
  leaves, diced
1/2 cup water
2 cups cooked, chopped
  vegetables, (broccoli, zucchini,
  or cauliflower)
1 teaspoon salt (or to taste)
1 teaspoon ground pepper (or
  to taste)
1 (12-ounce) can chicken broth
1/2 cup half and half

Simmer onion, carrot and celery in water for 10 minutes, or until vegetables are tender. In a blender or food processor, purée all vegetables. Add salt, pepper, chicken broth and cream. Heat before serving, but do not boil.

NOTE: This is excellent served with a tossed salad and garlic toast.

Astoria Seafood Soup
Serves: 6

1/4 cup butter
1 large onion, chopped
1 clove garlic, minced
6 mushrooms, sliced
5 cups chicken bouillon
1 cup Chardonnay
1/2 teaspoon tarragon
1/8 teaspoon dried dill weed
2 medium potatoes, peeled,
  and cut into ½-inch cubes
1 pound fish fillets (red
  snapper or ling cod), cut
  into ½-inch cubes
1 (6½-ounce) can minced
  clams, drained
1/4 pound shrimp
1/4 pound crab meat
1 lemon, cut into wedges
1 teaspoon parsley flakes
Freshly ground black pepper
  to taste

In an 8-quart pan, sauté onion, garlic and mushrooms in butter over medium-high heat, until tender. Add bouillon, wine, tarragon and dill. Bring to a boil. Add potatoes, cover and simmer until tender, about 20 minutes. Add cubed fish, cover and simmer until fish is opaque, about 3 minutes. Add clams, shrimp and crab meat. Cover and simmer until hot, another 3 minutes. Squeeze in lemon juice. Sprinkle with parsley. Add pepper to taste. Ladle into large soup bowls.

NOTE: This is great served with warm garlic french bread, tossed green salad with thousand island dressing and a glass of chardonnay.

Delicious Turkey Soup
Serves: 3 to 4

2 leeks, chopped
7 ounces shredded cabbage
2 tablespoons margarine
7 cups chicken broth
1 bay leaf
  Salt and pepper to taste
4 potatoes, chopped
1/2 to 1 cup chopped cooked
  turkey
Grated cheese
Chopped parsley

Sauté leeks and cabbage in a large pot with margarine, stirring constantly, until tender. Add broth, bay leaf, salt and pepper. Add potatoes and simmer until soft. Mix in turkey. Top with grated cheese of your choice and garnish with parsley.

Crab Bisque
Serves: 8

1/4 cup butter
1 large onion, chopped
1 cup chopped celery
6 potatoes, pared and
  cut in cubes
1/2 teaspoon salt
1/4 teaspoon pepper
1 bay leaf
1 quart chicken broth
1 quart milk
1 pound crab meat (may
  substitute shrimp meat)
3 tablespoons cornstarch
1/4 cup cold water

In a large soup pot, melt butter over medium heat. Add onion and celery; cook until onion is tender, stirring occasionally. Add potatoes, salt, pepper, bay leaf and chicken broth. Cover and cook until potatoes are tender. Stir in the milk, cover and cook, until soup is hot, but not boiling. Stir in crab. Blend cornstarch and water and add to the soup. Over medium heat, bring to a slow boil until soup thickens. Remove bay leaf before serving.

Wild Rice Soup
Serves: 6 to 8

Stock:

5 cups water
2 duck or chicken carcasses
or
2½ pounds chicken backs and necks
1 smoked ham bone
2 carrots, coarsely chopped
1 medium onion, chopped
2 stalks celery, chopped
1 bay leaf
Salt and fresh ground pepper to taste

Soup:

1/2 cup wild rice, rinsed well
3 cups water
1 tablespoon corn oil margarine or
1 tablespoon olive oil
1/2 cup finely chopped onion
1/2 cup finely chopped celery
1/2 cup finely chopped carrots
Stock from above, plus enough water to make 4 cups liquid, heated
1 cup lowfat milk (substitute half and half for richer soup or skim milk for a lighter taste)
1/2 teaspoon salt
1/8 teaspoon freshly ground pepper

For stock: Simmer ingredients for 1 to 2 hours, uncovered. Strain and discard fat. Reserve stock for soup.

For soup: Combine rice and water in a saucepan and bring to a boil. Cover and cook over low heat for 40 to 45 minutes, or until rice is tender. Drain off excess water. Melt margarine or heat olive oil in a large pot. Add vegetables and cook until tender-crisp, about 5 minutes. Add water if necessary to prevent scorching. In a blender or food processor, combine 1 cup cooked rice and 1 cup hot stock. Blend until smooth. Add to the vegetable mixture along with remaining stock and rice. Cook over medium heat for 30 minutes, stirring to prevent sticking. Just before serving, add milk, salt and pepper.

Elegant Mushroom Soup
Serves: 6

4 tablespoons butter or margarine
1 clove garlic, minced
6 to 8 green onions, green part
    only
4 tablespoons flour
3 cups chicken stock
2 cups mushrooms, cut up
1/2 cup milk or whipping cream
1/8 teaspoon tarragon
Sour cream (garnish)
Tarragon (garnish)

Melt butter, sauté garlic and onion tops, but do not brown. Stir in flour and chicken stock; bring to a boil and cook 2 minutes. Pour mixture into a food processor or blender. Add mushrooms and process. Pour into pan; add cream and tarragon and reheat, but do not boil. May be garnished with a spoonful of sour cream and a pinch of tarragon.

Stan's Sliced Onion Soup
Serves: 8

5 to 6 onions, thinly sliced in
    rings (white, yellow or bermuda)
3 tablespoons butter
1 tablespoon salad oil
1/4 teaspoon sugar
1 teaspoon salt (or to taste)
2 tablespoons flour
1½ quarts beef stock
    or
4 (14½-ounce) cans beef
    broth
1/3 cup dry red wine
1/2 teaspoon freshly ground
    pepper
8 slices rye bread, cut into a
    circular shape and toasted
1 cup grated Swiss cheese
2/3 cup grated parmesan cheese
3 tablespoons butter

In a large pot, sauté onion in butter and oil over low heat, cover and simmer for 15 to 20 minutes. Add sugar and salt; cook uncovered, over medium heat, for an additional 20 minutes, until the onions turn golden. Add flour, mix well; then add broth, wine and pepper. Simmer, uncovered, for 30 minutes. Preheat oven to 325 degrees 30 minutes before serving. Bring soup almost to a boil and pour into 8 oven-proof soup crocks. Float toast rounds on top, sprinkle each with cheese and drizzle with butter. Bake at 325 degrees for 20 to 30 minutes.

NOTE: You can never use too many onions!

Great Potato Soup

Serves: 4 to 6

3 cups diced potatoes
1/2 cup diced celery
1/2 cup diced onion
1½ cups water
1 tablespoon chicken bouillon
   granules
   or 2 chicken bouillon cubes
1/4 teaspoon salt
2 cups milk, divided
1 (8-ounce) container sour cream
   with chives
1 tablespoon flour

In a large saucepan, combine potato, celery, onion, water, bouillon and salt. Cover and cook about 20 minutes, or until vegetables are tender. Add 1 cup of milk; heat through. In a medium bowl, blend sour cream and flour, gradually add remaining 1 cup of milk. Pour ⅓ of the hot potato mixture into the sour cream mixture; stir and return to pan. Cook over medium heat until thickened.

Easy Minestrone

Serves: 6

1/4 cup extra virgin olive oil
1 large yellow onion, chopped
1 cup carrots, diagonally sliced
1 cup zucchini, diagonally sliced
1 cup fresh green beans
2 cups Swiss chard, coarsely
   chopped
1 cup canned plum tomatoes,
   crushed
8 cups chicken broth (homemade
   or canned)
Salt and pepper to taste
1 cup dried ziti pasta
1½ cups canned red kidney beans
   Freshly grated parmesan cheese

Heat olive oil in a large stock pot and sauté onions until soft and golden. Add carrots, zucchini, green beans, and Swiss chard, one at a time, (cooking each 2 minutes before adding the next). Add tomatoes, broth, salt and pepper. Cook on medium-low heat for about 20 minutes, or until vegetables are tender. Add pasta and cook until done. Add beans and heat through. Serve with parmesan cheese sprinkled on top of each bowl.

Savor
the
Flavor
of
SALADS

Sesame Seed Asparagus
Serves: 4

1 pound fresh asparagus
2 tablespoons sesame seeds
1 tablespoon sugar
2 tablespoons soy sauce

Wash and cook asparagus with a pinch of salt, until tender-crisp and a bright green color, (about 5-7 minutes). Do not overcook. Cut into diagonal slices. Drain and chill. Parch sesame seeds in a covered saucepan over medium-low until seeds begin to pop. Do not overheat as seeds will become bitter. Grind or mash seeds to bring out flavor and fragrance. Make a sweet sauce of sugar, soy sauce and parched sesame seeds. Pour sauce over asparagus and toss lightly.

NOTE: You may also use spinach, cauliflower, broccoli or beans with this marinade.

Romaine Salad
Serves: 6

5 slices white bread
2/3 cup olive oil, divided
2 cloves garlic, minced
3 heads romaine lettuce
1 teaspoon salt
1/2 teaspoon freshly ground
   black pepper
1 tablespoon Worcestershire sauce
2/3 cup salad oil
6 to 8 tablespoons grated romano
   or parmesan cheese
1 egg
1/2 cup lemon juice

Cut bread into small cubes and sauté in 2 to 2½ tablespoons olive oil, until browned and crisp. Remove from heat and set aside. Combine remaining olive oil and garlic. Let stand for 15 minutes. Wash and dry lettuce, break into pieces and put in a large salad bowl. Add croutons, salt, pepper, Worcestershire, garlic oil mixture, salad oil and cheese. Break an egg over the mixture and add lemon juice. Toss from the bottom and serve immediately.

Marianne's Spinach Salad

Serves: 4

1 pound spinach, cleaned and torn
   into bite-size pieces
1 red apple, sliced
5 slices bacon, cooked and
   crumbled, grease reserved
1/3 cup sliced almonds, toasted
   in bacon grease

Dressing:
1/4 cup oil
3 tablespoons white wine vinegar
1/8 teaspoon salt
   Pepper to taste
1 teaspoon sugar
1/2 teaspoon dry mustard
3 green onions, finely chopped

Toss spinach and apples, sprinkle with bacon and almonds; toss with dressing just before serving.

Asparagus Spear Salad

Serves: 4 to 6

1/2 pound fresh asparagus
1 (6-ounce) jar marinated artichoke hearts (reserve
   marinade)
1/2 cup sliced mushrooms
1/4 cup sliced green onions
1 tablespoon vinegar
1 teaspoon sugar
1 teaspoon toasted sesame seeds
1/4 teaspoon salt
   Tabasco to taste
   Lettuce leaves (garnish)

Steam asparagus until tender-crisp, cool quickly with cold water. Drain artichoke hearts, reserving marinade. Slice any large artichoke hearts in half. Arrange cooled asparagus on a 10 x 6 x 2-inch dish. Top with artichoke hearts and sprinkle mushrooms and onion over top. Combine reserved marinade with vinegar, sugar, sesame seeds, salt and Tabasco. Pour over vegetables and refrigerate several hours. At serving time, arrange on chilled plates over lettuce leaves.

NOTE: This is a good barbecue side dish.

Spinach-Bacon Salad
Serves: 6

1 pound (2 bunches) fresh spinach
1 red onion
1/2 pound bacon
2/3 cup salad oil
1/4 cup garlic wine vinegar
2 tablespoons sherry
1½ teaspoons soy sauce
1 teaspoon sugar
1 teaspoon dry mustard
1/2 teaspoon curry powder
1/2 teaspoon salt
Pepper to taste

Wash spinach and discard stems. Pat leaves dry on paper towels. Wrap in towels and refrigerate. Peel onion, slice and separate into rings. Fry bacon, drain, cool and crumble; set aside. Combine oil, vinegar, sherry, soy sauce, sugar, mustard, curry, salt and pepper in a jar. Shake until well mixed. Tear cold spinach into bite size pieces. Add onion and 3 to 4 tablespoons dressing and half of bacon. Toss lightly. Add more dressing if desired and toss with remaining bacon.

New American Potato Salad
Serves: 8

2½ pounds small red potatoes
1/3 cup chicken broth
1 teaspoon Dijon mustard
1/4 cup low-calorie Italian
   dressing
1/8 teaspoon ground black pepper
1 to 2 tablespoons white wine
   vinegar
3 to 4 green onions, thinly sliced
1/4 cup chopped parsley
1/2 cup sliced tomatoes

Steam potatoes until just tender. Let cool to handle. Quarter warm potatoes and toss with broth, mustard and dressing. Add pepper and adjust flavoring with vinegar. Cool for 1 to 2 hours, (tossing occasionally while cooling to blend flavors). When ready to serve, add green onions and parsley; toss gently. Garnish with sliced tomatoes.

Broccoli Bacon Salad
Serves: 4

3 stalks broccoli
1/4 pound sliced bacon, reserve 2
   teaspoons drippings for dressing
1 medium onion, diced
1 cup grated cheddar cheese

Dressing:
1/2 cup mayonnaise
1/4 cup sugar
3 tablespoons white wine vinegar
2 teaspoons bacon drippings

Cut broccoli flowerettes into bite size pieces. Peel stalks and cut into bite-size pieces. Cut bacon strips into ¼-inch pieces and fry until crisp; set aside. Mix together broccoli, onion, cheese and bacon.

For dressing: Combine mayonnaise, sugar, white wine vinegar and bacon drippings. Top the broccoli with dressing. Chill for 1 to 3 hours.

Summer Potato Salad
Serves: 8

3 pounds red potatoes, unpeeled
3/4 cup whipping cream, whipped
3/4 cup mayonnaise
2 tablespoons vinegar
3/4 teaspoon dry mustard
1/2 teaspoon salt, or to taste
1/4 cup snipped fresh chives
1/4 cup fresh minced parsley
1/4 cup finely minced shallots

Boil potatoes in salted water for 15 to 20 minutes, until tender but still firm. Drain and rinse under cold water. Refrigerate until cold. Cut the potatoes into cubes and set aside. Whip the cream until stiff. In a medium bowl, blend the mayonnaise, vinegar, mustard and salt. Fold in the whipped cream, chives, parsley and shallots. Fold the potatoes in carefully, just to coat. Cover and refrigerate for at least 2 hours. Garnish with a few more chopped chives, as desired and serve.

Mozzarella Salad with Green Herb Dressing
Serves: 8 to 10

1 bunch leaf lettuce
1 bunch escarole
1 bunch romaine
2 pints cherry tomatoes
1 pound mozzarella

Dressing:
1 egg
2 tablespoons green peppercorn
  mustard, Dijon style
2 teaspoons balsamic vinegar
1/4 cup champagne vinegar (may
  substitute red wine vinegar)
1/2 teaspoon salt
Freshly ground white pepper
3/4 cup extra virgin olive oil

Tear various lettuces into bite-size pieces and combine with cherry tomatoes (halved if large). Cube mozzarella and combine with lettuce and tomatoes; set aside.

For dressing: In a food processor bowl or blender, combine egg, mustard, vinegars, salt and pepper. Add olive oil in a thin steady stream. Process until emulsified. Toss the salad with just enough dressing to coat. Serve immediately.

Mandarin Salad
Serves: 6 to 8

2 bunches loose leaf lettuce
  (romaine, red leaf, etc)
1 to 2 (11-ounce) cans mandarin
  orange slices, drained
1/4 to 1/2 cup salted peanuts

Dressing:
3/4 cup granulated sugar
1 cup vegetable oil
1 teaspoon mustard (dry, Dijon or
  regular)
1 teaspoon salt
1/3 cup red wine vinegar
1½ tablespoons minced onion
2 tablespoons poppy seeds

Tear lettuce into bite-size pieces and combine with oranges and peanuts in a large bowl.

For dressing: Combine sugar, oil, mustard, salt, vinegar, onion and poppy seeds in a jar. Shake well to blend. Toss the salad with desired amount of dressing.

Marinated Vegetable Salad
Serves: 8

1/4 cup red wine vinegar
1½ cups cocktail vegetable
 juice
1 tablespoon honey
1 teaspoon dry mustard
1/2 teaspoon dried dill weed
2 cups diagonally sliced carrots,
 cooked tender-crisp
2 cups cauliflowerettes, cooked
 tender-crisp
1 cup green bell pepper, cut into
 rings
1 cup diagonally sliced
 asparagus, cooked tender-crisp
 (optional)
1 cup sliced radishes
1 cup sliced red onions

At least 8 hours before serving: In a large bowl, mix vinegar, vegetable juice, honey, mustard and dill. Add pre-cooked and raw vegetables to marinade, stir, cover and refrigerate for at least 6 to 8 hours. Stir occasionally.

Cauliflower Salad
Serves: 6

2 cups thin sliced raw cauliflower
1/2 cup sliced black olives
1/3 cup sliced green pepper, cut
 in thin strips
1/4 cup chopped red pimiento
1/2 bermuda onion, cut into small
 rings

Dressing:
1½ tablespoons lemon juice
1½ tablespoons red wine vinegar
4½ tablespoons salad oil
1/4 teaspoon sugar
1 teaspoon salt
1/8 teaspoon pepper (or to taste)

Toss all salad ingredients in a bowl. Mix dressing ingredients and pour over vegetables. Toss. Marinate in refrigerator for at least 1 hour before serving.

Berry Summer Salad
Serves: 6 to 8

2 bunches fresh spinach, washed,
   dried and torn
2 pints fresh strawberries,
   cleaned, hulled and halved

   Dressing:
1/3 cup sugar
2 tablespoons sesame seeds
1 tablespoon poppy seeds
1½ teaspoons minced onion
1/4 teaspoon Worcestershire sauce
1/4 teaspoon paprika
1/2 cup vegetable oil
1/4 cup cider vinegar

Place spinach and strawberries in a bowl; do not mix. Place dressing ingredients in a blender or food processor and blend until thoroughly mixed and thickened; do not over-mix. Just before serving, toss salad gently with dressing.

Mandarin-Almond Salad
Serves: 6 to 8

1/4 cup slivered almonds
1 tablespoon sugar

   Dressing:
1½ teaspoons salt
2 tablespoons vinegar
2 tablespoons sugar
1/4 cup salad oil
1 tablespoon parsley
Dash of pepper
Dash of Tabasco

2 bunches leaf lettuce
1 cup finely chopped celery
3 green onions, finely chopped
1 (11-ounce) can mandarin
   oranges, drained

Caramelize slivered almonds by mixing with sugar and stirring constantly over low heat until lightly browned. Cool on waxed paper and break into small pieces; set aside. Combine ingredients for dressing and mix well. Just before serving, tear lettuce into bite-size pieces and combine with celery, onions and mandarin oranges. Toss with dressing and nuts; serve immediately.

Tomato Salad with Basil
Serves: 6

6 ripe tomatoes, diced
1 yellow bell pepper, diced
1 large cucumber, diced
3 tablespoons balsamic vinegar
6 tablespoons olive oil
1/2 teaspoon salt
Freshly ground pepper to taste
1/4 cup chopped fresh basil leaves

Place diced tomatoes, bell pepper, and cucumber in a large bowl. Let mixture sit for 10 minutes; drain off excess tomato juice. In another bowl, add vinegar and slowly whisk in the olive oil; add salt, pepper and basil. Add dressing to the vegetables and toss well. Chill and serve on a bed of lettuce.

NOTE: To make this more of a meal, add ½ pound of baby shrimp.

Colorful Coleslaw
Serves: 8 to 10

3 cups chopped cabbage
1 cup chopped red cabbage
1 cup chopped celery
1 cup chopped cauliflower
1 cup mayonnaise
1 cup sour cream
1 tablespoon sugar
1 teaspoon salt
1 tablespoon tarragon vinegar
1/2 cup chopped cucumber
1/4 cup chopped green pepper
  (optional)
1/4 cup chopped onion
1 tablespoon butter
1/2 cup chopped peanuts
2 tablespoons grated parmesan
  cheese, divided

Mix cabbages, celery and cauliflower; chill. Mix mayonnaise, sour cream, sugar, salt, vinegar, cucumber, green pepper and onion; chill. Melt butter and brown peanuts over low heat. Remove from heat and stir in 1 tablespoon parmesan cheese. Mix vegetables and dressing. Top with peanut mixture and remaining 1 tablespoon of parmesan cheese. Toss again and serve.

Cauliflower and Pea Salad

Serves: 8

1 medium head cauliflower
3 celery stalks, chopped
1 (10-ounce) package frozen peas,
  scalded in boiling water
  or
2 cups fresh scalded peas
1 cup mayonnaise
1 small red onion, diced
3 to 4 tablespoons milk
1½ teaspoons seasoning salt
1/2 teaspoon pepper

Break cauliflower into bite size pieces, (do not cook); place in a bowl and add celery and peas. In another bowl, mix mayonnaise, onion, milk, seasoning salt and pepper. Pour dressing over vegetables and toss well. Cover and refrigerate for 1 to 2 hours to let the flavors blend.

Confetti Bean Salad

Serves: 8 to 10

1 (27-ounce) can red kidney beans
2½ cups chopped celery
2 tablespoons finely chopped
  onion
3/4 cup chopped walnuts
4 sweet pickles, chopped
1/3 cup salad oil
1/4 cup wine vinegar
1/2 teaspoon salt
1/2 teaspoon freshly ground
  pepper

Rinse and drain beans thoroughly. Combine beans, celery, onion, walnuts and pickles; set aside. In another bowl, mix oil, vinegar, salt and pepper. Pour over bean mixture, toss and refrigerate for ½ to 1 hour. Serve over lettuce leaves.

Classic Caesar Salad
Serves: 4 to 6

4 slices bacon
4 tablespoons margarine
4 slices white or french bread, cubed (crusts removed)
1 egg
1 large head romaine lettuce, washed and dried well
1/2 cup freshly grated parmesan or romano cheese
1 clove garlic, cut in half
1/2 teaspoon salt
1/4 teaspoon freshly ground pepper
1/4 teaspoon dry mustard
Juice of 1 lemon
3 tablespoons olive oil

Cook the bacon, drain on paper towels and dice. In a frying pan over low heat, melt margarine. Fry bread cubes, tossing often to brown and crisp on all sides. (Cubes should be firm when done). Coddle the egg by immersing egg in boiling water for 1 minute, removing and running under cold water until cool; set aside. Rub the inside of a salad bowl with garlic pieces and discard. Tear lettuce into bite-size pieces and add to the bowl along with the bacon, cheese, salt, pepper and mustard; toss well. Add the juice of 1 lemon and olive oil; toss again. Break the coddled egg into the salad. Toss again and add croutons. Serve immediately.

Spicy Black Bean Salad
Serves: 4 to 6

1 (15-ounce) can black beans
or
1½ cups black beans
1 small green pepper, chopped
1 small carrot, coarsely grated
1 tablespoon chopped red onion
1/4 teaspoon grated lime rind
3 tablespoons lime juice
1/4 teaspoon cumin or red pepper
2 tablespoons vegetable oil
1 clove garlic, minced
1/4 teaspoon ground pepper
1/4 teaspoon salt

Rinse and drain canned beans or cook black beans according to package directions. Add green pepper, carrot and red onion to cooled black beans. In another bowl, mix remaining ingredients and pour over bean and vegetable mixture. Let stand. Serve at room temperature.

Potato Salad with Bleu Cheese
Serves: 6 to 8

8 to 10 new potatoes, unpeeled
1/2 cup bleu cheese, crumbled
1 cup chopped celery
2 tablespoons chopped chives
2 tablespoons chopped scallions
3/4 cup sour cream
3/4 cup mayonnaise
3 tablespoons vinegar
1/4 teaspoon salt
1/4 teaspoon pepper

Wash potatoes. Cook in boiling water until tender; cool. Slice with skins. In a large bowl, combine bleu cheese, celery, chives and scallions; add cooled sliced potatoes. In a separate bowl, combine sour cream, mayonnaise, vinegar, salt and pepper. Stir until blended. Fold dressing into potato mixture and mix well. Chill thoroughly before serving.

Winter Vegetable Salad
Serves: 12 to 14

2 to 3 stalks broccoli (1½ pounds)
1 small head cauliflower (1½ to
   2 pounds)
1/4 cup chopped green onions
1/2 cup toasted slivered almonds
1½ cups grated cheddar cheese
1 pound bacon, cooked crisp and
   crumbled
   or
1 (3¼-ounce) jar imitation bacon
   bits

Dressing:
1½ cups lite mayonnaise
1/4 cup sugar
2 tablespoons red wine vinegar
Salt and pepper to taste

Cut broccoli and cauliflower into bite-size pieces and place in a mixing bowl. Add green onions, almonds, cheese and bacon.

For dressing: Combine mayonnaise, sugar and vinegar; mix well. Pour dressing over salad and toss well to coat. Add salt and pepper to taste. Let the salad stand for at least 2 hours for best results.

Spinach Salad with Chutney Dressing
Serves: 6

Dressing:
1/4 cup wine vinegar
2 to 3 tablespoons chutney
2 cloves garlic, crushed
2 tablespoons coarsely ground
French mustard
2 teaspoons sugar
1/2 cup vegetable oil

Salad:
1 pound fresh spinach, washed,
    dried and torn into bite-size
    pieces
6 fresh mushrooms, sliced
1 cup sliced water chestnuts
6 slices bacon, cooked crisp and
    crumbled
1/2 cup shredded gruyere cheese
3/4 cup fresh bean sprouts
1/4 cup thinly sliced red onion

For the dressing: In a blender, combine vinegar, chutney, garlic, mustard and sugar; blend until smooth. With machine running, slowly pour oil in and blend until thickened and smooth. Refrigerate at least 30 minutes before serving. To prepare salad, mix all salad ingredients, toss with dressing and serve.

Crunchy Coleslaw
Serves: 8 to 10

1 small head cabbage
1/2 cup chopped green onions
8 ounces sunflower seeds
2 teaspoons butter
1/2 cup slivered almonds
2 (3-ounce) packages oriental
    noodles
4 tablespoons sugar
1 cup salad oil
2 teaspoons salt
6 tablespoons rice vinegar

Finely chop cabbage and combine with green onions. Brown sunflower seeds in butter. Just before serving, add sunflower seeds, almonds and crushed top ramen noodles (do not use seasoning packet and do not cook). For dressing: Mix sugar, oil, salt and vinegar. Be sure the sugar is dissolved. Pour dressing over slaw mixture and toss well.

Vegetable Rice Salad
Serves: 4

1/2 cup uncooked rice
1 cucumber, diced
1 cup diced red bell pepper
2 green onions, chopped
1/4 cup grated parmesan cheese
1 tablespoon chopped fresh basil
2 tablespoons olive oil
2 tablespoons cider vinegar
2 tablespoons plain yogurt
1/2 teaspoon Dijon mustard

Cook rice according to package instructions; let cool. In a mixing bowl, combine cucumber, bell pepper, onion and rice. In a separate bowl, mix parmesan cheese, basil, olive oil, vinegar, yogurt and mustard; mix well. Pour over rice mixture, toss to coat and chill.

Pickled Coleslaw
Serves: 10 to 12

1 large head cabbage, shredded
2 large onions, chopped
3/4 cup sugar
1 teaspoon salt

Dressing:
1 cup white vinegar
1/4 cup sugar
2 teaspoons prepared mustard
1 tablespoon celery seed
3/4 cup salad oil

Toss cabbage, onion, sugar and salt. Let stand while making dressing.

For dressing: Mix all ingredients except oil in a saucepan and bring to a boil. Add salad oil when mixture bubbles. Mix well, remove from heat and pour over cabbage mixture. Chill overnight.

NOTE: This is a great salad for barbecues, picnics or potlucks.

Spinach Pasta Salad
Serves: 5 to 6

3/4 pound spinach noodles
1 tablespoon olive oil
4 tomatoes, chopped
1 red or green pepper, chopped
1 small onion, chopped
1 cup chopped parsley
1 (2½-ounce) can sliced black
  olives
1 (6½-ounce) jar marinated
  artichoke hearts, chopped and
  drained
8 ounces feta cheese, crumbled

  Dressing:
1/4 cup olive oil
1 tablespoon sugar
1/4 cup white wine
2 tablespoons lemon juice
1 teaspoon basil
1 teaspoon salt
1 teaspoon pepper

Cook noodles in water with olive oil until soft. Rinse with cold water and drain. In a mixing bowl, combine noodles, tomatoes, green pepper, onion, parsley, olives and artichokes.

For dressing: In a medium size mixing bowl, combine olive oil, sugar, wine, lemon juice, basil, salt and pepper. Fold vegetable-noodle mixture into dressing. Sprinkle feta cheese over top and serve.

Japanese Cucumber Salad
Serves: 6

2 large cucumbers, peeled
1/4 teaspoon salt
6 tablespoons cider vinegar
6 tablespoons sugar
2 tablespoons toasted sesame
  seeds

Cut cucumbers into very thin slices. Layer slices in a bowl. Sprinkle with salt. Let sit for 10 minutes. Rinse out salt from cucumbers. Add vinegar and sugar; toss. Refrigerate. Garnish with toasted sesame seeds.

Tomato-Mozzarella Platter
Serves: 6 to 8

Dressing:
1/2 cup mayonnaise
3 tablespoons white wine vinegar
2 tablespoons vegetable oil
2 tablespoons milk
1 teaspoon sugar

Salad:
1 teaspoon fresh minced basil
  or
1/4 teaspoon dried basil
3 medium tomatoes, sliced
1 medium cucumber, sliced
1 (8-ounce) package sliced
  mozzarella cheese
Fresh basil or spinach leaves
  (washed and dried)

Whisk together dressing ingredients in a small bowl and chill for 1 hour. Line a platter with the basil and/or spinach leaves. Arrange alternating layers of tomatoes, cucumbers and cheese (domino-style). Spoon dressing over salad and serve.

Green Bean and Walnut Salad
Serves: 4

1½ pounds fresh green beans
1/2 cup fresh mint leaves
3/4 cup olive oil
1/4 cup white wine vinegar
3/4 teaspoon salt
1/4 teaspoon pepper
1/2 teaspoon crushed garlic
1 cup coarsely chopped walnuts
1 cup red onion slices
1 cup feta cheese, crumbled

Blanch green beans for 4 to 5 minutes; chill. Chop mint leaves. Add to the green beans; set aside.

For dressing: Combine oil, vinegar, salt, pepper and garlic. Add walnuts, red onion and feta cheese to beans. Pour dressing over bean mixture and toss to coat. Chill until ready to serve.

Marinated Asparagus
Serves: 4

1/2 cup salad oil
4 tablespoons red wine vinegar
1 teaspoon salt
1 teaspoon dry mustard
1 tablespoon grated onion
1 tablespoon chopped pimiento
4 slices bacon, fried crisp and
   crumbled (optional)
1 pound asparagus, cooked to
   tender-crisp
Butter lettuce leaves
   (optional)

In a bowl or jar, combine oil, vinegar, salt, mustard and onion; shake or stir well. Add pimiento. Place cooked asparagus in a shallow dish, pour marinade over all. Marinate in refrigerator for a minimum of 4 hours (or overnight). To serve: Remove asparagus from marinade. Arrange stalks on plates or on a platter of butter lettuce leaves. Pour remaining marinade over asparagus and sprinkle lightly with crisp fried bacon crumbles.

Sunchoke Salad
Serves: 6

Lemon mayonnaise:
   (makes 1 cup)
1 egg
1/2 teaspoon grated lemon peel
1/2 teaspoon dry mustard
1/2 teaspoon salt
1/4 teaspoon oregano
2 tablespoons lemon juice
1/4 cup olive oil
3/4 cup salad oil

Salad:
6 Jerusalem artichokes
1/4 cup sliced green onion
1/4 cup shredded carrot
1 tablespoon capers
3/4 cup lemon mayonnaise
Red lettuce leaves

For lemon mayonnaise: Using a food processor blend egg, add lemon peel, mustard, salt, oregano, lemon juice and olive oil. Cover and blend on low, immediately removing top and slowly pouring in salad oil in a steady stream. Blend until smooth and thickened.

For salad: Peel sunchokes and shred coarsely. Toss with onion, carrot and capers. Blend in ¾ cup lemon mayonnaise. Chill mixture well. To serve: Line a bowl with red lettuce leaves. Put salad in center.

Antipasto Salad
Serves: 10 to 12

12 ounces rotini pasta
1/2 to ¾ bottle Bernsteins
  garlic cheese dressing
2 (6-ounce) jars marinated
  artichoke hearts, drained and
  cut in half
1 can black olives, drained
4 ounces feta cheese, crumbled
3 ounces dry sliced salami, cut
  in strips
1/2 green pepper, chopped
4 green onions, sliced
10 cherry tomatoes

Cook rotini pasta according to package directions. Mix all ingredients together and serve. (This can be made a few hours ahead of serving.)

Artichoke Wild Rice Salad
Serves: 6 to 8

1 (5-ounce) package wild and
  white rice mix
1 (6½-ounce) jar artichoke
  hearts, drained
12 to 15 cherry tomatoes
3 cups chopped green onions

  Dressing:
1/4 cup wine vinegar
1/2 cup oil
2 teaspoons minced parsley
1 teaspoon tarragon leaves

Cook rice according to package directions. Cut artichoke hearts into bite-size pieces. In a large bowl, combine rice, artichokes, tomatoes and onions. Cover and refrigerate overnight. Mix dressing ingredients, pour over salad, toss and serve.

Aspen Village Salad
Serves: 8

1 large head romaine lettuce,
   shredded
1 cup shredded medium cheddar
   cheese
8 ounces shredded Monterey Jack
   cheese
1/2 cup sliced, pitted black olives
12 ounces jicama, peeled and
   julienned
2½ pounds cooked chicken
   breasts, boned, skinned and
   shredded
1 cup fresh salsa (or canned
   picante sauce)
2 ripe avocados, peeled and cubed
1/2 cup mayonnaise
2/3 cup sour cream
1/2 teaspoon ground cumin
2 tablespoons fresh, chopped
   cilantro
2 medium tomatoes, seeded and
   chopped
2 cups tortilla chips (garnish)
Shredded medium cheddar cheese
   (garnish)

On a large plater, mound the following ingredients which have been gently combined with the salsa: Lettuce, cheeses, olives, jicama and chicken. Refrigerate for 2 hours, until well-chilled. Just before serving, add avocados to top of the salad mixture. Mix together mayonnaise, sour cream and cumin and pour over salad to cover. Sprinkle chopped cilantro and tomatoes over dressed salad. Garnish with tortilla chips around the platter. Sprinkle extra cheddar cheese around in a circle next to the tortilla chips.

Cabbage Salad Oriental

Serves: 6

1 (3-ounce) package chicken
flavor oriental noodles
4 cups shredded cabbage
1/4 cup chopped green onions
2 tablespoons sesame seeds

Dressing:
Seasoning packet from noodles
3 tablespoons vinegar
2 tablespoons sugar
2 tablespoons salad oil
1/2 teaspoon ground white pepper
1/4 teaspoon salt
1/2 cup toasted, slivered almonds
1 to 2 cups cooked chicken, cubed
(optional)

Crush noodles slightly; place in colandar. Pour boiling water over noodles to soften slightly. Drain well. In a large bowl, combine noodles, cabbage, onions and sesame seeds.

For dressing: Combine seasoning packet from noodles, vinegar, sugar, oil, pepper and salt; mix well. Pour over cabbage mixture and toss to coat. You may add the cubed chicken, if desired. Cover and chill several hours or overnight. Before serving, stir in almonds.

Cheese Tortellini Salad

Serves: 6

1 (9-ounce) package cheese
tortellini
1½ cups fresh broccoli florets
1/4 cup chopped fresh parsley
1½ tablespoons chopped pimiento
1 (6½-ounce) jar marinated
artichoke hearts, undrained
3 green onions, chopped
1/4 teaspoon dried basil
1/2 cup Bernsteins Cheese and
Garlic Dressing
10 cherry tomatoes, halved
1/4 to 1/2 cup grated parmesan
cheese
1 (4¼-ounce) can sliced ripe olives

Cook tortellini according to package directions. Drain and rinse with cold water. Place cooled tortellini in a 2 to 3-quart bowl and add broccoli, parsley, pimiento, artichoke hearts, green onions and basil. Pour salad dressing over all and toss to coat well. Cover and refrigerate for 3 hours or overnight. Just before serving, add tomatoes, parmesan cheese and olives, toss to mix.

Chicken Curry Salad
Serves: 6

1/2 cup rice
1 teaspoon curry powder
2 tablespoons salad oil
1 tablespoon vinegar
1/4 cup minced onion
2 cups cooked chicken, diced
2 cups chopped celery
1/4 cup diced green pepper
3/4 cup mayonnaise
1/2 teaspoon salt
Dash of pepper

Cook rice according to package directions and cool. Blend curry powder, salad oil, vinegar and mix with rice, onion and chicken. Chill. Just before serving, add celery, green pepper, mayonnaise, salt and pepper. Mix well. Serve on lettuce leaves.

Chinese Chicken and Won Ton Salad
Serves: 4

Dressing:
1/3 cup cider vinegar
4 teaspoons sugar
1 teaspoon salt or soy sauce
1/4 teaspoon pepper
1/3 cup vegetable oil
1/3 cup sesame oil

Salad:
1/4 cup sesame seeds
10 won ton skins
1/3 cup vegetable oil
3 cups cooked chicken breasts,
  cut into chunks
4 green onions, sliced
1 medium red pepper, seeded and
  diced
4 cups shredded romaine lettuce
Sesame seeds (garnish)

For dressing: Combine vinegar, sugar, salt or soy sauce and pepper. Whisk in vegetable and sesame oils. Cover and refrigerate. Toast sesame seeds and set aside.

Cut won ton skins in ½-inch strips. Heat next ⅓ cup vegetable oil in frying pan. Fry strips, a few at a time, until light brown. Drain on paper towels. Combine chicken, green onions, red pepper and lettuce. Pour ½ of the dressing over salad and toss gently. Add won ton strips and toss. Sprinkle with additional sesame seeds. Serve remaining dressing on the side.

Chinese Pasta Salad
Serves: 8 to 10

Dressing:
- 1 clove garlic
- 1 piece of fresh ginger (size of a quarter)
- 1 tablespoon sesame oil
- 1/3 cup soy sauce
- 1 teaspoon sugar
- 1 tablespoon fresh lemon juice
- 1 teaspoon grated lemon peel
- 1 to 2 teaspoons dry mustard
- 2 shakes Tabasco
- 3 tablespoons rice vinegar
- 1/2 cup salad oil

Salad:
- 3 whole chicken breasts
- 1 pound cooked fresh fettucine noodles
- 4 scallions, sliced thin with tops
- 2 to 3 stalks celery, sliced thinly on diagonal
- 1/4 to 1/2 cup finely chopped cilantro
- 1/4 cup chopped fresh parsley
- 1/4 cup toasted sesame seeds

For dressing: In food processor, with machine running, drop in garlic and ginger; pulse to mince. Add remaining ingredients, except salad oil and blend. With machine running, add oil slowly so it incorporates well. Store dressing in a covered jar in refrigerator.

For salad: Skin chicken breasts. Poach or cook in microwave. Cool chicken, remove from bones and cut into bite-size pieces. Refrigerate if prepared ahead. Cook pasta according to package directions; drain. (You may want to cut pasta into 6 to 8-inch lengths to make serving easier). Marinate chicken pieces in the dressing for 3 to 4 hours, but not overnight. To assemble the salad, put pasta in bowl, add scallions, celery, cilantro, parsley and all but 2 tablespoons of the sesame seeds. Add chicken and dressing. Toss to distribute evenly and coat with dressing. Sprinkle with reserved sesame seeds.

Curried Turkey and Grapes
Serves: 4

2¼ cups cooked turkey, cut
   in ½-inch cubes
1 cup thinly sliced celery
1 cup red seedless grapes
1 (8-ounce) can pineapple
   chunks, drained
1 cup chopped cashews or
   almonds
1½ teaspoons lemon juice
1/2 cup mayonnaise
1/2 teaspoon curry powder
1/2 teaspoon dry mustard
4 red lettuce leaves
4 cups salad greens, small pieces
4 tablespoons chopped cashews or
   almonds
4 small bunches grapes (garnish)

Combine turkey, celery, grapes, pineapple and nuts. In another bowl, combine lemon juice, mayonnaise, curry and dry mustard. Combine the two mixtures and mix well. Line 4 plates with red lettuce leaves and divide salad greens evenly. Mound the turkey mixture evenly on each of the 4 plates. Sprinkle with chopped nuts and garnish with bunches of grapes.

Dilled Bow-Tie Pasta Salad
Serves: 6

4 ounces uncooked farfalle
   (bow-shaped pasta)
1/2 cup grated cheddar cheese
1/2 cup sliced celery
1/2 cup sliced green pepper
2 tablespoons chopped pimiento
1/2 cup mayonnaise
1/2 teaspoon dill weed
1/8 teaspoon salt
   Pepper to taste

Cook pasta, drain and cool. In a large bowl, combine pasta, cheese, celery, green pepper and pimiento. In a separate bowl, combine mayonnaise, dill weed, salt and pepper. Pour dressing over pasta mixture. Toss lightly to coat. Chill and serve.

Dilly Chicken Salad

Serves: 6

Dressing:
1/3 cup mayonnaise
1/4 cup plain yogurt
1/4 cup chopped fresh dill
or
1 tablespoon dried dill weed
1/4 teaspoon salt

Salad:
2½ cups cubed cooked chicken
4 ounces fresh broccoli florets,
  blanched
2 medium tomatoes, cut in wedges
1 medium cucumber, peeled, seed-
  ed and chopped
4 ounces snow peas
1/3 cup chopped red onion
5 cups freshly torn spinach
1/2 cup toasted slivered almonds
  (optional)

For dressing: Mix mayonnaise, yogurt, dill and salt; set aside.

In a large bowl, mix chicken, broccoli, tomatoes, cucumber, snow peas and red onions; toss with dressing and chill. Arrange chicken salad on torn spinach and sprinkle with slivered almonds, if desired.

Ginger Chicken Salad

Serves: 4

3 pounds chicken breasts
4 green onions, cut into 4-inch
  lengths
5 slices of ginger root, cut into
  ⅛-inch slices
1 cup water
Cold water
1/2 cup Dijon mustard
1/2 cup oil
1 tablespoon sesame oil
1½ teaspoons sherry

Place chicken breasts in a large skillet, skin side down in a single layer. In a food processor, purée onions and ginger with 1 cup of water and pour over chicken. Add cold water to just cover the chicken. Bring to a boil, reduce heat and simmer until cooked through, about 25 minutes. Plunge chicken into ice water and cool quickly to room temperature. Skin and bone chicken cut cross-wise into diagonal pieces. In a bowl, whisk together mustard, oils and sherry. Spoon over chicken and serve on a bed of lettuce.

Metropol Chicken Salad

Serves: 3 to 4

1 pound boneless chicken breast
2 cups chicken stock
1 green apple, chopped
    Juice of ½ lemon
2 tablespoons minced celery leaves
1 tablespoon chopped parsley
1/2 cup chopped celery
2 green onions, sliced
1/2 cup mayonnaise
1/2 teaspoon oregano

Poach chicken in broth until just firm. Drain and save broth for other uses. When cool, slice chicken into ¼-inch pieces. Toss apple with lemon juice and add to chicken. Mix in celery leaves, parsley, celery, onions, mayonnaise and oregano. Stir well and chill.

Pasta Salad Primavera

Serves: 8 to 10

8 ounces rotelle or ziti pasta
2 to 3 cups broccoli florets
2 to 3 large tomatoes, diced
1 cup frozen tiny peas, thawed
1 cup Italian dressing (Bernsteins
    Cheese and Garlic)
1 tablespoon chopped fresh basil
    or
1 teaspoon dried basil
8 ounces mozzarella cheese, diced
1/2 cup grated fresh parmesan
    cheese
1/2 cup sliced ripe olives
Salt and pepper to taste

Cook pasta. Drain and rinse with cool water. Steam broccoli florets until tender crisp; cool. In a large bowl, combine tomatoes, broccoli, peas, Italian dressing and basil. Add cheeses and macaroni and toss lightly. Add olives and season to taste.

NOTE: Great for picnics or potlucks.

Five Spice Chicken Salad

Serves: 6 to 8

2 whole chicken breasts, skinned and boned

Marinade:
1/4 cup soy sauce
Dash of ginger
1 tablespoon oil
1 clove garlic, crushed
1 teaspoon lemon juice
1 teaspoon five spice

Dressing:
1½ tablespoons sugar
1/4 cup salad oil
1 teaspoon salt
1/2 teaspoon black pepper
3 tablespoons white vinegar
1 tablespoon soy sauce

Salad:
1/2 head cabbage, chopped
2 tablespoons sesame seeds, toasted
2 green onions, finely sliced
1 (3-ounce) package oriental noodles, broken up (without seasonings)

Place whole chicken breasts in marinade and marinate for 2 hours. Place chicken and marinade in a baking dish and bake at 325 degrees for 20 minutes. Cool and cut into bite-size pieces; set aside. Blend all dressing ingredients together and set aside. Mix together salad ingredients adding the chicken pieces. Pour dressing over salad and toss to coat evenly. Refrigerate for ½ hour before serving.

Winter Chicken Salad
Serves: 4

3 cups diced cooked chicken
1 (8-ounce) can sliced water
    chestnuts, drained
1/2 cup thinly sliced celery
2 tablespoons chopped green
    onion
1 egg, hard boiled and diced
3/4 teaspoon freshly grated
    lemon peel
1/2 cup mayonnaise
2 tablespoons orange juice
    concentrate
1/2 teaspoon salt
Lettuce leaves (garnish)
Avocado halves (optional)
Tomato halves (optional)

Mix chicken, water chestnuts, celery, onion, egg and lemon peel. Chill for 1 hour. Mix mayonnaise, orange juice concentrate and salt. Toss this dressing into chilled chicken mixture just before serving. Serve on a bed of lettuce, in avocado halves or tomato shells on lettuce leaves.

Greek Rotini Salad
Serves: 6 to 8

3 cups uncooked rotini
2 tablespoons lemon juice
1/2 cup olive oil
1/4 teaspoon salt
1/4 teaspoon pepper
1/4 teaspoon oregano
2 cloves garlic, minced
2 tomatoes, cut into wedges
1 cucumber, peeled and thinly
    sliced
1 cup thinly sliced green pepper
10 black or green olives
6 ounces feta cheese, crumbled
8 radishes, sliced
1/4 cup sliced green onions
2 tablespoons chopped parsley

Cook pasta, rinse with cold water and drain. In a small bowl, combine lemon juice, oil, salt, pepper, oregano, and garlic. Whip until thick and creamy; chill. In a large bowl, combine pasta, tomato, cucumber, green pepper, olives, feta cheese, radishes, green onions and parsley. Pour dressing over salad and toss gently. Serve immediately.

Pea Salad with Shrimp and Cashews

Serves: 6 to 8

1½ cups cashews
4 cups petite peas, thawed
    and drained
1 cup sliced green onions
2 stalks celery, chopped
3/4 pound salad shrimp
1 (6½-ounce) can sliced
    waterchestnuts

Dressing:
1/4 cup mayonnaise
1/4 cup sour cream
1 tablespoon lemon juice
1 tablespoon fresh dill, minced
    or
1 teaspoon dried dill weed
Salt and pepper to taste

Set aside 2 tablespoons cashews. In a large bowl, stir together remaining cashews, peas, onions, celery, shrimp and water chestnuts.

For dressing: In a bowl, mix mayonnaise, sour cream, lemon juice and dill. Add dill dressing to salad ingredients and stir. Season to taste with salt and pepper. Garnish with reserved cashews.

Peach Tortellini Salad

Serves: 4 to 6

12 ounces fresh or frozen
    cheese tortellini
2 fresh peaches
1/3 cup chopped parsley
1 cup sliced celery

Dressing:
5 tablespoons white vinegar
2 teaspoons fresh basil
2 tablespoons sugar
1½ teaspoons thyme
2 cloves garlic
3/4 teaspoon salt
1/4 teaspoon pepper
1/2 cup oil

Cook tortellini according to package instructions, rinse and drain. Peel and chop peaches into chunks. Mix tortellini, peaches, parsley and celery.

For dressing: In a blender, mix all ingredients, except oil. Slowly add the oil to the blended mixture and blend well. Pour dressing over tortellini mixture.

Pasta Spinach Salad
Serves: 6 to 8

Dressing:
1 egg
1 cup salad oil
1/2 cup grated parmesan cheese
1/4 cup white wine vinegar
1/2 to 1 teaspoon pepper
1/2 teaspoon salt
1/4 teaspoon ground cloves
1 to 2 cloves garlic, minced

Salad:
8 ounces corkscrew macaroni
10 ounces fresh spinach, torn
8 ounces mozzarella cheese, cubed
8 ounces mild pepper ham, cooked ham or thuringer sausage
1 (4-ounce) can diced green chili peppers, drained
Grated parmesan cheese (garnish)

For dressing: Place egg in blender; blend 5 seconds. With blender running, slowly add oil in thin stream, until mixture thickens. Add parmesan cheese, vinegar, pepper, salt, ground cloves and garlic. Blend until smooth.

Cook macaroni according to package instructions; drain. Toss macaroni with dressing. Add remaining ingredients and mix well. Cover and chill. Sprinkle 2 tablespoons parmesan cheese over each serving.

Pasta Spinach Salad

Peachy Chicken Salad
Serves: 3 to 4

1/4 pound snap peas or chinese
  pea pods, cooked
  or
1 (10-ounce) package frozen
  snow peas, thawed and cooked
1/2 cup fresh or canned
  pineapple, well-drained
1 cup seedless red grapes
4 medium fresh peaches (or
  nectarines), sliced
1/2 cup chopped pecans
1/3 cup lite mayonnaise
1/3 cup lowfat plain yogurt
1 tablespoon milk
1 teaspoon soy sauce
3 cups cooked chicken, cut in
  bite-size pieces
Watercress (garnish)
Freshly ground black pepper

Combine well-drained pea pods, pineapple, grapes, peaches and pecans in a mixing bowl. In another bowl, mix mayonnaise, yogurt, milk and soy sauce; mix well. Add dressing to the fruit mixture and toss to coat. Add chicken to the salad and toss to mix. To serve, mound salad on a bed of watercress and garnish with ground pepper. Cover and chill at least 30 minutes before serving.

Seafood Curry Salad
Serves: 6 to 8

1 (16-ounce) package frozen peas
1/2 pound small shrimp
1/2 pound fresh crab
2 cups chopped celery
1 cup bean sprouts
1 (8-ounce) can sliced water
  chestnuts, drained
3 green onions, chopped

  Dressing:
1 cup mayonnaise
1 tablespoon lemon juice
1 teaspoon soy sauce
1 teaspoon curry powder
Garlic, salt and pepper to taste

Rinse frozen peas in water and let drain in colander for ½ hour. Mix all salad ingredients and chill (overnight if necessary). Mix all dressing ingredients together and chill (overnight if necessary). Toss with salad and serve.

Scallop Salad
Serves: 6

1 (1-pound) package corkscrew
  pasta
1½ pounds small or medium bay
  scallops, rinsed and drained
1 cup fresh broccoli florets,
  cut in bite size pieces
1 small yellow bell pepper, thinly
  sliced
1/2 cup sliced mushrooms
1/2 cup grated carrot
1½ teaspoons cajun spice
1 (7-ounce) package Italian salad
  dressing mix

Cook pasta according to package directions; rinse, drain and set aside. Combine scallops, broccoli, bell pepper and mushrooms in a microwave safe dish. Cover and microwave for 5 to 8 minutes on high, stirring once. Scallops and vegetables should be just tender and not over-done; drain well. Place pasta in a large bowl and add scallop-vegetable mixture, carrots and cajun spice; mix well. Make the Italian dressing according to the package directions and add to the pasta mixture; stirring well to coat. Refrigerate for at least 1 hour before serving.

NOTE: This makes a great luncheon or summer dinner salad. You may use any combination of scallops, baby shrimp or crab to equal 1½ pounds.

Cranberry Waldorf Gelatin Salad
Serves: 12 to 18

1 (3-ounce) package red raspberry
  gelatin
1 envelope unflavored gelatin
1 teaspoon cinnamon
1/4 teaspoon salt
1/4 teaspoon ginger
2 cups boiling water
1 cup cold water
2 large apples, peeled and
  chopped
1 cup chopped nuts
1 (4 to 6-ounce) can whole
  cranberry sauce

In a large bowl, combine gelatins and spices. Stir until well mixed. Add boiling water and stir. Add cold water. Refrigerate until thickened, about 1 hour. Stir in apples, nuts and cranberry sauce; mix well so cranberry sauce is blended in. Pour into a 9 x 13-inch pan; chill several hours or overnight.

Crunchy Cranberry Mold

Serves: 10

1 (6-ounce) package cherry jello
1 cup hot water
3/4 cup sugar
1 tablespoon lemon juice
1 tablespoon plain gelatin
    (dissolved in water according
    to package directions)
1 cup pineapple juice
1 cup ground raw cranberries
1 orange, (rind ground fine)
1 cup crushed pineapple, drained
1 cup chopped celery
1/2 cup chopped pecans
Lettuce

Dissolve cherry jello in hot water; add sugar, lemon juice and pineapple juice-gelatin mixture. Stir until blended. Put mixture into a ring mold and chill, until partially set. Mix remaining ingredients and pour into ring mold. To serve, unmold on lettuce leaves.

NOTE: You may want to garnish with turkey or chicken salad. Try using grape leaves in place of lettuce.

Jello A La Grandma

Serves: 8 to 12

1 (11-ounce) can mandarin
    oranges, juice reserved
1 (12 to 16-ounce) can pineapple
    chunks or tidbits, juice reserved
Juice from 1 (6-ounce) can frozen
    orange juice concentrate,
    undiluted
Enough hot water to make 2 cups
    liquid when combined with
    juices
1 (3-ounce) package strawberry
    jello
1 (3-ounce) package orange jello
2 bananas, sliced

Combine juice from mandarin oranges, pineapple and orange juice concentrate. Add hot water to make 2 cups liquid. Make jello with juice mixture and let partially set. Add mandarin oranges, pineapple and bananas. Pour into a 9 x 13-inch pan and set until firm.

Strawberry Salad
Serves: 10

1 (6-ounce) package strawberry
  jello
1½ cups boiling water
1 small can crushed pineapple,
  with juice
2 cups frozen strawberries,
  defrosted, reserve juice
1 cup mashed bananas
1 pint sour cream (no
  substitutes)

Make jello with boiling water, then add juice from pineapple and strawberries. Add fruit. Pour ½ mixture in a 9 x 13-inch dish. Put in refrigerator to chill. Leave rest of mixture out. When mixture is set, layer 1 pint of sour cream over set jello. Pour remaining jello over sour cream. Set up overnight.

Sweet and Spicy French Dressing
Yield: 2 cups

1/2 cup sugar
1 tablespoon flour
1/2 cup cider vinegar
1 teaspoon salt
1 teaspoon Worcestershire sauce
1/2 cup finely chopped onion
1 clove garlic, split
1 cup oil
1/3 cup catsup
1 teaspoon celery seed

In a saucepan, combine sugar, flour and vinegar; cook over medium heat until mixture bubbles and thickens, stirring constantly. Pour into a blender and add salt, Worcestershire, onion and garlic. Whirl until smooth. With blender still running, add the oil in a steady stream. Then blend in catsup and celery seed. Cover and chill.

Italian Dressing
Yield: 1½ cups

1 cup oil
1/3 cup vinegar
2 tablespoons lemon juice
1 teaspoon garlic salt
1 teaspoon sugar
1/2 teaspoon dry mustard
1/2 teaspoon oregano
1/4 teaspoon basil
Freshly ground pepper to taste

Combine all ingredients in a screw top jar. Cover tightly and shake vigorously to blend well. Store in covered container in refrigerator.

Tarragon Dressing
Yield: 1½ cups

1/2 teaspoon dry mustard
1/2 teaspoon paprika
1/4 teaspoon salt
1/2 teaspoon celery seed
1/4 cup honey
1 tablespoon lemon juice
1/4 teaspoon grated onion
1/3 cup tarragon vinegar
1 cup vegetable oil

Mix mustard, paprika, salt and celery seed. Add honey, lemon juice, onion and tarragon vinegar; mix well. Add vegetable oil in a slow, steady stream, whisking constantly. Pour into a jar and store in refrigerator. Shake well before using.

Pat's French Dressing
Yield: 2 cups

1 cup sugar
2 teaspoons dry mustard
2 teaspoons salt
1/2 medium onion, grated
2/3 cup vinegar
2 cups safflower oil
3 tablespoons catsup
2 tablespoons celery seed

In a food processor bowl, mix sugar, mustard, salt, onion and vinegar. On medium speed, gradually pour in oil. Then add catsup and celery seed. Pour into a jar and store in refrigerator. Shake well before using.

Fruit Salad Dressing
Yield: 3/4 cup

1/2 cup plain yogurt
1 tablespoon sugar
1 teaspoon vanilla
1 tablespoon rum
1 tablespoon pineapple juice

Mix ingredients and pour over fruit.

NOTE: This is good over mandarin oranges, fresh pineapple, bananas, apples, peaches, etc.

Berry Honey Dressing
Yield: 1½ cups

1 (3-ounce) package cream cheese
1/4 teaspoon salt
2 tablespoons honey
1/4 cup sour cream
1/2 cup sliced strawberries

For smooth dressing, whip together the cream cheese, salt, honey, sour cream and strawberries. If desired, fold the sliced strawberries into the dressing instead of whipping. Refrigerate until ready to use.

NOTE: Serve over wedges of fresh pineapple, sliced peaches, orange segments or sliced apples.

Creamy Avocado Dressing
Yield: 1¼ cups

1 large ripe avocado, chilled,
    peeled and pitted
1/2 lemon, peeled and seeded
1/2 cup orange juice, unsweetened
2 teaspoons mayonnaise
1/4 teaspoon salt (optional)

Using a food processor with chopping blade or a blender on high speed, process the first 4 ingredients until mixture is smooth. Add salt to taste. Serve immediately. (If made ahead, chill immediately and stir vigorously before serving.)

NOTE: Serve over sliced tomatoes or citrus fruit slices arranged over a bed of lettuce.

Hazelnut Vinaigrette
Yield: 1 cup

1/2 cup toasted, coarsely
  chopped hazelnuts
1/3 cup olive oil
1/4 cup tarragon vinegar
1/4 teaspoon salt
1/4 teaspoon pepper
1/2 clove garlic, minced

Mix ingredients and serve over chilled greens.

Sweet and Sour Poppy Seed Dressing
Servings: 2 cups

1/2 cup fresh lime juice
1/3 cup honey
1 teaspoon poppy seed or
  celery seed
1 teaspoon dry mustard
1/2 teaspoon salt (optional)
1 cup vegetable oil

Place all ingredients, except oil, in a blender and mix well. With the blender on low speed, add oil a few drops at a time. Stop and scrape sides as necessary. When oil is completely incorporated, serve or refrigerate dressing immediately. If made ahead, stir before serving over salad of choice.

NOTE: Serve this dressing over mixed fruits or spinach leaves.

Savor
the Flavor
of
EGGS, CHEESE,
BRUNCH

❦ ❦ ❦

3-Cheese Breakfast Bake
Serves: 8

1/2 loaf french bread (16-ounces)
3 tablespoons unsalted butter,
  melted
1/4 pound Swiss cheese, grated
1/4 pound Monterey Jack cheese,
  grated
8 eggs
1½ cups milk
1/4 cup dry white wine
2 green onions, sliced
1 teaspoon Dijon mustard
1/4 teaspoon pepper
12 thin slices Genoa salami
3/4 cup sour cream
1/3 cup grated parmesan cheese

Lightly oil a 9 x 13-inch baking dish. Cut bread in small chunks and place in baking dish. Drizzle butter over bread and top with grated Swiss and jack cheese. Combine eggs, milk, wine, onions, mustard and pepper. Pour egg mixture over bread chunks and cheese. Top with salami slices. Cover with foil and refrigerate for at least one hour. Bake at 325 degrees for 1 hour. Remove foil and spread top with sour cream and parmesan cheese mixture. Return to oven and bake at 325 degrees for an additional 10 minutes. Allow to set slightly, cut and serve.

Baked Omelet
Serves: 8

1 pound bulk sausage or links,
  cooked
6 eggs
1½ cups milk
1 teaspoon salt
1 teaspoon dry mustard
1 (8-ounce) can sliced mushrooms,
  drained
1½ cups grated sharp cheddar
  cheese
1 tablespoon minced onions
6 slices bread, crusts only

Brown sausage, drain and cool. In a mixing bowl, beat eggs, add milk, salt, mustard, mushrooms, cheese and onions. Add cooked sausage. Cut crusts off of bread and cut into pieces. Add crusts to the egg mixture and mix well. Put in a greased 9 x 12-inch dish. Set overnight. Bake at 350 degrees until firm and brown around the edges, about 30 to 40 minutes.

Baked Sicilian Frittata
Serves: 8

5 medium potatoes, peeled and sliced
4½ tablespoons olive oil
1 cup chopped onion
1/4 cup chopped green pepper
3 cloves garlic, minced
4 cups frozen chopped broccoli
12 eggs
3/4 cup grated parmesan cheese
1/2 cup water
1 teaspoon basil
1/2 teaspoon salt
1/2 teaspoon pepper
1½ cups Monterey Jack cheese

In a skillet, cook potatoes in olive oil for 10 minutes. Add onion, green pepper and garlic; cook until onion is tender. Add broccoli and cook, covered for 5 minutes. In a separate bowl, mix together eggs, parmesan cheese, water, basil, salt, and pepper. Put potato mixture in a large baking dish. Pour egg mixture over top of potato mixture. Sprinkle with Monterey Jack cheese. Bake at 350 degrees for 30 to 35 minutes until eggs set.

Breakfast Pizza
Serves: 6

1 (8-ounce) tube crescent rolls
1 pound bulk sausage
1/4 cup chopped green onions
1/4 cup chopped green peppers
1/2 cup sliced mushrooms
1/2 cup sliced small zucchini
1/2 cup sliced ripe olives
5 eggs, beaten
Salt and pepper to taste
1/4 cup milk
1 cup shredded cheddar cheese

Press rolls into a 9 x 13-inch or 11 x 15-inch glass baking dish and round up on sides a bit. Brown sausage and drain, crumble on top of crust material. Sprinkle green onions, green peppers, mushrooms, zucchini and olives over the sausage. Mix beaten eggs, salt, pepper and milk and pour mixture over all. Top with cheese and bake at 350 degrees for 25 minutes.

NOTE: Great served with fresh fruit.

Breakfast Sandwiches

Serves: 6

12 slices bacon, fried crisp
1/4 cup chopped green onions
5 eggs, hardcooked and chopped
1 cup grated Swiss cheese
1/3 cup mayonnaise
1 tablespoon Dijon mustard
Salt and pepper to taste
Butter
12 slices bread

Crumble bacon. Combine with onions, eggs, cheese, mayonnaise, mustard, salt and pepper. Butter bread for grilling. Divide mixture among 6 slices of bread. Top with remaining bread and grill.

NOTE: This is great served after an evening of bridge, or for a late breakfast.

Buffet Eggs

Serves: 3 to 4

6 hard boiled eggs, shelled
1/2 cup melted butter or margarine
1/2 teaspoon Worcestershire sauce
1/4 teaspoon prepared mustard, regular or brown
2 to 3 green onions, finely chopped, including tops
1 tablespoon minced parsley
3 to 4-ounces sliced cooked ham, finely chopped
Salt and pepper to taste

White Sauce:
4 tablespoons butter
4 tablespoons flour
2 cups milk

Topping:
1 cup grated cheddar cheese
Minced parsley
Minced onion

Cut eggs lengthwise and remove yolks. Mash yolks with butter, worcestershire and mustard. Add onions, parsley and ham to the egg mixture. Season with salt and pepper. Spoon filling into the empty egg whites. Arrange eggs in a buttered casserole dish.

For white sauce: In saucepan, melt butter, add flour and milk; blend until sauce thickens. Pour warm white sauce over eggs. Sprinkle cheese over all. Top with extra minced parsley and/or onions, if desired. Bake, uncovered, at 325 degrees for 25 to 30 minutes.

Crabmeat Quiche

Serves: 6 to 8

Crust:
6 tablespoons butter
2 tablespoons shortening
1½ cups flour
3 to 5 tablespoons very cold water

Filling:
1/2 cup mayonnaise
2 tablespoons flour
2 eggs, beaten
1/2 cup milk
7½ ounces crabmeat, drained and flaked
8 ounces grated Swiss cheese
1/3 cup sliced green onions

For crust: Cut butter and shortening into flour until it resembles cornmeal. Make a well, add 3 tablespoons water. Blend with a fork or pastry blender. If it seems very crumbly, add more water. Roll into a ball, wrap in waxed paper and refrigerate for 15 to 30 minutes. Roll out dough to fit a 9-inch pie or quiche plate.

For filling: Mix the mayonnaise, flour, eggs and milk until well blended. Stir in crabmeat, cheese and onions. Pour into pastry shell. Bake at 350 degrees for 40 to 45 minutes.

Crab Brunch Casserole

Serves: 6

6 to 8-ounces fresh crab meat
2 tablespoons butter or margarine
1/2 cup chopped celery
1/2 cup sliced mushrooms
3 tablespoons flour
1/2 teaspoon salt
1/8 teaspoon pepper
1½ cups milk
1 cup shredded cheddar cheese
2½ cups cooked rice
1/2 cup toasted slivered almonds
1/4 cup buttered bread crumbs

In a heavy skillet, melt butter or margarine. Sauté celery and mushrooms until tender, about 5 minutes. Blend in flour, salt and pepper. Gradually add milk and cook, stirring constantly until thickened and smooth. Add cheese and cook over low heat until melted. Combine crab with cooked rice and almonds; stir into cheese sauce. Turn mixture into a greased baking dish. Top with buttered bread crumbs. Bake at 350 degrees for 35 to 40 minutes.

Crab Soufflé Sandwiches

Serves: 12

4 tablespoons butter
1/3 cup flour
1/4 cup mayonnaise
1 cup sliced mushrooms,
   sautéed in butter
1 pint half and half
6 eggs, separated
3 tablespoons dry sherry
1/2 teaspoon Worcestershire sauce
3/4 teaspoons salt
Freshly ground white pepper
   to taste
1/8 teaspoon cayenne pepper
2½ cups flaked crabmeat
12 slices thin-sliced bread,
   trimmed and buttered on one
   side
1/2 teaspoon salt
1/2 teaspoon cream of tartar
1 cup freshly grated parmesan
   cheese

Melt butter in a large heavy saucepan until foamy. Add flour, blend and cook for 3 minutes. Stir in mayonnaise. In a separate pan, sauté mushrooms (reserve juice); set aside. Add half and half to reserved juices to make 2 cups. Add to flour mixture, cook and stir until well blended and thickened. Remove from heat. In a bowl, beat the egg yolks and sherry together, stir in half the cream mixture, then add this back to the remaining cream sauce. Return pan to heat and stir for 3 minutes, (do not boil). Add worcestershire sauce, salt, pepper, cayenne, mushrooms and crab. Cut buttered bread slices in half diagonally. Place 12 half slices 2-inches apart on a large baking sheet and spread with half the cooled crab mixture. Cover with the other half of the bread and the rest of the crab mixture, (making a two layer, open-face sandwich). Chill. Beat the egg whites with salt until foamy. Add cream of tartar and beat until stiff but not dry. Spread on top and sides of each sandwich, covering each thoroughly. Sprinkle with freshly grated parmesan cheese. Bake at 375 degrees 15 to 20 minutes until lightly browned.

115

Italian Sausage Frittata
Serves: 6 to 8

1 (6-ounce) jar marinated artichoke hearts, liquid reserved

1 medium onion, chopped (about 1 cup)

1 clove garlic, minced

1/2 pound fresh mushrooms, sliced

5 large eggs, well beaten

1/4 teaspoon basil

1/4 teaspoon marjoram

1/4 teaspoon salt

1/4 teaspoon pepper

1 cup shredded mozzarella cheese

2 Italian sausages, skinned, browned, crumbled and well drained

1 (10-ounce) package frozen chopped spinach, thawed and well drained

1 cup freshly grated parmesan cheese

Butter a quiche pan or a 10-inch pie plate. Drain artichoke hearts, reserving 1 tablespoon marinade. Dry artichoke hearts between two paper towels. Sauté onion and garlic in reserved artichoke marinade for about 5 minutes, (until onions are soft). Add artichoke hearts and mushrooms. Cook for an additional 2 to 3 minutes; set aside. In a mixing bowl, combine eggs, basil, marjoram, salt, pepper and mozzarella; set aside. In the bottom of the prepared dish, evenly arrange crumbled sausage and well drained spinach. Evenly distribute cooked vegetables over the sausage and spinach, then pour the egg and cheese mixture over all. Sprinkle the parmesan cheese on top. Bake at 350 degrees for 35 minutes, or until knife inserted in center of fritatta comes out clean. Remove from oven and let stand for 5 to 10 minutes before cutting into wedges.

NOTE: Select sausages that are hot, medium or mild, according to your own taste. This is delicious as a brunch dish with fresh fruit, or as a dinner dish with a green salad and french bread.

JJ's Spinach Quiche Dijon
Serves: 8

Crust:
2 cups all-purpose flour
1/4 teaspoon salt
1/4 pound butter
1 egg
1 tablespoon lemon juice
1 egg yolk

Quiche filling:
1½ to 2 pounds fresh spinach
1/2 teaspoon salt
Nutmeg to taste
1 teaspoon dried tarragon, crushed
1/2 teaspoon lemon juice
1 to 2 tablespoons Dijon mustard
1/2 cup feta cheese, crumbled
1/2 cup minced onion
2 eggs
2 egg yolks
1 cup whipping cream
1 tablespoon chopped parsley

For crust: Sift flour and salt into a bowl. Add butter, cut into small pieces. Mix whole egg with lemon juice, add to flour mixture. Blend using pastry blender, heavy mixer or food processor until butter is incorporated and dough is stiff. Form dough into a ball and chill at least ½ hour. Roll dough for an 9-inch pie pan, trim and crimp edges. (If dough seems too dry or crumbly, it is too chilled, just let it rest briefly at room temperature). Place foil or waxed paper circle inside pie shell and weight it down with uncooked beans or rice. Bake shell at 425 degrees for 18 minutes, then remove beans/rice and foil/waxed paper. Using pastry brush, apply egg yolk to inside of crust. Bake at 425 degrees for an additional 3 minutes. This glazes the crust so it won't get soggy. Let crust cool a little before adding filling.

For filling: Wash spinach thoroughly, allow water to cling to leaves and place in a heavy pan. Cover and wilt spinach over medium heat. (Cook until water comes out and bulk is reduced). Drain spinach on paper towels, pressing out moisture. Chop coarsely and add salt, nutmeg, tarragon and lemon juice. Adjust seasonings to taste. Set aside. Brush inside of crust generously with dijon mustard. Be sure to brush sides of crust. Do not skimp on mustard. Arrange chopped spinach in crust shell and sprinkle crumbled feta cheese uniformly. Sprinkle minced onion over spinach and cheese. Beat eggs and yolks with cream, pour over spinach. Cover spinach but do not overfill shell. Sprinkle chopped parsley on top. Bake at 350 degrees for 35 to 40 minutes or until just set in center. Serve warm or chilled.

Mexican Brunch Casserole
Serves: 6

1 pound ground beef
1/2 cup chopped onions
1/2 teaspoon salt
1/4 teaspoon pepper
2 (4-ounce) cans whole green
   chiles, cut in half, crosswise
   and seeded
1½ cups grated sharp cheddar
   cheese
1/4 cup flour
4 eggs, beaten
1½ cups milk
1/4 teaspoon hot pepper sauce

Brown meat and onions; drain. Add salt and pepper. Place ½ of the chiles in a 10 x 6 x 1½-inch dish and sprinkle with cheese. Top with the beef mixture. Arrange remaining chiles over beef. Combine rest of ingredients and beat until smooth. Pour over chiles. Bake at 350 degrees for 45 to 40 minutes. Cool for 5 to 10 minutes, cut into squares and serve.

NOTE: This dish is great for a Cinco de Mayo brunch.

Rogue River Omelet
Serves: 6

1 pound bulk sausage
1/2 large onion, chopped
1 green pepper, chopped
5 potatoes, sliced or diced
   (skins can be on or off)
10 eggs, beaten
1 to 2 cups grated cheddar cheese

Cook sausage in large pan. Break into small pieces as cooking. Drain off majority of grease. Add onion and pepper. Add potatoes, continue frying all ingredients until potatoes are cooked. Add beaten eggs; continue cooking. When eggs are cooked, add the cheese and cook until melted.

NOTE: This is great for camping as it only takes one pan. It is very adaptable for any size group. For those who like spicy food, this is wonderful topped with salsa.

Sherried Eggs
Serves: 6 to 12

12 medium eggs
12 slices bacon
12 teaspoons dry sherry
12 teaspoons whipping cream
Salt and pepper to taste
12 teaspoons parmesan cheese

Butter a 12 cup muffin tin. Pre-cook bacon so it is limp, not crisp. Place one piece of bacon around inside of each muffin cup. Break an egg into center of cup. (It must be a small or medium egg, as large eggs will not leave enough room for remaining ingredients). Pour 1 teaspoon of sherry into each cup. Pour 1 teaspoon of cream into each cup over sherry. Sprinkle with salt and pepper and top each egg with 1 teaspoon of parmesan cheese. Place muffin tin on a cookie sheet. Bake at 350 degrees for 15 minutes. You may cook this longer depending on how you like your eggs done.

NOTE: This is great served with English muffins and fresh fruit. This can be made ahead. Cover with plastic wrap and place on a cookie sheet in the refrigerator until ready to bake.

Tofu Broccoli Bake
Serves: 6

10 to 12-ounces fresh broccoli,
    cut into florets
1 pound soft tofu
2 eggs
2 cups shredded cheddar cheese
1/2 teaspoon salt
Non-stick vegetable oil spray

Steam broccoli until tender-crisp; set aside. Place remaining ingredients in a food processor or blender and process until smooth. Stir in broccoli florets. Coat a 9-inch pie plate with non-stick vegetable oil spray. Pour mixture into pie plate and bake at 350 degrees for 30 to 40 minutes.

Spanakopita
Serves: 4 to 5

1 small onion, chopped
1 pound butter, divided
1/2 pint cottage cheese
1 pound feta cheese, crumbled
1/2 cup grated parmesan cheese
3 eggs, beaten
1 bunch fresh spinach, chopped
1 teaspoon lemon juice
1 tablespoon chopped fresh
  parsley
1/4 cup chopped scallions
1 (16-ounce) package phyllo dough
1/2 teaspoon fennel or dill

Sauté onion in ½ of the butter; set aside. In a large bowl, crumble cottage and feta cheeses together, mix in parmesan cheese. Add eggs and chopped spinach. Add sautéed onion to cheese, egg and spinach mixture. Add lemon juice, parsley and scallions. In another pan, melt the other ½ of the butter; set aside. Butter a 9 x 13-inch baking dish. Layer phyllo in bottom and up sides of baking dish topping each layer with melted butter. Repeat, making 8 layers. Top with a layer of the spinach mixture. Repeat with 8 more layers of phyllo and butter. Top with another layer of the spinach mixture. Repeat with phyllo, butter and spinach mixture, until you reach the top of the dish, (ending with phyllo). Mark with cross-cuts and sprinkle with fennel or dill. Bake at 350 degrees for 50 minutes or until golden brown. Allow to set for 5 minutes, then cut and serve.

Yogurt Pancakes with Blueberries or Fresh Fruit
Serves: 3

1 cup flour
1/2 teaspoon baking soda
1 tablespoon sugar
1 teaspoon baking powder
1/8 teaspoon nutmeg
1/2 cup plain yogurt
1/2 cup milk
1 tablespoon oil
1 egg
3/4 cup fresh blueberries or
  other fresh fruit

Mix all ingredients except fruit. Bake pancakes on a hot, well-oiled griddle. Serve pancakes with fresh fruit.

Swedish Pancakes

Serves: 4

1½ cups flour
3 tablespoons sugar
1/2 teaspoon salt
3 eggs
2 cups milk
2 tablespoons butter, melted
Maple Syrup
Strawberries
Whipped cream

Mix dry ingredients together. Add eggs and milk; mix well. Add melted butter; mix well. Batter will be thin. Cook pancakes in skillet or on a griddle. Serve with maple syrup or strawberries and whipped cream.

Poppy Seed Pancakes

Serves: 8

4 cups stone ground whole
   wheat flour
1/2 cup brown sugar, packed
1/2 cup poppy seeds
4½ teaspoons baking powder
1 tablespoon salt
6 eggs
3¾ cups milk
3½ teaspoons vanilla
1½ cups soybean oil

Mix first five ingredients in a large bowl. In another bowl, mix eggs, milk, vanilla and oil well with electric mixer. Pour into dry ingredients and mix well. Heat griddle to medium heat. Brush lightly with oil. Ladle ¾ cup batter onto griddle and cook until bubbles pop, about 3½ minutes. Turn and cook other side. Transfer to a baking sheet. Keep warm in oven. Serve immediately.

Orange-Vanilla French Toast
Serves: 8

2 cups orange juice
2 cups half and half
6 eggs
1/4 cup sugar
1½ tablespoons Grand Marnier
1/2 teaspoon vanilla
1 (1-pound) loaf of bread, sliced
Butter
Powdered sugar
Maple Syrup

Mix first 6 ingredients together in a large shallow baking dish. Soak each slice of bread thoroughly in the batter (about 30 seconds a side). Cook on a lightly-oiled griddle for about 4 minutes each side. Serve with butter, powdered sugar or maple syrup.

Stuffed French Toast
Serves: 4 to 6

1 (8-ounce) package cream cheese, softened
1 teaspoon vanilla
1/2 cup chopped walnuts
1 (16-ounce) loaf french bread
4 eggs, beaten
1 cup whipping cream
1/2 teaspoon vanilla
1/2 teaspoon nutmeg
1 (12-ounce) jar apricot or orange marmalade
1/2 cup orange juice

Beat cream cheese and vanilla on medium speed. Stir in walnuts. Cut french bread into 1½-inch slices. Cut a pocket in top of each slice. Fill each with 1½ tablespoons of the cheese mixture.

In a separate bowl, mix eggs, cream, vanilla and nutmeg. Dip bread into mixture and cook in a hot skillet. Top with mixture of jam and orange juice.

Jack's French Toast
Serves: 4

1 loaf stale french bread, uncut
4 eggs
3/4 cup Jack Daniel's whiskey
1 tablespoon sugar
Salad oil
Butter
Maple Syrup

Cut 8 slices of bread, ¾-inch thick. Mix eggs, whiskey and sugar. Dip bread in egg mixture. Deep fry in ½-inch deep mixture of ½ oil and ½ butter or fry in a frying pan ½-inch deep in mixture of ½ oil and ½ butter, until golden brown. Serve with maple syrup.

Savor
the
Flavor
of
VEGETABLES

Glazed Acorn Rings

Serves: 6

2 acorn squash
1/3 cup orange juice
1/2 cup brown sugar
1/4 cup corn syrup
1/4 cup butter
2 teaspoons grated lemon rind
1/8 teaspoon salt

Cut ends off of squash. Cut crosswise into 1-inch slices and remove seeds. Place in single layer in large, shallow baking dish and add orange juice. Cover and bake at 350 degrees for 30 minutes. Combine remaining ingredients in a small saucepan; simmer 5 minutes. Pour over squash and bake, uncovered, for an additional 15 minutes, basting occasionally.

Calico Beans

Serves: 8

1 pound bacon
1 cup chopped onion
2 garlic cloves, minced
1/2 cup catsup
3/4 cup brown sugar
1 teaspoon salt
1 teaspoon dry mustard
2 teaspoons vinegar
1 (15-ounce) can kidney beans, drained
1 (15-ounce) can lima beans, drained
1 (15-ounce) can butter beans, drained
1 (15-ounce) can baked beans, drained

Brown bacon, pour off half of the grease. Add onion and garlic, cook until onion is tender. Add catsup, brown sugar, salt, mustard and vinegar. Add drained beans. Mix well and bake in a covered dish, at 350 degrees for 40 minutes.

Broccoli Parmesan

Serves: 6

1½ pounds broccoli
2 tablespoons butter
1 tablespoon minced onion
2 tablespoons flour
1/2 teaspoon salt
Ground black pepper
1/2 teaspoon dry mustard
1/8 teaspoon marjoram
1 chicken bouillon cube
1½ cups milk
1/2 cup grated parmesan cheese
Paprika

Steam broccoli until tender. Meanwhile, heat butter in a saucepan. Add onion and cook until soft. Blend in a mixture of the flour, salt, pepper, mustard and marjoram; add bouillon cube. Add milk gradually. Heat until mixture bubbles, stirring constantly. Remove from heat and add ⅓ cup of cheese, stirring until melted. Arrange broccoli in a shallow baking dish. Pour sauce over broccoli, sprinkle with remaining cheese, then with paprika. Broil about 3-inches from heat for 4 minutes, until cheese is melted and bubbly.

Carrot and Onion Broil

Serves: 4

2 tablespoons butter or margarine
2 cups thinly sliced carrots
2 cups thinly sliced onions
Dill weed

Put butter into a shallow baking pan. Set 6 inches below the broiler and heat to melt butter. Add carrots and onions to melted butter. Toss, then put under broiler and cook for about 15 minutes, (tossing vegetables every 3 to 4 minutes). If carrots and onions begin to look dry, add a bit more margarine to keep them coated as they cook. When carrots are tender-crisp, sprinkle vegetables with fresh or dried dill weed and serve.

Ginger Glazed Carrots

Serves: 4

6 to 8 carrots (about ½ pound)
1/4 cup butter
1/4 cup honey
1 tablespoon chopped preserved
    ginger root (crystalized ginger)

Peel and diagonally slice carrots to ¼-inch thickness. Steam carrots until barely tender (about 10 minutes); drain. Sauté carrots, butter, honey and ginger over medium-high heat; stirring frequently until browned and well glazed (approximately 3 to 5 minutes).

Dilled Carrots

Serves: 8 to 10

2 pounds (5 or 6 large) carrots,
    cut in 1½-inch chunks
1 cup white vinegar
2 tablespoons sugar
2 teaspoons salt
1 teaspoon dried dill
Freshly ground pepper to taste
1 tablespoon chopped parsley

Steam carrots until just tender (about 10 to 15 minutes). Rinse with cold water to stop cooking, then place in a small bowl with cover. Combine remaining ingredients (except parsley) and pour over carrots. Cover and refrigerate overnight. Drain and serve topped with parsley.

Carrots with Pistachios

Serves: 6

2 tablespoons butter
1/2 cup shelled and skinned
    pistachio nuts
1/4 cup Cointreau, Triple Sec
    or Grand Marnier
1 pound carrots, peeled and cut
    into ¼-inch diagonal slices
3 tablespoons butter
3 tablespoons water
1 teaspoon salt

Melt butter in medium skillet. Sauté nuts for one minute. Stir in Cointreau. Remove from heat and set aside. Place carrots, butter, water and salt in a saucepan. Bring to a boil, reduce heat to medium-low and simmer for 5 minutes until carrots are barely tender. Transfer carrots to a heated serving bowl with a slotted spoon. Bring carrot liquid to a boil and reduce to 2 tablespoons liquid. Pour juice over carrots, add nut glaze and toss.

Cauliflower Soufflé
Serves: 6 to 8

1 large head cauliflower
3/4 cup grated cheddar cheese
4 eggs, separated
1 teaspoon sugar
1/2 teaspoon salt
1/8 teaspoon pepper
Paprika (garnish)

White Sauce:
1½ cups medium white sauce
3 tablespoons butter
3 tablespoons flour
1½ cups milk

Cook cauliflower until barely tender and cut into 1 to 2-inch bite-size pieces. In a saucepan over medium heat, melt butter, stir in flour and cook for 1 minute. While stirring, add milk and cook, stirring, until thickened. To sauce, add cheese, egg yolks, sugar, salt and pepper. Beat egg whites until stiff and fold into sauce mixture. Put cauliflower into a 1½ to 2-quart soufflé dish; pour sauce over the top. Bake, uncovered at 350 degrees for 20 to 30 minutes until soufflé is set. Garnish with paprika.

Eggplant Casserole
Serves: 6

1 eggplant (1½ pound)
1/3 cup vegetable oil
6 slices bacon
1 large onion, chopped
1 medium green pepper, chopped
1/2 pound mushrooms, sliced
1 clove garlic, minced
1 (1-pound) can tomatoes
1/2 teaspoon cumin
2 tablespoons brown sugar
1/2 teaspoon salt
1 cup shredded Monterey Jack
  cheese

Wash eggplant, peel and slice ½-inch thick. Grease cookie sheet and place eggplant slices in a single layer. Brush them with the oil and bake, uncovered, at 450 degrees for 20 minutes. Cook bacon until crispy; drain and crumble. Use 2 tablespoons of the bacon drippings to sauté onion, green pepper, mushrooms and garlic, until onion is tender. Stir in tomatoes (break up with spoon), cumin, brown sugar and salt. Cook over medium heat, uncovered, until most of the liquid has evaporated. Layer the baked eggplant, bacon and sauce in a 9 x 12-inch lightly greased casserole dish. Top with the cheese and bake, uncovered, at 350 degrees for 15 minutes.

Eggplant Parmigiana

Serves: 4 to 6

1 large eggplant
1 teaspoon salt
2 to 3 tablespoons oil
2 (8-ounce) cans tomato sauce
1 clove garlic, minced
1 teaspoon Italian seasoning
1/2 cup freshly grated parmesan
cheese
12 ounces mozzarella cheese,
sliced

Peel the eggplant and cut crosswise into ½-inch slices. Sprinkle with salt, then place in a colander to drain for 30 minutes or more. Pat dry with paper towels. Heat oil and sauté eggplant until browned on both sides. Place in a single layer in an oiled casserole dish. Mix tomato sauce, garlic and Italian seasoning; pour over and around the eggplant slices. Sprinkle with parmesan cheese and top with mozzarella slices. Bake at 350 degrees for 30 minutes.

Mushrooms in Wine Sauce

Serves: 4 to 6

1 pound fresh mushrooms
2 medium green bell peppers
1 medium onion
1/2 cup margarine

Sauce:
2 tablespoons Dijon-style mustard
1/2 cup brown sugar
2 tablespoons Worcestershire
sauce
3/4 cup mellow red table wine
1/8 teaspoon ground pepper

Wash mushrooms and cut in half. Cut peppers into 1-inch squares. Chop onion coarsely. Melt margarine and sauté onion until transparent. Add mushrooms and peppers to onions and sauté 10 to 15 minutes, stirring often. Mix together mustard, brown sugar and worcestershire until smooth. Add wine and pepper and stir well. Add wine sauce when mushrooms begin to brown and shrink. Simmer for 45 minutes or until sauce is much reduced and thickened. Mushrooms and peppers will be very dark.

NOTE: Good as a side dish with steak or roast beef or over fresh pasta as a main course.

Wonderful Onion Rings
Serves: 4

1 cup beer
1 cup all-purpose flour
3/4 teaspoon salt
2 large onions, cut into rings
Oil for frying

Mix the beer, flour and salt together well. Cover and let stand at room temperature for 3 hours. Put the onion rings in a bowl of ice water in the refrigerator for 2 hours. When you are ready to cook, drain and dry the onion rings. Dip them in the batter and fry in hot oil until golden brown.

NOTE: This batter is wonderful for cooking all vegetables and fish.

Potato and Broccoli Vinaigrette
Serves: 4 to 6

4 medium potatoes, peeled and
    cut into 1-inch cubes
1 bunch broccoli (1 to 1½
    pounds), trimmed and broken
    into small branches, blanched
1/2 cup oil
1/4 cup cider vinegar
1 clove garlic, minced
1½ teaspoon salt
1 teaspoon basil
1/8 teaspoon liquid hot pepper
    sauce
2 green onions, sliced
Cherry tomatoes (garnish)

In a saucepan over medium heat, cook potatoes, covered, in boiling water until tender. Drain and keep hot. In a small saucepan, combine remaining ingredients, except tomatoes. Bring just to boiling over medium heat, stirring. Arrange hot potatoes and broccoli in serving dish; pour hot vinegar mixture over and toss gently. Garnish with tomatoes.

Roasted Garlic Potatoes
Serves: 6 to 8

6 large potatoes, peeled and cut
  in quarters
2 tablespoons oil
6 cloves garlic, peeled and
  lightly crushed
Salt and pepper to taste

Place potatoes in water (to cover), and bring to a boil for 2 minutes. Drain thoroughly and cool. Preheat oven to 400 degrees. Spread oil over bottom of heavy large pan, which will hold potatoes in a single layer. Add crushed garlic cloves. Roast in oven for about 45 minutes, shaking pan and turning potatoes several times, until potatoes are golden brown and tender. Remove garlic cloves if they begin to turn dark brown. Sprinkle with salt and pepper, if desired. Add a little more oil if pan seems dry.

Potato Soufflé
Serves: 6 to 8

2 cups mashed potatoes
1 (8-ounce) package cream cheese,
  softened
2 eggs
1 small onion, diced
2 tablespoons flour
Salt and pepper to taste
1 (2-ounce) can French fried
  onions

When making mashed potatoes, use about ½ as much milk as usual. In a large bowl, combine potatoes, softened cheese, eggs, diced onions, flour, salt and pepper. Beat at low speed until fluffy and light. Pour into greased 9-inch round baking dish. Sprinkle French fried onions over top. Bake at 300 degrees for 35 minutes.

Cheddar Potato Bake

Serves: 10 to 12

6 medium potatoes, whole and
  unpeeled
1/3 cup chopped green onions
1/4 cup butter, melted
1 (10¾-ounce) can cream of
  chicken soup
1½ cups grated cheddar cheese
1 pint sour cream

Boil potatoes until firm, not soft. Grate potatoes. Mix all ingredients and put into a greased casserole dish. Bake at 350 degrees for 45 minutes.

Confetti Stuffed Potatoes

Serves: 8

4 medium size baking potatoes
3 tablespoons milk
1 cup plain yogurt
2 tablespoons sliced green onions
2 cups grated carrots
4 slices bacon, fried crisp and
  crumbled
Salt and pepper to taste
1 cup grated cheddar cheese

Clean potatoes and bake until just done. Cut potatoes in half lengthwise and scoop out leaving about ¼-inch shell. Set shells aside. Mash potatoes until smooth, then beat in milk and yogurt. Stir in onions, carrots, and bacon. Salt and pepper to taste. Mound mixture into skins and top with cheese. Heat at 400 degrees until hot and cheese melts.

Overnight Potatoes

Serves: 6 to 8

8 medium potatoes
1 pint sour cream
6 green onions, chopped
1½ cups grated cheddar cheese
Salt and pepper to taste
Paprika

Peel, boil and shred potatoes. Butter a 2-quart casserole dish. Add potatoes, sour cream, onion, 1 cup cheese, salt and pepper; mix well. Cover and refrigerate overnight. Uncover and sprinkle with paprika. Bake at 350 degrees for 45 minutes. Sprinkle with remaining ½ cup cheese and bake an additional 15 minutes.

Broiled Parmesan Potatoes
Serves: 4

2 tablespoons margarine or butter, melted
1 teaspoon dried basil, crushed
1/2 teaspoon paprika
1/4 teaspoon garlic powder
1/8 teaspoon pepper
2 medium potatoes, diagonally sliced to ¼-inch thick
1/4 cup grated parmesan or romano cheese

Stir together margarine or butter, basil, paprika, garlic powder and pepper. Place potato slices in a single layer on the unheated rack of a broiler pan. Brush margarine mixture over both sides of potato slices. Broil about 5-inches from the heat for 8 to 9 minutes until potatoes begin to brown. Turn potatoes, using a wide spatula. Sprinkle with cheese. Broil for an additional 4 to 6 minutes until potatoes are tender.

Mike's Barbecue Potatoes
Serves: 4

4 to 5 medium russet potatoes
2 to 3 carrots
1/2 onion
Non-stick vegetable oil spray
2 tablespoons vegetable oil
3 to 4 tablespoons dry onion soup mix
3/4 teaspoon lemon pepper
1/2 teaspoon seasoning salt
4 tablespoons margarine

Clean potatoes. Slice unpeeled potatoes lengthwise into ½-inch spears. Peel and slice carrots into spears. Peel and slice onion into ¼-inch thick rings. Spray a 12 x 24-inch piece heavy duty foil with non-stick vegetable oil spray. Cover foil with oil, then layer with potatoes, carrots and onion. Sprinkle with soup mix, lemon pepper, and seasoning salt. Dot with margarine. Bring edges of foil together and fold to make leakproof packet. Place on rack of barbecue 4 to 5-inches above coals. Cook until potatoes are tender, about 1 hour, or, bake in a 400 degree oven for about 1 hour.

Steamed Vegetable Medley
Serves: 4 to 6

6 small red new potatoes
   (each about 2¼-inches in
   diameter, 1 pound total weight)
3/4 pound carrots
3 fresh lemon slices
2 bay leaves
6 large cloves garlic, peeled
3/4 pound brussels sprouts
   (about 1-inch in diameter)
2 tablespoons margarine, softened
1 teaspoon chopped parsley
1 teaspoon chicken bouillon
   granules
   or
1 chicken bouillon cube
1/4 teaspoon savory
1/4 teaspoon dried mint (optional)
1/4 teaspoon coarsely ground
   black pepper

Scrub potatoes, do not peel; cut in half. Peel carrots and slice diagonally about ¼-inch thick. Layer potatoes and carrots in a steamer. Arrange lemon slices, bay leaves and garlic on top. Cover and steam for 20 to 30 minutes, until partially cooked. Add trimmed brussels sprouts and continue steaming for 10 to 15 minutes until vegetables are tender-crisp. Mix margarine, parsley, bouillon, savory, mint and pepper; set aside. Put vegetables in serving dish; discarding lemon and bay leaves, and reserving garlic. Mash two of the cooked garlic cloves and mix into the margarine mixture. Toss margarine mixture with vegetables until blended. Serve.

Summer Vegetable Pot
Serves: 6 to 8

4 ears fresh corn, cut from cob
5 medium fresh tomatoes, unpeeled, cut in ¼-inch slices
6 to 7 small zucchini, cut lengthwise into 4 pieces
2 medium onions, sliced in thin
   rings
2 cloves garlic, minced
Salt and pepper to taste
Lemon pepper to taste
1/2 cup butter

Put corn, tomatoes, zucchini and onions into a large earthenware casserole. Add garlic, salt, pepper and lemon pepper; mix vegetables carefully together. Dot with butter, cover and bake at 325 degrees for 45 minutes.

Steamed Vegetable Medley

Mixed Garden Vegetable Stir-Fry
Serves: 6

2 cups carrots, sliced
2 cups green beans, cut into thirds
2 cups cauliflowerettes
2 tablespoons cold water
2 teaspoons cornstarch
2 tablespoons soy sauce
1 tablespoon dry sherry or brandy
2 teaspoons sugar
2 tablespoons vegetable oil
1 medium onion, cut into wedges
1 cup zucchini, thinly sliced
Pepper to taste

Cook carrots and beans in boiling water for 3 minutes; add cauliflower, cook an additional 2 minutes. (Vegetables should be tender-crisp.) Remove from heat; drain and set aside. In a small dish, blend water and cornstarch. Add soy sauce, sherry, sugar and pepper; set aside. Preheat a large skillet or wok over high heat. Add vegetable oil. Stir fry onion for 1 minute, add previously cooked vegetables and zucchini; stir fry about 2 minutes until tender-crisp and heated through. Add cornstarch mixture to the vegetables. Stir well and cook for 3 to 4 minutes, until sauce bubbles and thickens. Serve at once.

Parmesan Spinach Casserole
Serves: 4 to 6

3 pounds fresh spinach
  or
3 (10-ounce) packages frozen
  chopped spinach
6 tablespoons grated parmesan
  cheese
6 tablespoons minced onion
6 tablespoons whipping cream
5 tablespoons butter, melted
1 teaspoon salt
1/8 teaspoon pepper
1/2 teaspoon monosodium
  glutamate (optional)
1/2 cup buttered bread crumbs

Cook spinach until tender in boiling water; drain thoroughly and place in a medium size mixing bowl. Add cheese, onion, cream, butter, salt, pepper and monosodium glutamate; mix well. Put spinach mixture into a shallow baking dish; top with buttered crumbs. Bake, uncovered, at 450 degrees for 10 to 15 minutes.

Orange Yams Colonial

Serves: 16

4 pounds yams
1 tablespoon butter
1 tablespoon honey
Salt, pepper and nutmeg to taste
Juice and grated rind of 2 oranges

Boil yams in a covered pan of water until tender. Drain; drop in cold water and slip off skins. Mash yams and blend in remaining ingredients. Spoon into buttered casserole and bake at 325 degrees for about 40 minutes until golden.

NOTE: Great for Holiday dinners!

Sweet Potato Cashew Bake

Serves: 8

2/3 cup brown sugar, packed
2/3 cup broken cashew nuts
1 teaspoon salt, or to taste
1/2 teaspoon ground ginger
6 to 8 medium sweet potatoes, cooked and sliced
2 cups diced canned peaches, drained
1/4 cup butter or margarine

In a small bowl, blend brown sugar, cashews, salt and ginger. In a 9 x 13-inch casserole, layer ½ of the potatoes, ½ of the peaches and ½ of the brown sugar mixture; repeat layers. Top with pats of butter or margarine. Cover with foil and bake at 350 degrees for 30 minutes. Uncover, and bake for an additional 10 to 15 minutes. Garnish with additional peach slices, if desired.

NOTE: This is great served with your traditional Holiday turkey dinner or with chicken, pork, or ham.

Bourbon Sweet Potatoes with Pecan Glaze

Serves: 8

7 medium sweet potatoes
1/4 cup butter
1/4 cup whipping cream
1/2 teaspoon salt
1/4 cup bourbon

Glaze:
1/4 cup butter
1/2 cup light brown sugar
1/2 teaspoon salt
1/4 cup water
1/2 to 1 cup chopped pecans

Carefully add sweet potatoes to boiling water, reduce heat and simmer, covered, for 30 to 35 minutes until tender. Peel potatoes and trim ends. Mash with butter, cream, salt and bourbon. Spread into casserole dish. In a skillet over medium heat, melt butter. Add sugar, salt and water; stir and cook until thick. Add pecans and pour on top of potatoes. Bake at 325 degrees for 30 minutes until warmed through.

Stuffed Zucchini

Serves: 4

2 zucchini (6 to 7-inches)
1 egg
1/2 cup grated sharp cheddar
   cheese
1/2 cup small curd cottage
   cheese
2 tablespoons chopped onion
2 tablespoons chopped parsley
Salt and pepper to taste
1/2 cup crushed saltines
1 tablespoon melted butter

Parboil whole zucchini in boiling water for 8 minutes. Cut zucchini in half lengthwise and blot on paper towels. Scoop out insides. Blot zucchini shells and drain insides on more paper towels. Chop the zucchini insides and save. Beat the egg. Add chopped zucchini, cheese, cottage cheese, onion, parsley and seasonings. Fill shells. Mix saltines and butter and sprinkle on top of stuffed zucchini. Bake at 350 degrees for 45 minutes.

Julie's Cheese Zucchini Casserole
Serves: 6 to 8

6 to 10 medium zucchini
1 medium to large onion, chopped
2 tablespoons butter or margarine
2 (6-ounce) cans tomato paste
1 (8-ounce) can tomato sauce
1/2 teaspoon salt
1/4 teaspoon pepper
1/2 teaspoon garlic powder
1/2 teaspoon Italian seasoning
1/2 teaspoon basil
1/2 teaspoon oregano
1½ cups grated cheddar cheese
1/2 cup shredded mozzarella
   cheese, (optional)

Wash zucchini and slice into ½-inch pieces. Steam for 5 minutes, do not overcook; set aside. Sauté onion in butter until tender; set aside. Mix tomato paste, sauce and seasonings. Grease a 9 x 13 baking dish. Layer half the zucchini, half the onion, half the sauce and half the cheddar cheese in casserole. Repeat. Top with mozzarella, if desired. Bake, uncovered, at 350 degrees for 30 minutes, until the vegetables are heated through and cheese bubbles.

Quick Garlic Zucchini
Serves: 4

4 medium zucchini
2 to 3 tablespoons olive oil
2 cloves garlic, minced
1 teaspoon thyme leaves
Salt and pepper to taste

Cut zucchini in half, lengthwise. Slice halves into 3/4-inch pieces. Heat oil in a frying pan. Add zucchini and sauté lightly tossing zucchini for 2 to 3 minutes, until lightly browned and tender-crisp. Remove from heat. Add garlic, thyme, salt and pepper to taste. Toss again and serve.

Italian Zucchini Stir-Fry

Serves: 2

1 zucchini (1½-inches in
   diameter, 10 to 12-inches long)
1 large tomato
1 tablespoon olive oil
1/8 teaspoon garlic salt
1/4 teaspoon Italian seasoning

Wash the zucchini and dry with a paper towel. Cut off the ends; cut into slices about ¼-inch thick. Peel the tomato; cut crosswise and press gently to remove seeds and juice (discard center). Cut the tomato into strips. Heat oil in a frying pan with a tight fitting lid. When oil is hot, add the zucchini slices and stir-fry over high heat until the slices just begin to show a little browning, stirring constantly to prevent burning. Add seasonings; stir well. Then add tomato strips. As soon as they start to release their juices, reduce the heat, cover tightly and simmer for 4 minutes, until translucent. It may be necessary to add a tablespoon of water if the tomato is not very juicy.

Zucchini Mediterranean

Serves: 4

4 zucchini
2 tablespoons olive oil
2 tablespoons, vinegar
1 clove garlic, mashed
1/2 teaspoon basil
1/2 teaspoon oregano
Salt and pepper to taste

Wash, trim and slice zucchini. Sauté in oil until slightly soft. Drizzle vinegar over zucchini while cooking. Add garlic, basil, oregano, salt and pepper. Toss to coat well. Serve hot or cold.

Zucchini Pie

Serves: 5 to 6

4 to 5 cups thinly sliced zucchini
1 large onion, chopped
1 clove garlic, minced
1/4 cup butter or margarine
1/2 cup chopped parsley
1/2 teaspoon salt
1/2 teaspoon pepper
1/2 teaspoon oregano
2 eggs, slightly beaten
2 cups grated mozzarella cheese
2 tablespoons Dijon-style mustard
1 (9-inch) pie crust, unbaked
   Balsamic vinegar

Sauté zucchini, onion and garlic in butter until tender. Stir in parsley, salt, pepper and oregano. Combine eggs and cheese; add to vegetables. Spread mustard on bottom of pie crust. Add the vegetable mixture. Bake at 375 degrees for 40 to 50 minutes until knife inserted in center comes out clean. Serve each slice with several drops of balsamic vinegar.

NOTE: The vinegar really makes the pie, it is a must!

Vegetable Sauce

Yield: 1 cup

1 cup sour cream
1 tablespoon Dijon mustard
1 tablespoon fresh lime juice
2 tablespoons fresh chopped
   parsley
Salt to taste
White pepper to taste

Blend all ingredients in a bowl. Spoon over hot vegetables, serve at once.

NOTE: This is excellent over asparagus, broccoli, carrots or green beans.

Savor
the Flavor
of
PASTA, RICE,
SIDE DISHES

❧ ❧ ❧

Scallop-Hazelnut Pasta

Serves: 4

5 tablespoons unsalted butter, divided
1 cup minced shallots
4 thin slices prosciutto, cut into thin strips
2½ tablespoons minced fresh basil
1 cup whipping cream
Salt and pepper to taste
6 ounces tagliolini pasta
12 ounces scallops
1/4 cup toasted hazelnuts, husked and coarsely chopped
3 tablespoons fresh snipped chives

Melt 4 tablespoons butter in a heavy large non-aluminum skillet over medium-low heat. Add shallots and ½ of the prosciutto; cook for 6 minutes until shallots are translucent, stirring frequently. Mix in basil and cook for 2 minutes. Pour in cream and simmer for 10 minutes until reduced by ¼. Season with salt and pepper.

Cook pasta in a large amount of boiling, salted water for 7 minutes, until just tender, but still firm to the bite. Bring cream mixture to a gentle simmer. Add scallops and cook (below a simmer) for 2 minutes until scallops are opaque, stirring frequently. Taste and adjust seasonings, as necessary.

Drain pasta well; return to pot. Mix in remaining 1 tablespoon butter, salt and pepper (if desired). Arrange in nests on 4 heated plates or on a large heated platter. Spoon scallop mixture into center of pasta and sprinkle with nuts and chives. Put remaining prosciutto strips on top and serve immediately.

Mushroom Stroganoff
Serves: 4

1/2 pound flat egg noodles
1 tablespoon margarine
1 onion, chopped
1 clove garlic, crushed
1/2 pound mushrooms, halved
1 tablespoon dried parsley
   or
2 tablespoons chopped fresh
   parsley
3 dashes Worcestershire sauce
1 cup sour cream
Salt and pepper to taste
Parsley (garnish)

Begin cooking the noodles according to package directions. In a saucepan over medium heat, melt margarine, and sauté onion, garlic, mushrooms and parsley. Stir in Worcestershire sauce and remove from heat. Stir in sour cream. Season with salt and pepper. Serve immediately over drained hot noodles. Garnish with additional fresh parsley.

Fettucini Broccoli
Serves: 4

1 medium onion, chopped
2 cloves garlic, minced
5 tablespoons butter, divided
2 bunches fresh broccoli (florets
   only, approximately 4-5 cups)
1 cup black olives, sliced
1 teaspoon oregano
1/2 teaspoon sweet basil
1/2 teaspoon salt
1/4 teaspoon freshly ground
   pepper
1 pound fresh fettuccine or
   linguine
1/2 cup freshly grated parmesan
   cheese

In a medium frying pan, sauté onion and garlic in 3 tablespoons butter, until golden brown. Add broccoli florets to pan, cover and cook over low heat for 15 to 20 minutes. (Broccoli should be tender-crisp and bright green, do not overcook.) Add olives during last 5 minutes of cooking time. During the final minute, add oregano, basil, salt and pepper. Meanwhile, cook pasta as recommended (time cooking to end as vegetables are done), drain and put into large bowl. Toss pasta with remaining 2 tablespoons butter and the parmesan cheese. Top with hot broccoli mixture. Serve immediately.

Rotini and Vegetables

Serves: 6

12 ounces rotini
2 cups fresh broccoli florets
3 large carrots, sliced
2 zucchini, sliced
1 cup sliced celery
1 tablespoon oil
1/2 teaspoon ground garlic paste
  or
1 clove garlic, finely minced
1/4 cup fresh chopped parsley
2 tablespoons grated parmesan
  cheese
Ground pepper to taste
1 cup low-fat cottage cheese

Cook rotini in boiling water 3 minutes. Add vegetables to pasta and continue cooking until pasta is done and vegetables are tender-crisp. Drain well. Toss drained pasta and vegetables with remaining ingredients. Serve immediately.

Spinach Pasta

Serves: 8

1 pound fresh spinach, washed
  and chopped
  or
1 (10-ounce) package frozen
  chopped spinach
2 cups cottage cheese
1 (6-ounce) package cream cheese
1/2 cup chopped onions
1 tablespoon butter
2 cups fresh sliced mushrooms
1/3 cup white wine
1/2 teaspoon thyme
Salt and pepper to taste
1 (6-ounce) can evaporated milk
1 (16-ounce) package spaghetti
  noodles
  or
1 (16-ounce) package fresh pasta
  noodles
Grated parmesan cheese (optional)

Cook spinach and drain. Beat cottage cheese and cream cheese till nearly smooth. Cook onions and mushrooms in butter until tender. Add, wine, thyme, salt and pepper. Stir in cottage cheese and cream cheese mixture, evaporated milk and spinach. Heat thoroughly and spoon over noodles. Garnish with parmesan cheese, if desired.

149

Pasta Monterey

Serves: 6

1 (16-ounce) package linguini or
  fettucine, cooked
2 cups thickly sliced fresh
  mushrooms
1/2 cup thinly sliced green or
  red bell pepper
1/3 cup thinly sliced green
  onions, including tops
3 tablespoons butter or
  margarine, divided
2 large cloves garlic, minced
1 tablespoon flour
2/3 cup whole milk
1/2 teaspoon seasoning salt
1/3 cup dry white wine
1/8 teaspoon white pepper
2 cups shredded Monterey Jack
  cheese, divided

Cook noodles according to package directions and set aside. In a large skillet, sauté mushrooms, green pepper and green onions in 2 tablespoons of butter. Cook for 5 minutes, add garlic and stir. Remove vegetables from pan and set aside. In the same pan, melt the remaining butter over medium heat, blend in flour, then gradually pour in milk. Stir until smooth and thickened. Blend in seasoning salt, wine, white pepper and 1 cup of the shredded cheese. Cook and stir until cheese melts. To the sauce, add the noodles and vegetables. Pour all into a 1½-quart casserole and top with remaining cheese. Bake, uncovered at 350 degrees for 20 minutes until bubbly.

NOTE: You may make this ahead of time, cover and refrigerate. Let stand for 30 minutes at room temperature before baking.

Conchiglie

Serves: 10

16 ounces large pasta shells

Filling:
2 pounds ricotta cheese
1/4 pound mozzarella cheese,
  grated
1/3 cup grated parmesan cheese
3 eggs, lightly beaten
1/4 cup fine bread crumbs
2 tablespoons finely chopped
  parsley
6 cups spaghetti sauce
  (jar or favorite homemade)
1/4 cup grated parmesan cheese

Cook shells in 6-quarts salted, boiling water for about 15 minutes. Drain shells and put back into a large kettle. Add enough cold water so shells can be handled comfortably. While shells are boiling, mix cheeses, eggs, bread crumbs and parsley. Pour a layer of spaghetti sauce on the bottom of a very large flat baking dish or one 9 x 13 and one smaller dish. Spoon filling into shells with a teaspoon and arrange in baking dish, one layer deep. Pour remainder of the sauce over and around the shells. Top with ¼ cup parmesan cheese. Cover and bake at 350 degrees for 30 to 45 minutes.

Cheese Stuffed Manicotti

Serves: 6 to 8

Sauce:
1 clove garlic, minced
1/2 onion, chopped
1 tablespoon olive oil
2 (8-ounce) cans tomato sauce
2 (16-ounce) cans tomatoes,
  chopped
1½ teaspoons oregano leaves
1 tablespoon chopped parsley

Filling:
2 cups low-fat cottage cheese
1 cup part-skim ricotta cheese
2 egg whites
3 tablespoons freshly grated
  parmesan cheese
2 tablespoons chopped parsley
Pepper to taste
1 teaspoon oregano
1/4 teaspoon nutmeg
8 ounces uncooked manicotti
  shells
1 cup water
Grated parmesan cheese (optional)

To prepare sauce: Sauté garlic and onion in olive oil. Add tomato sauce and tomatoes. Stir in oregano and parsley. Bring to a boil and simmer, covered, for 20 minutes to 2 hours, stirring occasionally.

To prepare filling: Combine the cheeses, egg whites, parsley, pepper, oregano and nutmeg. Spread 2 cups of the tomato sauce out in a 9 x 13 baking dish. Stuff uncooked manicotti shells. Arrange in a single layer side by side over sauce. Cover shells with remaining sauce and pour water over sauce. Cover dish with foil and bake at 375 degrees for 50 minutes. Remove foil and bake an additional 10 minutes. Sprinkle with parmesan cheese, if desired.

NOTE: Add 2 cups fresh sliced mushrooms to the sauce and/or 1 (10-ounce) package frozen chopped spinach to the filling. This enhances the presentation and the flavor!

151

Tofu-Spinach Manicotti
Serves: 6

Sauce:
2 small onions, chopped
2 cloves garlic, minced
1/4 cup olive oil
**2 (28-ounce) cans tomatoes,
   drained**
1/2 cup dry red wine
1 tablespoon basil
1 teaspoon salt
1 teaspoon oregano
1 teaspoon thyme

Filling:
10 ounces fresh spinach
1/4 cup olive oil
1 (1-pound) package tofu
2 eggs, beaten
**1 clove garlic, minced
   or**
1/2 teaspoon garlic powder
1 teaspoon salt
1/4 teaspoon pepper
**1 package large manicotti shells
   (14)**
Parsley (garnish)

For sauce: Sauté the onions and garlic in olive oil for 5 minutes. In a bowl, cut up the drained tomatoes and add to the onion mixture. Simmer uncovered for 30 minutes. Add wine and seasonings and simmer for an additional 5 minutes.

For filling: Wash spinach thoroughly. Chop spinach finely and sauté in olive oil until limp. Rinse, drain, and squeeze excess moisture out of the tofu; pat dry. In a medium bowl, crumble tofu and add beaten eggs, garlic, salt and pepper. Add the spinach and stir. Set aside.

To assemble: Pour one cup of the sauce into the bottom of a 9 x 13 baking dish. Stuff uncooked manicotti shells with the spinach and tofu mixture. Arrange the stuffed manicotti over the sauce in a single layer. Top with the remainder of the sauce, making sure to cover all the shells. Cover tightly with foil and bake at 350 degrees for 1 hour.

Hazelnut Manicotti

Serves: 6

1 package manicotti shells (8)

Filling:
1 cup coarsley chopped, pre roasted hazelnuts
1 package frozen chopped spinach,
thawed and drained
1 cup cottage cheese
1/2 cup sliced green onions
1 teaspoon garlic salt
1/4 teaspoon nutmeg
1/4 teaspoon pepper
2 eggs, slightly beaten
2 to 3 cups spaghetti sauce
1/2 cup grated parmesan cheese

Precook manicotti in boiling water for about 5 minutes, until partially softened; drain. Mix hazelnuts, spinach, cottage cheese, onions, seasonings and eggs. Fill manicotti shells. Cover the bottom of a 2-quart baking dish with one cup of spaghetti sauce. Arrange filled manicotti shells in a single layer in baking dish. Cover with remaining sauce and sprinkle with parmesan cheese. Cover and bake at 375 degrees for 40 to 45 minutes.

NOTE: Hazelnut-spinach mixture can also be placed in large, hollowed tomato halves and baked.

Spaghetti Carbonara

Serves: 4

3/4 pounds spaghetti
6 slices bacon, diced
1/2 cup dry white wine
3 eggs, at room temperature
2/3 cup grated parmesan cheese
Pepper to taste

Sauté bacon slightly, do not brown. Add wine and cook down. Keep warm. Beat eggs slightly, add cheese and bacon, blend. Cook spaghetti and drain. Add hot bacon oil to the spaghetti immediately. Add egg and cheese mixture so that hot oil will cook eggs. Toss with black pepper and serve immediately.

NOTE: This recipe is the real thing, very classic and simple. It is wonderful for camping trips. The bacon, egg and cheese mixture can be made ahead. Also great for trips when cooking facilities are limited. Will serve more people by simply increasing by 1 egg, ⅓ cup cheese and more bacon.

Carbonara
Serves: 4

1/4 pound pepper ham
1/4 pound Italian sausage
4 tablespoons butter, divided
8 ounces fresh linguine or
   spaghettini
Boiling water with dash of olive oil
1/2 cup fresh chopped parsley
3 eggs, well beaten
1/2 cup grated parmesan cheese
   Freshly ground black pepper
   to taste
Grated parmesan cheese (garnish)

Finely chop ham and break Italian sausage into small bits. Melt 2 tablespoons of butter into a 10-inch frying pan. Add sausage and ham, cook and stir for about 10 minutes, until sausage is browned and ham is curled and slightly browned. Cook pasta in a large kettle of boiling water until al denté and drain. Add pasta to hot meat mixture. Add remaining butter and parsley. Mix quickly to blend. Remove from heat. At once, pour in the eggs and quickly lift and mix the pasta to coat well with egg. Sprinkle in the parmesan cheese and a dash of pepper, mix again and serve. Garnish with extra parmesan cheese, if desired.

Sausage Pasta Parmesan
Serves: 4 to 6

1 pound fresh linguine
1/2 pound Italian sausage
1 clove garlic, minced
3 carrots, thinly sliced on
   diagonal
2 cups frozen or fresh broccoli, cut
   in bite size pieces on diagonal
1/2 cup frozen peas
1 cup grated parmesan cheese

Prepare linguine according to package instructions. Meanwhile, crumble sausage into a large frying pan, add garlic and cook until sausage is lightly browned. Add vegetables to sausage mixture, cover and cook over low heat until vegetables are tender, but not overcooked (about 10 to 15 minutes). Remove from heat, add parmesan cheese and toss. Add prepared pasta to sausage mixture and toss again.

NOTE: Serve with fruit salad and french bread.

Pistachio Pasta
Serves: 5 to 6

1 clove garlic, minced
1/4 cup minced onion
2 tablespoons olive oil
1/2 cup coarsely chopped
   pistachio nuts
1/4 cup chopped olives
1/4 cup minced parsley
1 teaspoon lemon juice
   or
1/2 teaspoon grated lemon
   peel
1/8 teaspoon pepper
1/4 teaspoon crushed basil
8 ounces pasta, cooked and
   drained
1/3 cup grated parmesan cheese

In a large saucepan, sauté garlic and onion in oil until onion is tender. Add nuts, olives, parsley, lemon juice, pepper, basil and pasta. Toss and heat over medium heat for 2 to 3 minutes. Add parmesan cheese, toss again and serve.

Hot Carrot Pasta
Serves: 6 to 8

2½ cups thinly sliced carrots
1/2 cup chopped onion
1/2 cup butter
1 pound fresh pasta
1/4 cup minced parsley
1/2 cup grated parmesan cheese
1/4 teaspoon salt
1/4 teaspoon pepper

Sauté carrots and onions in butter until tender, but not browned. Cook pasta and drain. Add pasta, parsley, parmesan, salt and pepper to cooked carrots. Toss lightly and serve immediately.

Barley Casserole
Serves: 6 to 8

1 cup uncooked barley
3 tablespoons butter
1 large onion, finely chopped
1/2 pound fresh mushrooms,
  sliced
2 cups chicken broth
1 tablespoon soy sauce
1/2 teaspoon salt
1/4 teaspoon pepper
1 tablespoon minced fresh
  parsley (optional)

In a saucepan over medium heat, brown barley in butter, add onions and sauté until tender. Add remaining ingredients. Pour into a greased 2-quart casserole. Bake, uncovered, at 300 degrees for 1½ to 2 hours, stirring occasionally. Sprinkle with parsley before serving.

Mushroom-Barley Pilaf
Serves: 8

2 medium onions, chopped
1/2 pound fresh mushrooms,
  sliced
1/4 cup butter, divided
1¼ cups pearl barley
1 quart chicken stock
  or
6 chicken bouillon cubes
  and 4 cups water
Salt and pepper to taste

Melt 3 tablespoons butter, sauté onions and mushrooms. Remove and place in a large casserole. Melt remaining butter and brown barley until golden, stirring constantly. Add to mushrooms and onions. Pour 1⅓ cups of chicken stock over all, cover and bake at 350 degrees for 30 minutes. Remove lid, season with salt and pepper and add another 1¾ cups of stock. Cover and bake an additional 30 minutes. Uncover and cook an additional 10 to 15 minutes, adding more stock if dry.

Armenian Pilaf

Serves: 4 to 6

1/4 cup butter
1/2 cup finely broken
  vermicelli
1 cup rice
2 cups boiling hot beef
  broth
Salt and pepper to taste

In a 1½ to 2-quart saucepan over medium heat, melt butter. Add vermicelli and cook until brown, stirring frequently. Add the rice and cook 2 to 3 minutes, stirring well. Add the beef broth, salt and pepper. Reduce heat to low, cover and cook for 20 minutes, until all the liquid is absorbed.

Nutty Wild Rice

Serves: 6

1/3 cup slivered almonds or
  pine nuts
1 teaspoon olive oil
1 large onion, chopped
1 large carrot, chopped
1 large clove garlic, chopped
1 cup fresh mushrooms, sliced
1 cup wild rice (uncooked)
2½ cups chicken broth
1/4 cup sherry
1/2 teaspoon salt
Pepper to taste
1/2 teaspoon oregano
1 teaspoon basil
1/3 cup chopped parsley

In a non-stick frying pan or toaster oven, slowly toast almonds. Set aside. In a large non-stick frying pan, heat oil over medium heat, add onion, carrot, garlic and mushrooms; sauté until tender. Add rice and cook until lightly browned. Add broth, sherry, salt, pepper, oregano and basil. Bring to a boil and simmer, covered, for 45 minutes. Remove from heat and let stand for 10 minutes. Toss with nuts and parsley and serve.

NOTE: A variation of this recipe could be fun. Try using ⅓ cup white rice, ⅓ cup brown rice and ⅓ cup wild rice or any combination of other grains adding up to 1 cup.

157

Artichoke Rice

Serves: 4 to 6

1 (6-ounce) package chicken
  flavored rice mix
2 (6 1/2-ounce) jars marinated
  artichoke hearts (with liquid)
1/3 cup mayonnaise
3/4 teaspoon curry powder
4 green onions, sliced
1/2 green pepper, chopped
12 stuffed green olives,
  sliced

Cook rice according to package instructions, remove pan from heat. Drain and chop artichokes; reserve marinade. In a small container, blend marinade, mayonnaise and curry.

Stir marinade mixture into rice. Add chopped artichokes, onions, peppers and olives; toss well. May be served warm or cold.

Green Rice

Serves: 6

1 pound fresh spinach, washed
  and chopped
  or
1 (10-ounce) package frozen
  chopped spinach
1/4 cup butter or margarine
3 cups instant rice
2⅓ cups water
2 teaspoons salt
1/2 teaspoon oregano
6 green onions, sliced
2 tablespoons chopped parsley
2 tablespoons lemon juice
1/2 cup grated parmesan cheese

If using fresh spinach, drain well. If using frozen spinach, thaw and drain well. In a large pan, sauté spinach in butter for 2 to 3 minutes. Stir in rice, water, salt and oregano; bring to a boil. Cover and simmer until all liquid is absorbed, about 5 minutes. Stir in onion, lemon juice and parsley; heat through. Sprinkle with parmesan cheese when serving.

Saffron Rice

Serves: 6

1 medium onion, chopped
2 tablespoons butter
2 cups white rice (uncooked)
4 cups boiling chicken stock
1/4 teaspoon saffron
1 cup chopped mushrooms
4 tablespoons butter
1/2 cup grated parmesan cheese

Sauté onion in butter until browned. Add uncooked rice and brown about 1 minute. Add chicken stock, mushrooms and saffron; stir and bring to a boil. Cover, reduce heat and simmer about 20 minutes. When cooked, add remaining butter and parmesan cheese; stir and serve.

Seasoned Rice Pilaf

Serves: 4

1 to 2 tablespoons margarine
   or butter
2 tablespoons chopped onion
1½ cups chicken broth
1 cup instant rice (uncooked)
1/2 bay leaf
1/2 teaspoon thyme
2 dashes Tabasco
   Pepper to taste

Preheat oven to 450 degrees. Melt butter in a large saucepan, add onion and cook for 2 to 3 minutes over medium heat. Add broth, rice and seasonings. Increase heat, bring mixture to a boil. Remove from heat and put all into a 1½-quart baking dish. Bake, uncovered, at 450 degrees for 17 minutes. Remove bay leaf and serve.

Spicy Spanish Rice

Serves: 4 to 6

3 or 4 cups cooked rice
1/2 pound hamburger
1 medium onion, chopped
1 cup celery chopped
1 large green pepper, chopped
1 teaspoon chili powder
1/4 teaspoon black pepper
1 teaspoon salt
2 (14-ounce) cans tomatoes,
   chopped

Cook rice according to package directions; set aside. Brown hamburger, add onion, celery, and green pepper; cook until tender. Add chili powder, black pepper, salt and tomatoes. Simmer, covered, for 20 minutes. Add rice and cook an additional 10 minutes.

Wild Rice Casserole
Serves: 6

1 cup wild rice (uncooked)
3 cups boiling water
1/2 pound mushrooms, sliced
1/2 cup chopped onion
1/2 cup butter
1 (16-ounce) can tomatoes
1/4 teaspoon salt
1 cup shredded cheddar cheese
1 teaspoon salt
1 cup hot water

Cook rice in boiling, salted water until nearly tender (about 40 minutes). Drain (if necessary). Sauté mushrooms and onions in butter for about 5 minutes. In a large bowl, toss rice with all ingredients. Add 1 cup hot water. Place in buttered 2-quart casserole. Cover and bake at 350 degrees for 1 hour.

Italian-Sausage Sauce
Yield: 3½ to 4 cups

1 pound low-fat bulk Italian
    sausage
Olive oil
1 medium onion, coarsely chopped
1 clove garlic, minced
1 (15-ounce) can tomato sauce
1 teaspoon oregano leaves
1/4 teaspoon thyme leaves
1/4 teaspoon pepper
1/3 cup minced fresh parsley
2 tablespoons catsup
8 ounces fresh linguine or
    fettucine
Chopped fresh parsley (garnish)
Grated parmesan cheese

In a large frying pan, brown sausage in a small amount of olive oil. Add onion and garlic and continue to cook, stirring occasionally until onion is tender. Add tomato sauce, oregano, thyme, pepper, parsley and catsup. Simmer uncovered for 30 minutes to blend flavors. Cook pasta in a large kettle of boiling water until al dente; drain. Turn pasta onto a large platter; top with sauce. Garnish with chopped parsley and pass parmesan at the table.

Pico DeGallo Sauce
Serves: 6 to 8

1½ cups diced tomatoes
  (about 4 small tomatoes)
1 tablespoon cilantro
1/4 teaspoon salt
2 tablespoons chopped green
  onions
1 tablespoon fresh jalapeno
  pepper, chopped and seeded

Mix all ingredients together, cover and refrigerate at least four hours. This may be refrigerated overnight.

Red Pasta Sauce
Serves: 4 to 6

1/2 pound extra-lean ground
  beef
2 teaspoons olive or vegetable
  oil
1 medium onion, minced
2 cloves garlic, minced
1 (28-ounce) can plum tomatoes
  with juice or puree
1 (6-ounce) can tomato paste
1 (4¼-ounce) can chopped black
  olives
1 teaspoon sugar
1 teaspoon dried basil, crumbled
1/2 to 1 teaspoon oregano,
  crumbled
1/4 teaspoon cardamon
1/4 teaspoon salt, if desired
1/4 teaspoon freshly ground black
  pepper
Several dashes of Tabasco
  or
Ground cayenne pepper to taste

In a large skillet, lightly brown beef, crumbling into very small bits. Remove beef to a plate lined with paper towels. Pour off any fat and wipe pan out. Heat oil briefly in pan. Add onion and garlic; sauté for 2 minutes, until transluscent. Add tomatoes with liquid, breaking them into pieces, if necessary. Add tomato paste, olives, sugar, basil, oregano, cardamon, salt, peppers and reserved cooked beef. Bring sauce to a boil over medium-high heat. Reduce heat to low and simmer for 30 minutes or until desired consistency is reached.

NOTE: For a change, you may want add 1 cup of finely sliced mushrooms, ½ cup diced celery or ½ cup diced red or green pepper after the onions are done and cook another minute.

Tomato Sauce
Yield: 2 cups sauce

1 onion, chopped
2 tablespoons vegetable oil
1 teaspoon garlic salt
1 carrot, grated
1/2 green pepper, chopped
1/2 teaspoon ground bay leaves
1 teaspoon oregano
1/2 teaspoon thyme
1/2 teaspoon basil
2 tablespoons fresh chopped
  parsley
2 cups tomatoes, fresh or
  canned
1 (6-ounce) can tomato paste
1/4 teaspoon brown sugar
1/8 teaspoon pepper

Sauté onion in oil. Add garlic salt, carrot, green pepper, bay leaves, oregano, thyme, basil, parsley, tomatoes, tomato paste, brown sugar and pepper. Stir together and simmer for ½ hour. Serve or refrigerate.

NOTE: If you freeze sauce, allow air space for expansion.

Pat's Pesto Sauce
Yield: 1 cup

1 cup olive oil
2 medium cloves garlic
1/2 cup pine nuts or walnuts
3 cups fresh basil leaves
1 cup fresh Italian parsley
  leaves
3/4 cup grated parmesan or
  romano cheese
1 teaspoon freshly ground pepper
Salt, if desired
Fresh linguine
Oil

Blend oil and garlic in blender at high speed until smooth. Gradually add nuts and process until well blended. Add basil leaves a few at a time, following with parsley leaves. Blend until smooth. Add grated cheese and pepper, continue to blend to a smooth consistency. Taste for salt. For immediate use, cook linguine in salted water with a little oil. Drain well and add a little bit of butter to hot linguine. Mix with a small amount of pesto sauce and place in a warm serving dish. Top with a generous amount of pesto. (A little boiling water from pasta may be added to pesto sauce to thin, if desired.)

NOTE: Pesto sauce should be at room temperature when served; if heated, cheese may lump.

Savor
the Flavor
of
FISH &
SEAFOOD

❧ ❧ ❧

Salmon Florentine

Serves: 4

1 pound fresh salmon fillets
1 tablespoon margarine or butter
2 teaspoons lemon juice
1/8 teaspoon salt
1/8 teaspoon pepper
1 cup instant rice
3/4 cup water
1/2 teaspoon instant chicken
  bouillon
1/8 teaspoon nutmeg
1 (10-ounce) package frozen
  chopped spinach
1/4 cup sliced green onion
3 tablespoons grated parmesan
  cheese
Lemon slices (garnish)
Green onion tops (garnish)

Place the butter, lemon juice, salt and pepper in a microwave-safe glass container. Melt the mixture on full power for 30 to 40 seconds; set aside. In a 8 x 8 x 2-inch microwave-safe dish, combine rice, water, bouillon and nutmeg. Cover with microwave-safe plastic, vent and cook on full power for 2 minutes. Stir in spinach, green onions and cheese; spread evenly in dish. Arrange salmon fillets on top of rice. Top with melted butter mixture and cover with microwave-safe plastic; vent. Cook on full power for 6 to 8 minutes, until fish flakes with a fork. Garnish with lemon slices and green onion tops.

Barbecued Salmon

Serves: 8

1/2 fresh salmon
  or
3½ pounds of salmon fillets
1/4 cup butter, melted
1/4 cup soy sauce
1/2 tablespoon Worcestershire
  sauce
1/2 teaspoon garlic powder

Put salmon, skin side down on grill. Mix remaining ingredients and use to baste salmon frequently. Cook until salmon changes color, (it will lighten). Turn over and peel off skin. Baste frequently and cook until done, about 15 to 20 minutes.

Mustard Baked Red Snapper

Serves: 4

4 red snapper fillets
4 tablespoons Dijon mustard
1 tablespoon grated onion
1 teaspoon garlic powder
1 tablespoon salad oil
1 tablespoon basil
1 tablespoon lemon juice
4 tomato slices
Parsley (garnish)

Mix first 6 ingredients together in a small bowl. Spread ¼ of the mixture on each piece of fish. Package each serving in aluminum foil and seal. Bake at 550 degrees for 15 minutes.

Herb Grilled Tuna

Serves: 6

1 to 2 pounds tuna steaks
  (1¼-inches thick)
3 tomatoes, peeled, seeded
  and chopped
1½ cups extra virgin olive
  oil
3 tablespoons fresh lemon juice
3 cloves garlic, minced
3/4 teaspoon salt
1/2 cup finely chopped mixed
  fresh herbs (chervil, chives,
  tarragon and parsley)

In a medium bowl, stir together tomatoes, olive oil, lemon juice, garlic and salt. Set aside and allow flavors to blend for 2 hours. Light a grill or preheat broiler. Stir the fresh herbs into the tomato sauce. Grill or broil the tuna 4-inches from the heat, turning once, for 3 minutes on each side (until charred outside and slightly pink inside). Transfer the tuna to a large platter and cut into thick strips. Top with ½ of the fresh tomato sauce and pass the remainder at the table.

NOTE: The sauce is known as Mediterranean "Sauce Vierge". Serve with a green salad, french bread and red wine.

Teriyaki Tuna
Serves: 6

1½ to 2 pounds fresh tuna
1 cup low-sodium soy sauce
2 tablespoons sugar
2 cloves garlic, crushed
2/3 cup dry sherry
1 tablespoon finely chopped
   ginger root
   or
1 teaspoon ginger powder

Mix first 5 ingredients together in a 9 x 13-inch pan. Add tuna and marinate for 2 hours, turning every ½ hour in refrigerator. Grill on barbecue 5 minutes on each side.

NOTE: Served cold, this makes an excellent appetizer.

Oven Fried Snapper
Serves: 6

2 pounds pacific snapper or
   perch fillets
1/2 cup olive oil
1 teaspoon salt
1/2 teaspoon ground white pepper
2 to 3 cloves garlic, minced
1 cup grated parmesan cheese
1 cup finely crushed dry herbed
   bread crumbs

Rinse fish with cold water and pat dry with paper towels. Cut fish into equal size serving portions. Combine oil, salt, pepper, and garlic in an oblong glass baking dish. Place fish in mixture. Let marinate 10 minutes, turn, and marinate an additional 10 minutes. Remove fish from marinade. Combine cheese and crumbs and roll fish in this mixture. Place on a well-greased cookie sheet. Bake at 500 degrees for 12 to 15 minutes until fish flakes easily when tested with a fork.

Halibut Onion Crunch
Serves: 4

4 halibut fillets or steaks
3 tablespoons cooking oil
1½ teaspoons lemon juice
1/2 teaspoon salt
1/8 teaspoon pepper
1/8 teaspoon dry mustard
1/4 teaspoon marjoram
1/4 teaspoon garlic salt
1/3 cup canned, French fried
  onions, crumbled
3 tablespoons grated parmesan
  cheese

Combine oil, lemon juice, salt, pepper, mustard, marjoram and garlic salt. Pour over halibut. Marinate 20 minutes, turning once. Transfer fish to buttered baking dish. Sprinkle with onions and cheese. Bake at 450 degrees for 20 minutes or until fish flakes with fork.

Beer Poached Salmon
Serves: 4

4 salmon steaks, 1-inch thick
12 ounces beer
2 tablespoons lemon juice
1 medium onion, chopped
1 celery stalk, chopped
1 teaspoon salt
1 bay leaf
3 or 4 peppercorns

Tarragon Mayonnaise:
1/2 cup mayonnaise
1/4 teaspoon dried tarragon
1 teaspoon minced chives
1 teaspoon chopped green onion
1/4 teaspoon Tabasco
1 teaspoon minced parsley

In a skillet, combine beer, lemon juice, onion, celery, salt, bay leaf and peppercorns, bring to a boil and simmer for 10 minutes. Add salmon steaks, cover and simmer 15 minutes.

Combine ingredients for tarragon mayonnaise and serve with salmon.

Salmon In Puff Pastry
Serves: 8

2 salmon fillets, 1½ to
  2 pounds each
1½ cups fresh spinach, stems
  removed
6 hard-cooked eggs, chopped
1/3 cup chopped fresh parsley
1/3 cup chopped onion
Salt and freshly ground pepper
1 pound puff pastry dough
1 egg, slightly beaten

Spinach Sauce
3 shallots, chopped
1/4 cup fish stock or clam juice
1½ cups dry vermouth
1 cup white wine
2 cups sour cream
Salt and white pepper
3 cups finely chopped fresh
  spinach
3 egg yolks
Lemon juice

Lay 1 fillet on waxed paper. Finely chop spinach by hand or in food processor. Spread over fillet. Mix together eggs, parsley and onion. Spread evenly over spinach. Season with salt and pepper to taste. Cover with other fillet. Roll out puff pastry to a thickness of ¼-inch, making one long piece large enough to wrap fish. Cut off ends and save for decorations. Wrap fish in pastry by placing pastry on cloth or several layers of waxed paper, add fish and filling, wrap with pastry, seal edges with beaten egg. Cut small leaves, flowers, diamonds or other patterns from left-over pastry dough. Carefully turn over salmon and place on an ungreased baking sheet, seamside down. Cut diagonal slits about 2-inches apart down the center. Decorate with cut-outs, using beaten egg as "glue". Bake at 425 degrees for 30 to 40 minutes. Lower oven to 375 degrees and bake for an additional 15 minutes. Allow to stand a few minutes before slicing. To serve, cut into 1½-inch slices. Serve with warm spinach sauce.

Spinach Sauce: Combine shallots, fish stock, vermouth and wine in a 2-quart saucepan. Cook over medium heat until reduced to about ½ cup, about 45 minutes. Add cream, salt and white pepper to taste. Cover and cook over medium heat, stirring frequently for 10 minutes. Add spinach and heat for 3 to 4 minutes. Beat egg yolks. Remove sauce from heat and stir a little of it into yolks. Then slowly stir yolk mixture back into sauce. Return to heat and cook 3 to 4 minutes. Season with lemon juice to taste.

Halibut with Orange Glaze
Serves: 4

2 pounds halibut steaks
2 tablespoons margarine, melted
2 tablespoons orange juice
1/8 teaspoon pepper

Glaze
2 tablespoons cornstarch
1 cup orange juice, divided
1/4 cup margarine
1/3 cup sliced almonds
1/4 cup dry white wine
1/4 cup apple jelly
1/4 cup lemon juice
1/4 teaspoon Tabasco sauce
1/4 teaspoon salt
1 (11-ounce) can mandarin
  oranges, drained

Rinse steaks in cold water, pat dry with paper towels. Lightly oil broiler pan. Place steaks on broiler pan. Combine melted margarine and orange juice; brush over steaks. Sprinkle steaks with pepper. Broil 4-inches from heat source for about 6 minutes. During that time, prepare glaze.

Combine cornstarch with ¼ cup orange juice; set aside. In a 2-quart saucepan, melt margarine over medium heat. Add almonds and sauté until lightly browned. Add remaining orange juice, wine, jelly and lemon juice. Stir in cornstarch mixture. Continue cooking, stirring constantly until mixture thickens. Add Tabasco, salt and orange sections; mix well. After 6 minutes broiling time, baste fish with glaze. Continue cooking for 2 to 4 minutes or until fish flakes easily with a fork. Keep glaze warm until fish is done, and serve fish with remaining warm glaze.

Garlic Grilled Halibut
Serves: 2

2 large halibut steaks, 1-inch thick
2 cloves garlic, finely chopped
2 tablespoons olive oil
1 teaspoon dried basil
3/4 teaspoon salt
1 teaspoon freshly ground pepper
1 tablespoon lemon juice
1 teaspoon chopped parsley

Combine garlic, oil, basil, salt, pepper, lemon juice and parsley. Add fish and marinate for at least 2 hours. Remove from marinade and reserve liquid. Lightly oil broiler pan or grill. Broil for about 5 minutes on each side. Brush with remaining marinade and heat another minute.

Halibut with Orange Glaze

Salmon Souffle
Serves: 4 to 5

1 pound cooked salmon, flaked
1 cup soft bread crumbs
1½ cups hot milk
3 tablespoons butter or margarine,
  melted
2 tablespoons chopped parsley
2 teaspoons chopped green onion
1½ cups grated sharp cheddar
  cheese
1/2 teaspoon salt
Dash pepper
Dash paprika
3 eggs, beaten
Lemon wedges

In a large bowl, mix bread crumbs, milk and butter. Stir well. Add remaining ingredients; mix well. Butter a 2-quart round baking dish. Put salmon mixture into the dish. Set casserole in a pan of water in a 350 degree oven and bake for 1 hour. Serve with lemon wedges.

Salmon Sauté
Serves: 4

1½ pounds skinless salmon
  fillets
6 tablespoons butter, divided
1/4 cup white wine
2 tablespoons lemon juice
2 tablespoons tarragon vinegar
2 tablespoons capers, drained

Cut the salmon fillets into desired serving sizes. Melt ½ of the butter in a sauté pan over medium-high heat. Cook the salmon pieces only until they flake (do not overcook), turning as necessary. Put on serving plate. Keep warm. De-glaze the pan with wine, lemon juice and vinegar. Remove from heat and cool slightly; whisk in remaining butter. Stir in capers and spoon over warm fish.

NOTE: A very elegant yet easy way to serve a Northwest favorite!

Oregon Marinated Salmon Steaks

Serves: 8

8 salmon steaks
1/4 cup olive oil
1/4 cup vegetable oil
1/2 cup soy sauce
1 clove garlic, minced
1/2 teaspoon ginger powder
Juice of one lemon
3 tablespoons seafood seasoning

Combine oils, soy sauce, garlic, ginger, lemon juice and seafood seasoning. Blend well. Pour marinade into a 9 x 13-inch glass dish. Place steaks in marinade, cover and refrigerate for about 12 hours, turning occasionally. Broil steaks for 8 minutes on each side.

Fillet of Sole Gourmet

Serves: 6

6 sole fillets
1 (6-ounce) package white and
    wild rice
1½ pounds fresh asparagus
    or
1 (9-ounce) package frozen
    asparagus
1 cup finely chopped celery
3 tablespoons butter
3 tablespoons flour
1 cup milk
1 teaspoon Worcestershire sauce
1 tablespoon fresh lemon juice
1/2 teaspoon celery salt
1/8 teaspoon white pepper
1 cup sour cream, at room
    temperature
Juice of ½ fresh lemon
2 tablespoons grated parmesan
    cheese
2 tablespoons sliced almonds

Cook rice according to package directions; spoon into buttered baking dish. Cook asparagus until tender-crisp; drain. Meanwhile, sauté celery in butter. Stir in flour and cook 1 minute. Add milk all at once and cook, stirring until sauce thickens. Add Worcestershire, lemon juice, celery salt and white pepper. Empty sour cream into medium bowl; gradually add hot sauce, stirring constantly. Sprinkle fillets lightly with lemon juice and salt to taste. Roll each fish fillet around 3 asparagus spears; arrange roll-ups on top of rice, lapped edge down. Spoon sour cream sauce over fish and sprinkle with cheese and almonds. Bake at 350 degrees for 25 minutes or just until fish becomes milky white and flakes easily with fork.

Stuffed Sole
Serves: 5 to 6

6 large, thin sole fillets
3 to 4 mushrooms, finely chopped
1 stalk celery, finely chopped
1/2 teaspoon parsley
1/2 teaspoon tarragon
1/4 cup finely chopped onion
3 tablespoons butter
5 to 6 shrimp, coarsely chopped
2 tablespoons flour
1/4 cup milk
1/4 cup dry white wine
1/2 cup grated cheese (may use
any desired cheese)
1/2 cup cracker or bread crumbs
1 tablespoon lemon juice
1/2 teaspoon pepper
Chopped fresh parsley (garnish)

Sauté mushrooms, celery, seasonings and onion in butter until soft. Add shrimp and cook over medium heat until shrimp change color. Stir in flour then milk. Stir until smooth. Add wine, then cheese and cook until cheese melts and sauce is very thick. Remove from heat. Add crumbs and set aside for 10 minutes. Spread 1 to 2 tablespoons stuffing in center of each fillet. Roll fillet up and arrange in buttered casserole with a cover. Sprinkle with lemon juice and pepper. Cover and bake at 400 degrees for 25 minutes. Remove cover and bake for an additional 10 minutes. Garnish with chopped parsley.

Grilled Swordfish
Serves: 4

4 swordfish steaks
Juice from 2 to 3 limes
1/2 cup dry vermouth
1 tablespoon salad oil
2 tablespoons soy sauce
1/4 teaspoon salt
1/2 teaspoon ground ginger

Combine lime juice, vermouth, oil, soy sauce, salt and ginger. Marinate steaks in this mixture for about 1 hour in the refrigerator. Grill steaks for 5 to 7 minutes on each side brushing frequently with marinade.

Baked Sesame Fish

Serves: 2

2 orange roughy, red snapper or
    halibut fillets (about 6-ounces
    each)
2 tablespoons orange juice
1 tablespoon ketchup
1 tablespoon soy sauce
1/2 tablespoon lemon juice
1/2 teaspoon sesame oil
1/2 tablespoon brown sugar
Non-stick vegetable oil spray
1 tablespoon sesame seeds

Place fish in a single layer in a glass baking dish. In a small bowl, combine orange juice, ketchup, soy sauce, lemon juice, sesame oil and brown sugar. Pour over fish. Cover and marinate in refrigerator for 2 hours, turning once. Remove fish and reserve marinade. Coat broiler pan with vegetable spray or oil. Put fish on pan and broil about 4 minutes on each side. Heat remaining sauce and pour over fish on serving plate. Top with sesame seeds.

Seasoned Orange Roughy

Serves: 3 to 4

1 pound orange roughy
1/4 cup butter
2/3 cup finely crushed dry
    seasoned bread crumbs
1/4 cup grated parmesan cheese
1/2 teaspoon basil
1/2 teaspoon oregano
1/2 teaspoon salt
1/2 teaspoon garlic powder
1 tablespoon white wine
1 tablespoon lemon juice
1/2 cup sliced mushrooms
1/4 cup slivered almonds

In a 9 x 13-inch pan, melt butter in oven. In a separate pan, combine bread crumbs, cheese, basil, oregano, salt and garlic powder. Dip fish in melted butter, then in crumb mixture. Arrange coated fish in 9 x 13-inch pan. Sprinkle with wine and lemon juice. Sprinkle mushrooms and almonds on top. Bake covered at 350 degrees for 25 minutes.

Fish Broil
Serves: 4 to 6

2 pounds white fleshed fish fillets
  (red snapper, ling cod or halibut)
Vegetable oil
3 tablespoons butter or margarine
1/4 pound mushrooms, sliced
2 tablespoons minced green
  onions
1/2 teaspoon salt
1/2 teaspoon basil leaves
1/4 teaspoon lemon pepper
1 medium tomato, chopped
1 cup shredded cheddar cheese
1 egg, beaten

Place fish on lightly greased baking sheet. Drizzle the top of each fillet with ½ teaspoon of vegetable oil. Bake at 500 degrees for 5 to 8 minutes until fish flakes. Remove from oven and drain off juices. Return to baking sheet. Meanwhile, melt butter in fry pan; add the mushrooms and green onions. Cook until liquid evaporates. Remove from heat and stir in the salt, basil, lemon pepper, tomato, cheese and egg. Spoon mixture over the fillets. Broil 5-inches from heat until cheese melts.

Seafood Fettucine
Serves: 8

1 pound cooked shellfish (crab,
  shrimp, scallops, or a
  combination)
1 pound spinach fettucine, cooked
  and drained
1 large onion, thinly sliced
2 leeks, thinly sliced (white
  part only)
1/2 cup dry white wine
1/2 cup chicken broth
2 tablespoons flour
1/8 teaspoon cayenne pepper
1 cup lowfat milk (hot)
1 teaspoon fresh lemon juice
1/2 cup grated parmesan cheese

Combine onion, leeks and wine; cook until onion is tender. In a bowl, combine cold broth and flour; add to onion mixture. Add pepper and hot milk; simmer, uncovered, stirring frequently, until thickened. Remove from heat, add lemon juice and shellfish; mix well. Put 1 cup of cooked fettucine noodles in the bottom of 8 individual baking dishes and pour equal amounts of fish sauce over each. Bake at 350 degrees for 10 minutes. Sprinkle with parmesan cheese and serve.

Crab Casserole

Serves: 10 to 12

5 cups crab (2½-pounds)
3/4 pound sliced fresh mushrooms
5 teaspoons chopped onions
2/3 cup butter
2/3 cup flour
5 cups milk
1 teaspoon salt
1/4 teaspoon pepper
2½ teaspoons parsley flakes
1¼ teaspoons dry mustard
1/3 cup sherry
2/3 cup pimiento
5 cups cooked rice
2/3 cup grated parmesan cheese

Sauté mushrooms and onions in 2 tablespoons butter. Add remaining butter and blend in flour. Add 4 cups milk, stirring constantly. When thick, stir in seasonings and 1 cup milk. Add pimiento and crab; spoon over cooked rice in casserole. Sprinkle with cheese. Bake at 425 degrees for 30 minutes until bubbly and cheese is browned.

Shrimp Eleganté

Serves: 4

1 pound medium shrimp, peeled
  and de-veined
2 tablespoons minced onion
2 tablespoons butter
1/4 pound sliced mushrooms
1 teaspoon salt
1/8 teaspoon pepper
3 tablespoons chili sauce
1⅔ cups water
1⅓ cups uncooked instant rice
1 cup sour cream
1 tablespoon flour
1 tablespoon chopped chives
  (garnish)
1 tablespoon chopped parsley
  (garnish)

Sauté onion in butter until golden. Add shrimp and mushrooms and sauté until shrimp are pink. Combine salt, pepper, chili sauce and water. Add to shrimp mixture and bring to a boil. Stir in rice, cover and simmer for 5 minutes. Combine sour cream and flour. Add to the shrimp and rice mixture and heat gently (do not bring to a boil). Divide between plates, garnish with chives and/or parsley and serve.

Shrimp with Feta Cheese and Tomatoes

Serves: 2 to 3

1 pound jumbo shrimp, peeled and
  de-veined
2 tablespoons olive oil
2 to 3 tomatoes, peeled, seeded
  and chopped
2 cloves garlic, minced
1/2 teaspoon oregano, crumbled
4 ounces feta cheese, crumbled

Sauté shrimp in olive oil for 5 to 6 minutes, until pink. Add tomatoes, garlic, oregano and cheese. Stir over medium heat for another 5 minutes. Add salt and pepper to taste. Serve over rice or fresh pasta.

Sherried Scallops

Serves: 4

1 pound scallops
2 to 3 tablespoons butter
2 garlic cloves, minced
Pinch tarragon
Pinch oregano
Pinch paprika
Pepper to taste
Juice of ½ lemon (5 teaspoons)
2 tablespoons sherry
1 tablespoon chopped parsley

Melt butter over medium heat. Stir in garlic, tarragon and oregano. Add scallops; season with paprika and pepper. Squeeze lemon juice over scallops and sauté 4 to 5 minutes. Remove scallops. Increase heat to high. Add sherry and cook, stirring constantly, until liquid is almost evaporated. Return scallops to sauce and heat briefly. Garnish with chopped parsley and serve immediately.

Soy Snapper
Serves: 4

1½ pounds red snapper
1 tablespoon brown sugar
2 tablespoons vegetable oil
1 tablespoon cider vinegar
1/2 teaspoon ground ginger
1 clove garlic, crushed
1 tablespoon parsley
2 tablespoons soy sauce

Combine ingredients for marinade. Add snapper and marinate at least 30 minutes to an hour. Broil or barbecue approximately 3 minutes on each side.

Shrimp in Mustard-Dill Sauce
Serves: 4

20 large shrimp, shelled and de-veined
1/2 lemon
2 cups whipping cream
2 tablespoons stone ground mustard
1 teaspoon dried dill weed
Salt to taste
20 broccoli florets, steamed tender-crisp

Boil shrimp with lemon for 2 to 3 minutes until firm and pink. Drain, discard lemon and keep warm. In skillet, boil cream over high heat for 2 to 4 minutes until it has thickened. Stir in mustard, dill weed and salt. Remove from heat. Divide sauce among heated serving plates and swirl to cover the bottom. Arrange shrimp and broccoli decoratively and serve.

Seafood Pilaf

Serves: 6

1/2 pound bay scallops
1/2 pound shrimp, peeled and
  de-veined (may be frozen)
2 tablespoons olive oil
8 scallions, thinly sliced,
  including tops
1 small onion, minced (1/3 cup)
1 large clove garlic, finely
  minced (1 teaspoon)
2⅓ cups dry white wine
2/3 cup bottled clam juice
2 teaspoons tomato paste
4 to 5 plum tomatoes, chopped
  or
2 to 3 medium tomatoes, chopped
1½ cups long-grain brown rice
1 tablespoon minced fresh mint
  or
1 teaspoon dried mint
1/2 cup minced fresh parsley,
  divided
Fresh ground pepper to taste
Lemon wedges

In large saucepan, heat oil and cook scallions, onion and garlic over medium heat until soft. Transfer mixture to bowl with slotted spoon, leaving as much oil as possible in pan. To remaining oil, add scallops and shrimp (if using frozen shrimp, add first, and then add scallops as soon as shrimp defrost) and cook until shrimp turn pink. Transfer seafood to bowl with scallion mixture. Add wine and clam juice to pan. Bring the liquid to a boil, add rice, tomato paste, and tomatoes; stir. Cover pan, reduce heat to low and cook rice 30 to 40 minutes or until liquid is absorbed and rice is tender. To serve, add seafood mixture, mint (if desired), 2 tablespoons parsley and pepper to cooked rice. Fluff rice with fork and reheat over low heat (if necessary). Sprinkle remaining parsley on top and serve with lemon wedges.

Shrimp Diane

Serves: 3 to 4

Shrimp Dish:

**1½ pounds large shrimp, shelled
and de-veined**
6 tablespoons shrimp stock
3/4 cup unsalted butter, divided
1/4 cup chopped green onions
3/4 teaspoon salt
1/2 teaspoon minced garlic
**1/2 teaspoon ground cayenne
pepper**
1/4 teaspoon ground white pepper
1/4 teaspoon ground black pepper
**1/4 teaspoon dried sweet basil
leaves**
1/4 teaspoon dried thyme leaves
1/8 teaspoon dried oregano leaves
1/2 pound mushrooms, sliced
**3 tablespoons freshly chopped
parsley**

Shrimp Stock:

**1½ pounds rinsed shrimp heads
and shells**
2 quarts cold water
**1 medium onion, unpeeled and
quartered**
**1 large clove garlic, unpeeled and
quartered**
1 rib celery

For shrimp: Rinse and peel shrimp. Use shells and heads to make shrimp stock. In a large skillet, melt ½ cup butter over high heat. When almost melted, add green onions, salt, garlic, ground peppers, basil, thyme and oregano; stir well. Add shrimp and sauté, shaking the pan in a back and forth motion until they turn pink, about 1 minute. Add mushrooms, 4 tablespoons stock, and the remaining ¼ cup butter in chunks and continue cooking, shaking the pan. Before the butter chunks are completely melted, add parsley and remaining 2 tablespoons stock and continue cooking and shaking the pan until all ingredients are mixed thoroughly and butter sauce is the consistency of cream. Serve immediately over fresh cooked linguine or rice.

For stock: Place all ingredients in stock pot, bring to boil over high heat, then gently simmer 4 to 8 hours, replenishing the water as needed to keep about 1 quart of liquid in the pan. Strain, cool and refrigerate until ready to use. (The stock can be made in considerably less time; i.e., boiling for 30 minutes is better than just using water for broth.)

Seafood Kabobs

Serves: 4 to 6

1 pound raw shrimp (30 or 40
   to a pound)
1 pound sea scallops
1 pound red snapper or halibut
1/2 cup olive oil
1/4 cup fresh lemon juice
2 cloves garlic, crushed
12 mushrooms
12 cherry tomatoes
12 green onions, cut in 3-inch
   lengths

Shell and de-vein shrimp. Mix olive oil, lemon juice and garlic. Place seafood in oil and lemon mixture. Cover seafood and refrigerate for 2 hours. Place seafood alternating with vegetables on bamboo or barbecue skewers. Cook over barbecue coals for 8 to 10 minutes. Baste with marinade while cooking.

Clam Linguine

Serves: 4

36 small clams, opened
   or
2 (6 1/2-ounce) cans chopped
   clams, with juice
2 tablespoons vegetable oil
3 cloves garlic, chopped
6 green onions, chopped
3/4 cup fresh sliced mushrooms
1/4 cup dry white wine
1/4 cup fresh chopped parsley
1/4 teaspoon oregano
1/4 teaspoon basil
1/4 teaspoon pepper
1 pound linguine, cooked and
   drained
1/2 cup grated parmesan cheese

Remove clams from shells, reserving juice; or drain canned clams, saving juice. In a skillet, heat oil and sauté garlic, green onions and mushrooms over medium heat until golden. Add clams and stir until clams are just cooked, about 5 minutes. Add clam juice, wine, parsley and spices and simmer 5 minutes. Place hot cooked pasta on serving plates, top with clam sauce and sprinkle with parmesan cheese.

Shrimp and Scallop Linguine

Serves: 4

1 pound bay shrimp
1 pound scallops
1/2 sweet red pepper, chopped
1/2 green pepper, chopped
1 small zucchini, sliced
1 tablespoon butter
1 tablespoon olive oil
2 tablespoons white wine
3 cups whipping cream
Salt and pepper to taste
Juice of one lemon
1 cup grated parmesan cheese
1 pound fresh linguine or spinach
  linguine

Sauté peppers and zucchini in butter and olive oil for 3 minutes, add shrimp and scallops, continue cooking until seafood is just cooked through (approximately 3 minutes). Remove from pan; set aside. Add white wine and whipping cream. Increase heat to medium-high. Allow cream to bubble and begin to thicken. Boil water in large pot and cook noodles for approximately 5 minutes. To the cream mixture, add scallops, shrimp and vegetables, salt, pepper and lemon juice. Remove from heat and add cheese. Serve the sauce over the pasta.

Twice-Baked Crab Potatoes

Serves: 8

2 cups crabmeat
4 large baking potatoes
4 tablespoon butter
1/2 cup chopped onion
1/2 cup sliced mushrooms
Salt and pepper to taste
1 cup dry vermouth
1/4 cup sour cream
1/4 cup half and half
3/4 cup grated Jarlsberg cheese

Scrub and bake potatoes. Cool slightly and cut in half, lengthwise. Scrape pulp into bowl, leaving a 1/4-inch shell. Reserve skins and mash pulp. Melt butter in skillet and sauté onion until lightly colored (about 25 minutes). Add mushrooms and sauté 5 minutes. Add crab meat and season with salt and pepper. Add vermouth and bring to a boil. Stir frequently. Cook until liquid is absorbed. Remove from heat and stir in sour cream and half and half. Combine crab and onion mixture, potato pulp and ½ cup cheese. Add additional salt, pepper or cream if necessary. Mound the mixture into potato skins. Sprinkle with additional ¼ cup cheese. Bake at 400 degrees until cheese bubbles.

Shrimp Spaghetti
Serves: 8

1½ pounds shrimp meat, cooked
6 ounces spaghetti
2 tablespoons butter or margarine
1 large onion, chopped
1 (10¾-ounce) can cream of
  mushroom soup
1 cup half and half
1 tablespoon Worcestershire sauce
1 tablespoon Dijon mustard
2 hard boiled eggs, sliced
1 (5-ounce) can water chestnuts,
  sliced and drained
1 (2-ounce) jar pimientos
Salt and Tabasco to taste
2/3 cup shredded cheddar cheese

While spaghetti cooks, melt butter over medium heat, add onions and cook until tender. Add soup, then blend in half and half, Worcestershire sauce and mustard. Add cooked spaghetti and mix well. Stir in shrimp, eggs, water chestnuts and pimientos. Season to taste. Put mixture in a 9 x 13-inch baking dish and sprinkle with cheese. Bake at 350 degrees for 30 minutes.

NOTE: Great casserole for a crowd.

Seafood and Artichoke Pasta
Serves: 4

1/2 pound medium size shrimp
1 pound steamer clams
1 can artichoke hearts, drained
2 cloves garlic, chopped
1/4 cup olive oil, divided
1 (1 quart) can tomatoes
1 (6-ounce) can tomato paste
Salt and pepper to taste
3/4 pound spaghetti or fresh pasta
2 tablespoons butter
1/2 cup chopped parsley

Sauté garlic in 2 tablespoons olive oil; set aside. Remove seeds from tomatoes (reserve liquid); chop tomatoes. Add chopped tomatoes, juice and tomato paste to the garlic; simmer for 30 minutes. Wash clams, peel and de-vein shrimp. Sauté shrimp in remaining olive oil for 5 minutes, until shrimp are light pink in color. Stir in clams and heat until clams open. Add the shrimp, clams and artichokes to the tomato sauce mixture. Add salt and pepper to taste. Cook spaghetti or pasta according to instructions; drain well. Return to pan and add butter. Serve pasta on a large, warmed platter and pour the seafood mixture over the pasta. Sprinkle with parsley and serve.

Crab and Artichoke Croissants

Serves: 6

1/3 pound crabmeat
1/3 cup mayonnaise
1/4 teaspoon dill weed
1 clove garlic, minced
2 tablespoons chopped parsley
Dash of cayenne pepper
4 ounces cheddar cheese, shredded
1 (2¼-ounce) can ripe olives,
   sliced
1 artichoke heart, cut up
3 croissants

In a small bowl, mix together the mayonnaise, dill, garlic, parsley and cayenne pepper. Stir in the crab, 3-ounces of the cheese, olives and drained, cut up artichoke hearts. Split croissants in half, horizontally. Place them, cut side up, on a baking sheet. Spread crab mixture on croissant halves. Sprinkle each equally with remaining cheese. Broil sandwiches about 4-inches from heat, until topping is melted, approximately 3 to 5 minutes.

Spinach Cream Sauce

Serves: 8

1 (10-ounce) package frozen
   chopped spinach
2 tablespoons butter
2 tablespoons flour
1/2 teaspoon salt
3/4 cup milk
1/2 pint sour cream

Cook spinach and drain thoroughly; set aside. In a saucepan, melt butter and cream in flour to form a paste. Add salt and milk, stirring constantly, until it comes to a boil and is smooth and thick. Add sour cream and cooked spinach. Reheat and serve with salmon or lamb.

Tartar Sauce

Yield: 1/2 cup sauce

1/2 cup mayonnaise
6 pitted green olives
1 slice onion
2 sweet pickles, cut into
   1-inch pieces
1 tablespoon capers

Place all ingredients in a blender or food processor and process at low until pickles and olives are finely grated. Serve with seafood.

Savor
the
Flavor
of
MEATS

❧ ❧ ❧

Burgers in a Roll

Serves: 8

2 pounds extra lean ground beef
8 (unsliced) French, sourdough, or
    Kaiser rolls
Garlic powder to taste
1/2 cup thinly sliced green onions
1/2 cup chili sauce
1/2 teaspoon dry mustard
1 cup grated cheddar cheese

Cut a thin slice from the top of each roll. Using your fingers, pull out the inside bread dough, leaving a shell about ½-inch thick. Sprinkle a little garlic powder inside each prepared roll. Mix ground beef, onions, chili sauce, dry mustard and cheese. Divide mixture evenly among rolls and place on a baking sheet. Bake at 350 degrees for 15 minutes without the tops, add extra cheddar cheese (if desired). Replace tops and bake an additional 20 minutes until rolls are crispy and filling is firm.

NOTE: Serve with potato salad and fresh fruit.

Gourmet Hamburgers

Serves: 4

1 pound lean ground beef,
    lightly salted
1/4 cup bleu cheese
1 tablespoon burgundy wine
1 teaspoon Worcestershire sauce
2 teaspoons mayonnaise
1/2 teaspoon mustard

Shape salted beef into 8 thin patties of equal size. Mix cheese, wine, Worcestershire, mayonnaise and mustard; spread evenly over 4 patties, but not all the way to the edge. Place a patty on top of each prepared patty and pinch edges together to seal and shape into one thick patty. Broil to taste, turning patties gently. Serve alone or on a bun.

NOTE: This is perfect for those bleu cheese lovers!

Mexican Tortilla Casserole

Serves: 4

1 pound ground beef
1/2 cup chopped onion
1 teaspoon salt
1 tablespoon chili powder
1/2 teaspoon oregano
1/4 teaspoon basil
1 (15-ounce) can tomato sauce
5 (8-inch) flour tortillas
2 cups shredded cheddar cheese

Garnish: (optional)
Sour cream, green onions,
  sliced black olives, avocado,
  tomatoes or salsa

Brown ground beef and onion. Drain. Add salt, chili powder, oregano, basil and tomato sauce; simmer for 10 minutes. In a greased round casserole, layer the tortillas, meat sauce and cheese, repeating until ingredients are gone. Bake at 350 degrees for 15 minutes. Cut into wedges and serve. Garnish, if desired.

Korean Meatballs

Serves: 4

1 pound lean ground beef
1 tablespoons soy sauce
1/8 teaspoon ground pepper
1 green onion, chopped
2 tablespoons toasted sesame
  seeds
Flour
1 egg, beaten
1 tablespoon water
1 to 2 tablespoons salad oil

Dipping Sauce:
4 tablespoons soy sauce
4 teaspoons vinegar
2 teaspoons honey or brown sugar
Cayenne pepper to taste
2 teaspoons toasted sesame seeds

Mix beef, soy sauce, pepper, onion and sesame seeds. Shape into 16 meatballs. Lightly coat meatballs with flour. Beat together egg and water. Dip meatballs in egg, let drain briefly. Heat frying pan and cook meatballs in salad oil for 5 to 7 minutes, turning several times. Remove and drain on paper towels. Transfer to a serving platter and keep warm in a 150 degree oven until ready to serve. Mix dipping sauce ingredients. Pass sauce while serving meatballs.

Swedish Meatballs

Serves: 6

Meatballs:
1 small onion, finely chopped
2 tablespoons butter
1 pound extra lean ground beef
2 eggs, beaten
1 cup mashed potatoes
1/4 teaspoon nutmeg
1 teaspoon salt
1/4 teaspoon pepper
1/2 teaspoon Tabasco sauce
1/3 cup whipping cream
1/4 cup dry bread crumbs
Oil for frying

Sauce:
3 tablespoons butter
3 tablespoons flour
1/4 cup chicken broth
3/4 cup whipping cream
1/4 teaspoon nutmeg
2 teaspoons chopped parsley

For meatballs: Sauté onions in butter until soft. In a medium bowl, combine onions, meat, eggs, potatoes, nutmeg, salt, pepper, Tabasco, whipping cream and bread crumbs. Form into 1½-inch balls and roll each in flour. Brown meatballs, a few at a time, in hot oil. Place in a greased baking dish.

For sauce: Melt butter and blend in flour. Slowly stir in broth, whipping cream, nutmeg and parsley. Cook over medium heat stirring constantly with wire whisk until smooth and thickened. Pour over meatballs and bake at 350 degrees for 10 to 15 minutes.

NOTE: This can be served as a main dish or as an appetizer. This makes approximately 24 meatballs.

Soccer Season Stew
Serves: 4 to 6

1½ pounds stew beef
2 or 3 potatoes, cut in
  1-inch chunks
3 or 4 carrots, cut in
  1-inch slices
1 medium onion, chopped
1 can artichoke hearts, drained
10 fresh mushrooms
1 tablespoon chopped parsley
1 (10¾-ounce) can golden
  mushroom soup
1/2 cup burgundy wine
1 teaspoon Worcestershire sauce
2 bay leaves

Line a 3-quart casserole with foil, leaving 4 to 5-inches hanging outside the edges. Layer meat, potatoes, carrots, onions, artichokes, mushrooms and parsley in casserole. Pour soup over all. Rinse the soup can with the wine and Worcestershire sauce and pour into casserole. Add bay leaves. Seal casserole well, pulling extra foil up over the lid. (At this point, casserole may be refrigerated for up to 24 hours until ready to bake.) Bake at 375 degrees for 3 hours.

NOTE: Serve with green salad and french bread.

The Barber's Chili
Serves: 4

1/2 pound top sirloin, cut
  in ½ to 1-inch cubes
1/2 pound pork, cut in ½
  to 1-inch cubes
3 tablespoons salad oil or
  bacon fat
1 medium onion, sliced
1 clove garlic, minced
1 tablespoon chili powder
1/4 teaspoon ground ginger
Salt and pepper to taste
2 cups tomato sauce
1 (15-ounce) can red kidney or
  chili beans, drained
1 tablespoon chili powder
1/4 teaspoon ground ginger
1/4 teaspoon rosemary
Salt, pepper and paprika to taste
Chopped onion (garnish)
Shredded cheddar cheese (garnish)

Heat the oil or bacon fat in a skillet; add onion and cook 2 minutes. Add the meat, garlic, chili powder, ginger, salt and pepper; cook, stirring until meat is browned. In a saucepan, simmer the tomato sauce, beans, chili powder, ginger, rosemary, salt, pepper and paprika. Simmer for 5 minutes. Add the meat mixture and simmer until thick, about 1 hour. Serve with chopped onions and grated cheddar cheese.

NOTE: This is great served with sesame cheese muffins. (See index; breads)

Deurmyer's Chili
Serves: 10 to 12

1½ pounds pork
(cut in 1-inch chunks)
1½ pounds lean beef
(cut in 1-inch chunks)
1/4 cup olive oil
1 quart water
2 bay leaves
3 to 6 tablespoons chili
powder (according to taste)
3 teaspoons salt
10 cloves garlic, chopped
1 teaspoon ground cumin
1 teaspoon oregano, crumbled
1 teaspoon cayenne pepper
1/2 teaspoon black pepper
1 tablespoon sugar
1 tablespoon paprika
3 tablespoons flour
6 tablespoons corn meal

Heat olive oil in a 6-quart pot; add meat and sear over high heat. Stir constantly until gray, not brown. Add 1-quart of water and simmer, covered for 1½ to 2 hours. Add bay leaves during last 15 to 20 minutes. Add all remaining ingredients except the flour and corn meal. (If you prefer milder chili, use about ½ of the chili powder indicated.) Simmer for an additional 30 minutes. Mix flour and corn meal with enough cold water to make a medium-thick paste and add to the pot. Cook for 5 minutes to determine if more water is necessary for desired consistency. Stir to prevent sticking.

NOTE: Chili is better if it sits overnight. Water may be added when reheating.

Black Tie Chuck Steak Barbecue
Serves: 6 to 8

2 to 3 pounds chuck steak
(1½-inches thick)
2 cloves garlic, minced
2 tablespoons olive oil
1/2 cup red wine vinegar
1/3 cup catsup
1 tablespoon Worcestershire sauce
1 teaspoon sugar
1 teaspoon dried basil

Mix together ingredients for marinade. Slash fat edges of steak at one inch intervals. Put meat in a shallow pan and cover with marinade. Marinate meat for 6 hours or overnight, turning several times. Drain meat and pat dry, reserving marinade. Grill meat over medium coals for 25 minutes, brushing occasionally with marinade. Turn and grill an additional 20 to 25 minutes for medium rare, brushing occasionally with marinade.

Ed's Chili
Servings: 14 to 18

2½ **pounds ground beef**
1 **pound pork chorizo**
2 **medium onions, chopped**
1 **green pepper, chopped**
1 **(28-ounce) can peeled tomatoes**
1 **(28-ounce) can tomato sauce**
1 **cup hearty red wine (optional)**
2 **cloves garlic, crushed**
1 **bay leaf**
1 **teaspoon cayenne pepper**
1 **teaspoon oregano, crumbled**
1 **teaspoon ground cumin**
1 **teaspoon salt**
1 **teaspoon pepper**
1 **tablespoon chili powder**
2 **(27-ounce) cans kidney beans,
   drained (reserve liquid)**
1 **(30-ounce) can small red beans,
   drained (reserve liquid)**

Toppings (optional):
**Grated cheddar cheese, chopped
   green onions, sour cream**

Brown hamburger and drain. Brown chorizo in separate pan and drain. Combine cooked meat in a large soup pot. Add onions and peppers to meat and cook until softened (about 5 minutes). Add tomatoes, tomato sauce and red wine (if desired). Add spices and reheat until mixture comes to a boil; cover and simmer several hours. Add beans 30 minutes before serving. If more moisture is needed, add the reserved bean liquid or more red wine. Garnish with toppings, if desired.

NOTE: Serve with corn bread and raw vegetable platter.

Curt's Hearty Spaghetti Sauce
Serves: 10 to 12

1 pound Italian sausage (4 to 5 links)
1½ pounds lean ground beef
1 tablespoon leaf oregano, crumbled
1 tablespoon basil, crumbled
1 tablespoon thyme, crumbled
2 cloves garlic, minced
1 tablespoon Italian seasoning, with savory
1 medium onion, chopped
2 (28-ounce) cans crushed tomatoes
3 (6-ounce) cans tomato paste
1 cup water
1/4 cup red wine
1/4 cup grated parmesan cheese
1 tablespoon salt
1/2 teaspoon ground pepper

In a small fry pan, parboil sausages for 10 minutes. Drain and rinse sausages. Cut each sausage into 4 to 5 equal size chunks and brown thoroughly over medium heat. In a 4-quart sauce pot, brown ground beef thoroughly over medium-high heat. Add oregano, basil, thyme, garlic, Italian seasoning and onion during the final minutes of browning. Reduce to low heat. Add tomatoes, tomato paste, and water to ground beef; mix well. Add wine, cheese, salt and pepper to ground beef; mix well. After browning thoroughly, add sausages to all other ingredients. Simmer at least 2 hours over low heat, stirring occasionally.

NOTE: It is recommended that you cool and refrigerate overnight, remove any surface grease and reheat before serving. This is good served over fresh pasta, ravioli, tortellini or as a sauce for lasagna. It gets better and better as it ages.

Poor Man's Steak Kabobs
Serves: 6 to 8

3 to 4 pounds boneless chuck
  roast
1½ to 2 teaspoons meat tenderizer

Marinade:
2 teaspoons garlic powder
2 tablespoons brown sugar
1 teaspoon ground ginger
1 teaspoon black pepper
1 teaspoon monosodium glutamate
  (optional)
2 tablespoons cooking oil
1/4 cup soy sauce
1/4 cup water

Vegetables:
Mushrooms, cherry tomatoes,
  onions, green peppers

Sprinkle tenderizer over roast (about ½ teaspoon per pound). Pierce roast deeply and leave at room temperature for 30 to 60 minutes. Cut roast into 1½-inch cubes. Mix marinade and pour over cubes. Let stand, covered, at room temperature for 2 hours (or in refrigerator for 4 hours) stirring occasionally. Drain meat and reserve marinade. Thread cubes onto skewers alternating with favorite vegetables. Barbecue over medium-hot coals for 10 to 15 minutes, basting with remaining marinade.

Steak Southwest
Serves: 6

2½ pounds flank steak
2 onions, chopped
2 cloves garlic, minced
1/4 cup butter
1/2 cup dark rum
1 tablespoon chili powder
1 teaspoon crushed oregano
1 teaspoon salt (optional)

With tip of sharp knife, score both sides of steak about ⅛-inch deep in diamond pattern. Sauté onions and garlic in butter. Add rum, chili powder and oregano. Bring to boil, cover and simmer for 5 minutes. Pour into large shallow baking dish. Let cool until warm. Coat both sides of steak in marinade. Let stand at room temperature for 30 minutes or longer, occasionally turning steak. Remove steak and pat dry, reserving onions. Place steak on broiler pan or barbecue grill and sprinkle with salt, if desired. Broil or grill 4 minutes on first side. Turn steak, top with onions and cook for an additional 4 minutes.

Ginger Beef Stroganoff

Serves: 4 to 6

1/2 cup soy sauce
1/3 cup sherry
1½ tablespoons fresh ginger, grated
1/2 tablespoon sugar
1 clove garlic, crushed
2½ pounds sirloin, cut in 1¼-inch chunks
2 tablespoons butter
1/2 cup chopped onion
1 pound fresh mushrooms, sliced
Water
1½ tablespoons flour
1/4 teaspoon salt
 Freshly ground pepper to taste
1/2 cup sour cream or yogurt
2 to 3 tablespoons fresh snipped parsley

Combine soy, sherry, ginger, sugar and garlic; mix well. Pour over sirloin chunks and marinate at least 4 hours. Drain beef and reserve marinade. Sauté onions and mushrooms in butter; remove from pan (reserving liquid); set aside. In same pan, sauté beef for 2 to 3 minutes (rare beef). Remove from pan and keep warm. Add water to reserved marinade to make one cup. In another sauté pan, stir flour into 1 tablespoon of the reserved onion-mushroom liquid and gradually add the one cup marinade. Cook until thickened. Add beef, onions, mushrooms, salt, pepper and sour cream (do not boil). Add parsley and serve over hot buttered noodles.

Curried Lamb Kabobs
Serves: 4

2 pounds boneless lamb, well
 trimmed of fat, cut into 1½-inch
 cubes
1/3 cup olive oil
1/3 cup Dijon mustard
1/4 cup grated onion
1/4 cup white wine vinegar
1 tablespoon Worcestershire sauce
1 tablespoon curry powder (scant)
2 cloves garlic, crushed
1½ teaspoons marjoram leaves
1 teaspoon salt
1/2 teaspoon pepper
1/2 pound fresh mushrooms
1 large green pepper
2 onions, cut into 8 pieces each,
 or,
8 to 12 small boiling onions
4 cherry tomatoes

In a glass bowl, beat oil, mustard, onion, vinegar, Worcestershire, curry, garlic, marjoram, salt and pepper. Place lamb cubes into marinade and toss until well coated. Cover with plastic wrap and marinate at room temperature at least 2 hours or in refrigerator for 3 to 4 hours. Clean mushrooms, cut pepper into 12 pieces, cut onions into 16 pieces. Skewer lamb, mushroom, pepper and onion, repeating until all are gone, ending with a lamb piece on 4 skewers. Broil 15 minutes or less, basting with remaining marinade during broiling, turning once or twice. Add cherry tomatoes at skewer ends during last 5 minutes.

Pork Chops with Pear Chutney
Serves: 4

4 pork chops (3-ounces each)
3/4 cup orange juice
1/4 cup cider vinegar
1/8 teaspoon cinnamon
1/8 teaspoon ground ginger
1 teaspoon slivered orange peel
2 pears, peeled, cored and
 chopped fine
1 tablespoon raisins
1 teaspoon diced candied ginger

Place orange juice, vinegar, cinnamon, ground ginger and orange peel in a sauce pan. Bring to a boil and add pears and raisins. Cook over medium heat until the mixture becomes syrupy, about 10 to 15 minutes. Remove from heat and add candied ginger. Grill pork chops or cook over medium-high heat for 10 minutes. Turn and cook for an additional 5 minutes. Smother with the pear chutney and serve.

Lamb Curry
Serves: 4

1 pound lamb, cubed
1/4 cup vegetable oil
2 medium size tart, unpeeled
   apples, diced
2 small onions, diced
1 tablespoon flour
1 cup cold water
1 beef bouillon cube
2 teaspoons curry powder
1/2 teaspoon salt
1/4 teaspoon pepper
1/4 teaspoon cinnamon
1/4 cup raisins
1/4 cup green pepper, diced
1/4 cup peanuts, chopped
1 cup uncooked rice, cooked
   (makes 3 cups)

Brown meat in oil. Remove meat and add apples and onions to meat drippings cooking until tender. In separate sauce pan, blend flour in cold water. Add bouillon cube and bring to a boil. Add bouillon mixture, curry, salt, pepper, and cinnamon to apples and onions; heat to a boil to thicken. Reduce heat, add meat. Simmer for 15 minutes. Add raisins and green pepper; simmer an additional 15 minutes. Garnish with peanuts. Serve over hot cooked rice.

Marinated Pork Chops
Serves: 4

1 pound pork chops

Marinade:
1/4 cup lemon juice
1/2 cup olive oil
1 teaspoon salt
   freshly ground pepper, to taste
1/4 teaspoon fine herbs
1 large clove garlic, puréed

Mix together ingredients for marinade. Pour over pork chops and marinate overnight (or as long as possible); drain and reserve marinade. Grill or broil pork chops, basting with marinade, until the meat is no longer pink inside (about 10 to 15 minutes). Use one marinade recipe for every pound of pork you prepare.

NOTE: Serve with baked potato, fresh steamed carrots and rolls.

Pork Chops in Sour Cream
Serves: 6

6 center cut pork chops, about
   1 to 1½-inch thick, fat
   removed
2 tablespoons flour
2 tablespoons butter or margarine
6 cloves (optional)
2 tablespoons flour
1 (12-ounce) can beef consommé
2 bay leaves
2 teaspoons vinegar
1½ cups sour cream (may use
   light)

Dust chops with flour and brown in butter on both sides in a dutch oven. Remove and put a clove in each chop. Make a gravy with remaining drippings by adding the flour, consommé, bay leaves and vinegar; cook over low heat, until thickened. Remove from heat and add sour cream. Put chops in gravy, cover and bake, at 350 degrees for 1½ hours.

NOTE: Serve with broiled tomatoes and a tossed salad.

Smoked Pork Tenderloin with Sesame Pepper Jelly
Serves: 8 to 10

2 to 3 pork tenderloins
2/3 cup olive oil
1/4 cup sesame seeds
2 teaspoons freshly grated
   ginger root
1/2 teaspoon ground pepper
1/2 teaspoon paprika

Sesame Pepper Jelly:
1 package unflavored gelatin
1/4 cup boiling water
1 cup brown sugar
3 medium red bell peppers,
   seeded and finely chopped
1/4 cup red wine vinegar
2 ounces toasted sesame seeds

Preheat indoor grill or outside barbecue. Rub tenderloins with olive oil. Sprinkle with sesame seeds, ginger, pepper and paprika. Place a meat thermometer in middle, place on grill and cook, basting occasionally with jelly, until temperature reaches 180 degrees. Slice and serve with remaining jelly.

For Sesame Pepper Jelly: Soften gelatin in water until dissolved. Add brown sugar and bring to a boil, stirring constantly. Add peppers and vinegar and bring back to a boil. Turn off heat. Add sesame seeds and let mixture cool. Refrigerate for 2 hours, until mixture sets.

Spiced Sweet and Sour Pork
Serves: 4 to 6

1 pound lean boneless pork loin
1/2 teaspoon garlic powder
1/4 teaspoon cinnamon
1/4 teaspoon cloves
1/8 teaspoon nutmeg
1/8 teaspoon red cayenne pepper
1 tablespoon olive oil, divided
2 medium Rome beauty apples,
  cored and sliced
1 tablespoon cornstarch
1/2 cup apple juice
1 tablespoon teriyaki sauce
1 tablespoon cider vinegar
1 (8-ounce) can pineapple
  tidbits, with juice
2 cups cooked rice

Partially freeze pork. Slice diagonally across grain into thin slices; set aside. Combine garlic powder, cinnamon, cloves, nutmeg and pepper in a small mixing bowl. Add pork to spice mixture and toss well. Heat 1½ teaspoons oil in skillet over medium heat. When oil is hot, add pork and cook, stirring constantly for approximately 5 minutes, until browned. Remove pork from skillet, and reserve drippings. Add 1½ teaspoon oil and sliced apples to skillet; cook for 3 or 4 minutes until lightly browned. Return pork to skillet. Mix cornstarch, apple juice, teriyaki sauce and cider vinegar together; add pineapple (with juice). Pour mixture into skillet. Cook and stir for a few minutes, until sauce thickens. Serve over rice.

Oriental Pork
Serves: 6

1 to 1½ pounds pork tenderloin,
  visible fat removed
1/3 cup low sodium soy sauce
1/4 cup Safflower oil
1/8 teaspoon ground black pepper
1/2 teaspoon garlic powder
1/2 teaspoon ground ginger
2 tablespoons brown sugar
Parsley (garnish)

Mix together ingredients for marinade. Place meat in dish and turn so that all areas are covered with marinade. Marinate for 24 to 48 hours in the refrigerator, turning often. Bake in a covered casserole dish 45 minutes per pound at 325 degrees. Remove the cover from the baking dish during the last 15 minutes. To serve, drain and discard juice, cut meat diagonally into ½-inch slices and arrange on a serving platter. Garnish with parsley.

NOTE: Serve with rice pilaf and steamed broccoli or asparagus.

Spareribs in Blackberry Wine Marinade
Serves: 6

5 to 6 pounds pork spareribs
1 (1/5th) bottle blackberry wine
1 bottle hickory flavor barbecue
  sauce
1 (8-ounce) jar pineapple rings,
  with juice
1 large jar maraschino cherries,
  with juice
2 tablespoons Worcestershire
  sauce
2 tablespoons soy sauce
1/2 onion, chopped

Put pork spareribs in large pan, cover with water and blackberry wine. Simmer for up to 3 hours (checking after 2 hours). Remove ribs and discard cooking liquid. Wash pan and line completely with foil. Return ribs to pan. In a food processor; combine barbecue sauce, juices from pineapple and cherries, 10 cherries, Worcestershire sauce and soy sauce; blend. Sprinkle chopped onions on ribs, cover with sauce and arrange pineapple rings and remaining cherries on top. Bake, covered, at 375 degrees for 1 hour, uncover and cook an additional 30 minutes.

NOTE: Serve with rice and tossed salad.

Shredded Potato and Ham Pie
Serves: 6

Filling:
4 eggs, beaten
1 cup frozen mixed vegetables
1 cup chopped ham, beef or
  chicken
1 cup shredded cheddar cheese
1/2 cup milk
1/4 teaspoon dried onion

Crust:
2 medium potatoes, peeled and
  shredded (about 2 cups)
1/2 cup shredded cheddar cheese

For filling: Combine eggs, vegetables, chopped meat, cheese, milk and onion.

For crust: Combine potatoes with cheese and press into bottom and up sides of a 9-inch pie plate. Pour filling into crust and bake immediately at 350 degrees for 45 to 50 minutes. (Potatoes will turn brown if left unbaked.)

Ham Potato Scallop
Serves: 8

1½ cups diced cooked ham
1 medium onion, finely chopped
3 tablespoons butter or margarine
3 tablespoons flour
1 teaspoon salt
1/8 teaspoon pepper
1/2 teaspoon dry mustard
1½ cups milk
3/4 cup shredded sharp cheddar
    cheese
4 medium potatoes, sliced ¼-inch
    thick
1/2 cup sliced celery
1/2 cup finely chopped green
    pepper

Sauté onion in melted butter until tender. Stir in flour, salt, pepper and mustard. Gradually pour in milk, stirring constantly, until sauce is thickened. Add cheese and stir until blended. In a greased 1½-quart casserole, alternate layers of sliced raw potatoes, ham, celery and green pepper; cover with ½ of the cheese sauce. Continue to arrange ingredients in layers until all are used. Pour remaining cheese sauce over all. Bake, covered, at 350 degrees for 1 hour; remove cover and continue baking for an additional 30 minutes, or until potatoes are tender and lightly browned on top.

NOTE: Serve with fresh green beans and french bread.

Hazelnut Phyllo Squares
Serves: 6 to 8

1 cup finely chopped ham
4 cups chopped fresh spinach
1 cup sliced fresh mushrooms
1/2 cup chopped green onions
1/4 cup chopped parsley
2 cloves garlic, minced
2 cups grated Swiss cheese
3 eggs, slightly beaten
1/2 teaspoon dill weed
1 cup pre-roasted, finely
    chopped hazelnuts
8 ounces (½ package) phyllo
    dough

Combine spinach, mushrooms, onions, parsley and garlic in a large sauce pan. Cover and cook until spinach is wilted. Remove from heat, mix in cheese, eggs and dill weed. Place one sheet of phyllo in a buttered 2 quart pan (9 x 13 x 2). Brush with butter, repeat with 7 sheets of phyllo, buttering each sheet. Top with spinach mixture, then sprinkle with hazelnuts and meat. Top with remaining 7 sheets of phyllo, brushing each sheet with butter. Bake at 325 degrees for 45 minutes or until golden brown.

NOTE: This is also delicious without the ham for a "meatless" entree.

Stuffed Ham Rolls

Serves: 6

12 thin slices of ham
1 (10-ounce) package frozen
  chopped spinach, thawed and
  squeezed dry
2 cups packaged corn bread
  stuffing
2 cups sour cream

  Cream Sauce:
1/2 cup butter
1/2 cup flour
4 cups milk
1/4 teaspoon salt
1/2 teaspoon paprika
1/2 cup grated parmesan cheese
1 cup grated sharp cheddar cheese

Combine spinach, stuffing, and sour cream; chill overnight. Roll stuffing with hands into pencil shape and roll up in ham slices, making 12 ham roll ups. Put ham rolls in a 9 x 13 baking dish.

For cream sauce: Over medium heat, melt butter. Add flour and mix until well blended. Slowly add milk, salt and paprika; stirring until thick. Add cheeses and heat until melted. Pour sauce over ham rolls. Sprinkle any left over stuffing mixture over top. Bake covered at 350 degrees for 15 minutes, remove cover and bake an additional 15 minutes.

Low-Fat Italian Sausage

Yield: 2 pounds

2 pounds boneless pork,
  well trimmed
4 cloves garlic, crushed
1 teaspoon ground black pepper
2 teaspoons fennel seed
1/4 teaspoon cayenne
1 teaspoon oregano
1 teaspoon sage
1 teaspoon paprika

Peel garlic cloves. Using metal blade of food processor, process garlic until chopped. Add one pound of the meat, pepper, fennel seed and cayenne. Chop meat until coarsely ground. Empty work bowl into mixing bowl. Process the second pound of meat with oregano, sage and paprika. Add this to the other meat in the mixing bowl. Using your hands, mix meat until all herbs are thoroughly blended. This is best made one day ahead for flavors to blend.

NOTE: Since this sausage is virtually fat free, brown in a small amount of olive oil when cooking with it. This product freezes well. This can be added to Italian sauces or made into patties for breakfast.

Savor
the
Flavor
of
POULTRY

Chicken Kiev

Serves: 8

4 whole chicken breasts, split,
  skinned and boned
1/2 pound butter
2 tablespoons chopped chives
2 tablespoons chopped parsley
1 clove garlic, minced
1/2 teaspoon salt
1/4 teaspoon white pepper
1/2 cup flour
2 eggs, beaten
Dry bread crumbs
Oil for frying

Pound chicken breasts to ¼-inch thickness. Divide butter into 8 equal parts and form into balls. Roll balls in mixture of chives, parsley, garlic, salt and pepper. Place 1 ball in center of breast and roll so butter is completely enclosed. Secure with a toothpick. Dust chicken with flour, brush with egg and roll in bread crumbs. Preheat oil in deep fryer or electric skillet to 325 degrees. Fry for 5 to 7 minutes until golden brown.

NOTE: Serve with fresh pasta, spinach salad and crusty french bread.

Grilled Sesame Chicken

Serves: 4

2 whole chicken breasts, split,
  skinned and boned
  (equivalent to 1 pound)

  Marinade:
1/2 cup white grape juice
1/4 cup reduced-sodium soy sauce
  (may use regular)
1/4 cup dry white wine
1½ tablespoons sesame seeds
2 tablespoons vegetable oil
1/4 teaspoon garlic powder
1/4 teaspoon ground ginger

Combine ingredients in a shallow dish; mix well. Add chicken, turning to coat, cover and marinate in refrigerator 2 to 3 hours. Remove chicken, reserving marinade. Grill 4 to 5-inches from medium-hot coals, turning and basting with reserved marinade, for about 15 minutes total.

NOTE: Serve with wild rice and tossed salad.

Swiss Chicken Cutlets
Serves: 10

5 whole chicken breasts, split,
  skinned and boned
Salt to taste
2 eggs, beaten
1 cup finely crushed dry
  seasoned bread crumbs
2 tablespoons vegetable oil
  (more as needed)
3 tablespoons butter
1/4 cup flour
1/2 teaspoon salt
1/8 teaspoon pepper
2½ cups milk
1/2 cup dry white wine
1 cup shredded Swiss cheese
Avocado slices
Tomato wedges

Pound each chicken breast half to about ¼-inch thickness. Sprinkle lightly with salt. Dip in egg, then in bread crumbs. In a skillet, heat 2 tablespoons oil. Brown cutlets a few at a time for 2 minutes on each side, adding more oil as needed. Set chicken aside. In a saucepan, melt butter, blend in flour, salt and pepper. Add milk all at once; cook and stir until thickened and bubbly. Remove from heat and stir in wine. Pour half of the sauce into the bottom of a 9 x 13-inch baking dish. Arrange cutlets on top, overlapping cutlets. Top with remaining sauce. Cover and chill several hours or overnight. Bake, covered, at 350 degrees for 50 minutes, until heated through. Sprinkle with cheese. Top with avocado and tomato. Return to oven for 2 minutes or until cheese melts.

Note: Serve with wild rice, steamed broccoli and sourdough bread.

Indonesian Peanut Chicken

Serves: 4

2 whole chicken breasts, skinned and boned

Marinade:
**1/2 cup cream of coconut
3 tablespoons lime juice
1 tablespoon vegetable oil
2 teaspoons soy sauce
2 cloves garlic, crushed
1/8 teaspoon ground red pepper**

Peanut Sauce:
**1/3 cup chunky peanut butter
1/3 cup water
2 tablespoons soy sauce
1 tablespoon cider vinegar
1/8 teaspoon ground red pepper
2 cloves garlic, crushed**

In medium bowl, combine all marinade ingredients until well blended. Slice chicken in ¾-inch strips. Place in marinade and stir until well coated. Cover and refrigerate at least 4 hours, or up to 24 hours. Skewer chicken on thin wooden skewers. Preheat broiler or grill.

For peanut sauce: Blend sauce ingredients together in a small bowl; set aside. Broil chicken in pre-heated broiler or grill over medium-hot coals for 2 to 3 minutes on each side. Serve chicken with peanut sauce.

NOTE: Skewers can be soaked in water for 1 hour before using to prevent them from burning on the barbecue. This is good served with rice and a fruit salad.

Lemon Chicken Breasts

Serves: 2 to 4

**2 whole chicken breasts, skinned and boned
1 cup mushrooms, sliced
1 clove garlic, minced
1 tablespoon olive oil
2 tablespoons flour
1/2 teaspoon rosemary
1/4 cup lemon juice
1/4 cup chicken broth
2 tablespoons parsley**

In a frying pan over medium heat, sauté mushrooms and garlic in oil for 3 to 5 minutes. Remove from pan. Sprinkle chicken with flour and rosemary and brown on both sides. Add lemon juice and broth to pan and scrape browned bits from the bottom. Return mushrooms to pan. Lower heat to simmer, cover pan and cook for 15 minutes. Sprinkle with parsley.

NOTE: Serve over brown rice or fettucine noodles.

Barbecued Skewered Chicken

Serves: 6

3 whole chicken breasts, split,
  skinned and boned
1/4 cup soy sauce
3 tablespoons dry white wine
2 tablespoons lemon juice
2 tablespoons vegetable oil
3/4 teaspoon rosemary, crushed
1/2 teaspoon ground ginger
1 clove garlic, minced
1/8 teaspoon ground pepper

Cut chicken breasts into strips about 1½-inch long and ¼-inch thick. Combine remaining ingredients in a glass dish. Stir chicken into marinade. Cover and chill for 3 to 6 hours. Drain off marinade and thread chicken strips lengthwise onto skewers. Grill over hot coals for 3 to 4 minutes on each side.

NOTE: Serve with corn on the cob and potato salad. Mushrooms, cherry tomatoes and green, yellow or red pepper pieces could also be added to each skewer.

Java Chicken Barbecue

Serves: 8

2 chicken fryers, cut up
  (approximately 3½ pounds each)

  Marinade:
1 cup brown sugar
1½ cups strong black coffee
1/2 cup vinegar
1/4 onion, chopped
1½ tablespoons dry mustard
1 tablespoon salt
1/2 teaspoon pepper
3 tablespoons butter

Rinse chicken and pat dry. In a large skillet or dutch oven, mix all marinade ingredients and bring to a boil. Add chicken parts, stirring to coat each piece with marinade. Reduce heat, cover and simmer (do not boil) for 35 to 40 minutes, or until chicken is just tender. Remove pan from heat and let chicken cool in marinade, then refrigerate 1 to 2 hours or overnight. To glaze chicken before serving, remove pieces from marinade and set aside. Boil liquid to reduce quantity and to thicken slightly. Brush over chicken and grill over hot coals until heated through and skin is crisp and golden. (May be broiled in oven).

Barbecued Skewered Chicken

Chicken-Mushroom Skewers

Serves: 4 to 6

4 whole chicken breasts, skinned
  and boned
1/3 cup olive oil
3 tablespoons lemon juice
4 cloves garlic, minced
2 tablespoons chopped parsley
1 tablespoon dried mint leaves
  or
1 tablespoon basil
1 teaspoon salt
3/4 teaspoon pepper
16 small mushrooms

Combine oil, lemon juice and seasonings in a large, shallow dish. Cut chicken breasts into bite size pieces. Skewer chicken alternately with mushrooms. Place skewers in marinade and turn to coat thoroughly. Cover and refrigerate several hours, turning occasionally. Remove chicken from marinade and reserve. Broil or grill 12 to 15 minutes, brushing with marinade, turning once. Heat reserved marinade and serve with chicken.

NOTE: Serve with rice and steamed carrots.

Chicken Fajitas

Serves: 4 to 6

1½ pounds chicken breasts,
  skinned and boned
2 large onions, cut in ¼-inch
  slices
1 green pepper, cut into small
  cubes
2 tablespoons soy sauce
8 flour tortillas

Garnishes: (optional)
Salsa, Monterey Jack cheese,
  chopped tomato, sour cream or
  plain yogurt.

Grill chicken over hot coals, 4 to 5 minutes per side, until barely done. Cut into ½-inch strips and set aside. Stir-fry onions and pepper in a non-stick fry pan with soy sauce until onions are very soft. (Add 1 tablespoon water if needed to prevent burning). Add chicken to onion and pepper mixture and stir. Divide among 8 flour tortillas, add suggested garnishes, if desired, and serve.

NOTE: Serve with Spanish rice and tossed salad.

Chicken Asparagus
Serves: 6

3 whole chicken breasts, skinned
and boned
1 pound fresh asparagus spears
1½ cups chicken broth, divided
2 tablespoons cornstarch
1/3 cup lite mayonnaise
1/3 cup plain non-fat yogurt
2/3 cup evaporated-skim milk
1/3 cup grated part-skim cheddar
cheese
1 teaspoon lemon juice
1/2 teaspoon curry powder
Non-stick vegetable oil spray

Coat a skillet with non-stick cooking spray and lightly brown chicken breasts. Steam asparagus for 2 to 3 minutes until tender-crisp. Arrange asparagus in baking pan and top with chicken. In a saucepan, bring 1 cup of chicken broth to a boil. Combine remaining ½ cup cold broth with cornstarch and gradually add to boiling broth. Cool slightly, then add mayonnaise, yogurt, milk, cheese, lemon juice and curry powder. Pour over chicken and bake, uncovered, at 350 degrees for 25 to 30 minutes.

NOTE: Serve with pasta, fruit salad and french bread.

Italian Chicken and Artichokes
Serves: 6

2¼ pounds chicken breasts,
boned, halved and skinned (if
desired)
2 tablespoons butter or margarine
1 clove garlic, minced
1 (10¾-ounce) can cream of
chicken soup
1 cup sour cream
1/2 cup shredded mozzarella
cheese
1/4 cup dry white wine
2 tablespoons grated parmesan
cheese
1 (6 ounce) jar marinated
artichoke hearts, drained and
halved
2 tablespoons chopped parsley

Rinse chicken and pat dry. In skillet, melt butter or margarine and cook garlic for 15 seconds. Add chicken, cook 2½ minutes, on each side until lightly browned. In a bowl, mix together soup, sour cream, mozzarella cheese, wine and parmesan cheese. Add mixture to skillet, cover and cook 5 to 7 minutes until chicken is tender. Add artichokes, cover and cook an additional 1 to 2 minutes until heated through. Sprinkle with parsley.

NOTE: Serve with garden pasta spirals, tossed salad and rolls.

Stuffed Italian Chicken
Serves: 2

2 whole chicken breasts, skinned and boned
3/4 cup tomato juice
1 clove garlic, minced
Salt and pepper to taste
1/2 teaspoon Italian seasoning
1/2 cup cottage cheese
1/8 teaspoon Italian seasoning
1/4 cup shredded mozzarella cheese

In a saucepan over medium heat, bring tomato juice, garlic, salt, pepper, and ½ teaspoon Italian seasoning to a boil. Reduce heat to low and simmer tomato juice mixture for 10 minutes. Meanwhile, on a cutting board, pound chicken breasts with mallet to about ¼-inch thickness. In a small bowl, combine cottage cheese and ⅛ teaspoon Italian seasoning. Spoon half of the cottage cheese mixture onto center of each chicken breast. Roll in a jelly roll fashion. Spoon half of the tomato juice mixture into a 2-quart baking dish, then arrange chicken rolls seam side down. Spoon remaining tomato mixture over chicken. Top with mozzarella cheese. Bake, uncovered, at 350 degrees for 45 minutes. Spoon pan juices over chicken rolls and serve.

Parmesan Yogurt Chicken
Serves: 4

3 pounds chicken, cut up
2 tablespoons lemon juice
Salt and pepper to taste
1 cup plain yogurt
1/2 cup mayonnaise
2 tablespoons Worcestershire sauce
2 tablespoons Dijon mustard
1 teaspoon thyme
1/4 to ½ teaspoon cayenne pepper
1/2 cup thinly sliced green onion
1/2 cup grated parmesan cheese

In a baking dish, arrange chicken pieces skin side up in a single layer. Drizzle with lemon juice; sprinkle with salt and pepper. In a bowl, blend yogurt, mayonnaise, Worcestershire sauce, mustard, thyme, cayenne pepper and green onions. Spread this mixture over chicken and bake, uncovered, at 350 degrees for 50 minutes. Sprinkle with parmesan cheese and broil for 3 minutes until cheese melts.

NOTE: Serve with rice and fresh green beans.

214

Chicken Risotto
Serves: 6

3/4 pounds chicken breasts,
  skinned and boned
Salt, ground pepper and
  paprika to taste
1 tablespoon vegetable oil
1½ cups diced jicama
1/2 cup diced green pepper
1 tablespoon margarine
3/4 cup chopped onion
1 cup uncooked rice
1/2 cup dry white wine
2 cups chicken broth
3 cups water
1/4 cup fresh cilantro
1/4 cup grated parmesan cheese

Cut chicken breasts into chunks. Season chunks with salt, pepper, and paprika. In an electric or large non-stick skillet, heat oil over medium-high heat. Cook chicken, jicama, and green pepper until chicken is no longer pink. Remove chicken mixture and set aside. Melt margarine, add onion and cook until tender. Add rice and cook 2 or 3 minutes, stirring frequently. Add white wine to rice and stir until absorbed. Stir in one cup of broth and cook, uncovered, until absorbed, stirring frequently. Gradually add remaining 1 cup broth and water, allowing each cup to be absorbed before adding another, until rice is tender and mixture has a creamy consistency. (It takes about 1 hour for all the liquids to be absorbed). Stir in cilantro, parmesan cheese, and chicken mixture; heat through.

NOTE: Serve immediately with fresh steamed vegetables, salad and french bread.

Mandarin Chicken with Broccoli

Serves: 4

2 whole chicken breasts, split,
  skinned and boned
1 (10-ounce) package frozen
  broccoli spears, thawed and
  drained
1/4 cup flour
1/2 teaspoon garlic powder
1/4 teaspoon paprika
3 tablespoons margarine
3/4 cup orange juice
2 tablespoons white wine
1 tablespoon freshly chopped
  tarragon
  or
1 teaspoon dried tarragon
1 teaspoon cornstarch
1/2 teaspoon grated lemon peel
1 (11-ounce) can mandarin orange
  segments, drained
2 tablespoon sliced almonds,
  toasted

Flatten chicken breasts by pounding lightly. In a small bowl, combine flour, garlic powder, and paprika; coat chicken. Melt margarine in a skillet, brown chicken pieces on both sides. Remove from pan. Place chicken in a 2-quart baking dish. In same skillet combine orange juice, wine, tarragon, cornstarch and lemon peel. Cook over medium heat until mixture boils and thickens. Pour sauce over chicken. Bake, uncovered, at 350 degrees for 15 minutes. Divide broccoli into 4 equal portions and arrange on top of each chicken breast. Top with mandarin orange segments and sprinkle with almonds. Cover and continue to bake for 15 minutes.

NOTE: Serve with steamed rice and green salad.

Chicken Salsa

Serves: 4 to 6

1 chicken fryer, skinned, boned
  and cut into pieces
  or
2 pounds chicken breasts, skinned
  and boned
1 (14-ounce) container fresh salsa
1 cup shredded Monterey Jack
  cheese
1/4 cup chopped fresh cilantro

Arrange chicken pieces in a 9 x 13-inch baking dish. Spoon salsa over chicken. Cover pan with foil and bake at 325 degrees for 1 hour. Remove foil and continue cooking for 20 minutes. Sprinkle cheese over chicken pieces and return to oven for an additional 10 minutes. Sprinkle with chopped fresh cilantro before serving.

NOTE: Serve with spanish rice and tossed salad.

Chicken Breasts with Mustard Persillade
Serves: 8

4 whole chicken breasts, split, skinned and boned
1/3 to ½ cup Dijon mustard

 Persillade:
4 cloves garlic, minced
2 cups fresh bread crumbs (4 slices)
1/2 cup margarine or butter
2/3 cup chopped fresh parsley
Salt and pepper to taste

For persillade: Sauté garlic and bread crumbs in margarine. Add parsley and mix well. Cool crumb mixture. Brush chicken breasts liberally with mustard. Dip into persillade and press crumbs into chicken on both sides. Bake in a 9 x 13-inch pan, uncovered, at 425 degrees for 20 to 25 minutes until juices run clear and top is deep brown.

NOTE: Combining the garlic and bread in a food processor makes easy work of this dish. Serve with pasta and fresh green beans.

Lemon-Cream Chicken
Serves: 8

4 whole chicken breasts, split, skinned and boned
4 tablespoons butter
2 tablespoons white wine
1 lemon peel, grated
2 tablespoons lemon juice
1/4 teaspoon salt
1/4 teaspoon pepper
1 cup whipping cream
1½ cups fresh sliced mushrooms
1/3 cup grated parmesan cheese
Parsley (garnish)

Melt butter in fry pan, add chicken and sauté over medium heat for 10 minutes until chicken is browned on both sides. Remove chicken to a 9 x 13-inch oven-proof dish. Drain butter from pan and add wine, lemon peel, and lemon juice. Cook for 1 minute, then add salt, pepper, and cream. Stir and heat, but do not boil. Pour sauce over chicken and sprinkle with mushrooms and parmesan cheese. Bake, uncovered, at 325 degrees for 30 minutes. Garnish with parsley.

NOTE: Serve with fettucine, fresh steamed zucchini and tossed salad.

Nice 'n Spicy Chicken
Serves: 4 to 5

8 to 10 chicken legs
or
1 chicken fryer, cut in pieces
and skinned

Marinade:
1 teaspoon basil
1 teaspoon oregano
1 teaspoon rosemary
1/2 teaspoon cracked pepper
1 package onion soup mix
(1.2-ounces dry weight)
2 tablespoons olive oil, divided
1/3 cup red or white wine
2 cups chopped celery
1 jalapeno pepper, chopped
1 cup chopped onion
2 tablespoons minced garlic
1 (6-ounce) can tomato paste
1 (14½-ounce) can chopped
tomatoes
1 ¾ cups chicken broth
Grated parmesan cheese (garnish)

Place basil, oregano, rosemary, cracked pepper, onion soup mix, 1 tablespoon oil and wine in casserole. Pierce chicken and place in marinade, making sure marinade covers as much chicken as possible. Marinate at least ½ hour, turning occasionally. Remove chicken from marinade. In non-stick frying pan brown chicken in remaining oil on both sides, return to casserole. Add celery, pepper, onion and garlic to sauté pan. Sauté vegetables until tender, about 5 minutes. Add tomato paste, tomatoes and chicken broth to the sautéed vegetables. Cook until mixture is thick and reduced by about half. Pour sauce over browned chicken in the casserole. Bake at 350 degrees for 45 to 60 minutes. Garnish with grated parmesan cheese.

NOTE: Serve over fresh pasta with tossed salad and french bread.

Honey Curry Chicken
Serves: 4

1 chicken fryer, cut into pieces
1/2 cup honey
1/2 cup Dijon mustard
1 teaspoon curry powder
2 tablespoons soy sauce
1/2 teaspoon paprika

Place chicken, skin side down, in a 9 x 13-inch baking dish. In a small bowl, combine honey, mustard, curry and soy sauce. Pour over chicken and marinate 6 hours. Turn chicken so skin side is up. Cover dish with foil and bake at 350 degrees for 1 hour. Uncover and sprinkle paprika over chicken. Bake, uncovered, for an additional 15 to 20 minutes.

NOTE: Serve with baked potato and glazed or steamed carrots.

Kiss O'Lime Yogurt Chicken

Serves: 3 to 4

1 whole chicken fryer, skinned and
  cut into pieces
2 tablespoons lime juice
  Cayenne pepper to taste
1 cup plain yogurt
1 tablespoon flour
2 tablespoons sweet-hot or
  Dijon style mustard
1/4 teaspoon Worcestershire sauce
1/2 teaspoon thyme leaves,
  crushed
1/4 cup minced green onions
  (including tops)

Place chicken in baking dish lightly coated with vegetable spray. Sprinkle lime juice and cayenne pepper over chicken pieces. Combine yogurt, flour, mustard, Worcestershire sauce, and thyme leaves in bowl. Spoon sauce over chicken pieces and sprinkle with onions. Bake, uncovered, at 350 degrees for 1 hour. Watch carefully to see that sauce doesn't start browning.

NOTE: Serve with rice, marinated asparagus and rolls.

Naranja Chicken

Serves: 4

1 (3-pound) broiler fryer, cut in
  serving pieces
1 cup freshly squeezed orange
  juice
1/2 cup soy sauce
1/3 cup packed brown sugar
10 thin slices fresh ginger root
3 stalks celery, sliced in small
  pieces
2 tablespoons cornstarch, mixed
  with ½ cup water

Arrange chicken skin side up in single layer in a large shallow baking dish. Mix orange juice, soy sauce and brown sugar; pour over chicken. Sprinkle ginger root and celery around chicken. Bake in preheated 350 degree oven for 50 minutes. Remove chicken and stir cornstarch mixture into pan juices. Return chicken to baking dish, skin side down. Bake an additional 10 minutes until sauce thickens and chicken is tender when pierced.

NOTE: Naranja is Spanish for Orange.

Homemade Chicken Pot Pie

Serves: 4

2 whole chicken breasts, split,
  skinned and boned
3 cups water
4 tablespoons butter or margarine
1 cup sliced celery
1/4 cup finely chopped onion
1 cup diced carrots
8 ounces quartered fresh
  mushrooms
1/2 cup peas
1/2 cup flour
1 cup evaporated milk
1 package ready rolled puff pastry
Salt and pepper to taste

Grease 4 oven proof 14 to 18-ounce bowls. Boil chicken breasts in water for 20 minutes. Remove and reserve broth, cool and chop; set aside. In a large skillet, melt margarine, sauté celery, onion, and carrots, until onion is transparent. Add mushrooms and peas; toss lightly. Sprinkle flour over vegetables, stir and cook over low heat for 5 minutes. Gradually add chicken broth, bring to a boil, cook for 1 minute stirring constantly. Stir in evaporated milk and chopped chicken. Simmer until desired thickness is reached. Salt and pepper to taste. Spoon equal amounts into each bowl.

Puff Pastry: Cut 4½-inch strips, lightly brush with water and press onto edge of bowls forming a ring. Lightly brush ring with water and lay remaining square on top pressing down edges to seal like a pie crust. Trim edges and slit top to allow steam to escape. Bake 425 degrees for 25 to 30 minutes or until golden brown.

NOTE: A favorite pie crust recipe may be substituted for Puff Pastry.

Curried Chicken Breasts

Serves: 4 to 6

3 whole chicken breasts
1/2 teaspoon seasoned salt
  Dash of paprika
1 (4-ounce) can sliced mushrooms,
  liquid reserved
1 chicken bouillon cube
1/4 cup dry white wine
2 tablespoons minced fresh onion
1/4 teaspoon curry powder
1/8 teaspoon freshly ground
  pepper

Skin, bone and halve the chicken breasts, lengthwise. Sprinkle chicken with salt and paprika and place in a 11 x 7 x 1½-inch baking pan. In a small saucepan, drain the liquid from the mushrooms; add the bouillon cube. Heat and stir until bouillon is dissolved. Add mushrooms, wine, onion, curry powder and pepper; pour over chicken. Cover with foil and bake at 350 degrees for 40 minutes. Uncover and bake for an additional 20 minutes. Serve with pan juices.

Sour Cream Chicken Breasts

Serves: 6 to 8

6 whole chicken breasts
2 cups sour cream
1/4 cup lemon juice
4 teaspoons salt
4 teaspoons Worcestershire sauce
2 teaspoons paprika
4 cloves garlic, crushed
1/2 teaspoon pepper
1¾ cups dry bread crumbs
1/2 cup butter, melted

Cut whole chicken breasts in half. Mix together the sour cream, lemon juice, salt, Worcestershire sauce, paprika, garlic and pepper. Marinate chicken in sour cream mixture overnight, making sure each piece is well-coated. Remove chicken pieces from the marinade and roll in bread crumbs, to cover. Place chicken in a baking dish in one layer. Pour melted butter over all. Bake at 350 degrees for 30 minutes.

Mexican Chicken Lasagna
Serves: 8 to 10

4 cups cooked chicken, cubed
1 (16-ounce) carton small curd
  cottage cheese
1/3 cup chopped fresh parsley
1 (4-ounce) can diced green chiles
2 tablespoons salad oil
1 medium onion, chopped
2 cloves garlic, minced
1 red bell pepper, chopped
2 (16-ounce) jars mild salsa
1 tablespoon chili powder
1½ teaspoons ground cumin
1 (10-ounce) package lasagna
  noodles, uncooked
Non-stick vegetable oil spray
2 cups shredded Monterey Jack
  cheese
2 cups shredded cheddar cheese

Combine cottage cheese, parsley and chiles; set aside. Heat oil in a 4 to 5-quart saucepan. Add onions, garlic and bell pepper. Cook over medium heat for 10 minutes, until onion is tender. Add salsa, chili powder and cumin. Bring to a boil then reduce heat and cook, uncovered, for 10 minutes. Meanwhile, cook lasagna noodles according to package directions. Drain well. Spray a 9 x 13-inch pan with non-stick vegetable oil spray. Arrange a layer of cooked noodles on the bottom. Spread ½ of cottage cheese mixture then ½ of chicken over noodles. Spread ⅓ of salsa mixture then ⅓ of cheese over chicken. Repeat layers with noodles, ½ cottage cheese mixture, ½ chicken, ⅓ salsa then ⅓ cheese. Finish with remaining noodles, salsa and cheese. Bake, covered, at 375 degrees for about 45 to 50 minutes. Let stand for 5 to 10 minutes before serving.

NOTE: This is even better prepared the day before to let the flavors blend.

Chicken Taco Casserole
Serves: 6

1 pound boneless, skinned chicken breasts
1 (35-ounce) can tomatoes
1 cup chopped onion
1 tablespoon vegetable oil
2 cloves garlic, crushed
1 (8-ounce) can tomato sauce
1 (4-ounce) jar pimientos, drained and sliced
3 tablespoons chopped parsley
1 teaspoon ground coriander
2 teaspoons ground cumin
1/4 teaspoon black pepper
Non-stick vegetable oil spray
4 (½-ounce) taco shells
6 ounces (1½ cups) shredded Monterey Jack or cheddar cheese

Drain tomatoes, reserve ½ cup liquid. Chop tomatoes and set aside. In a large skillet, sauté onion in oil until tender. Add garlic, sauté 1 minute. Stir in chopped tomatoes and liquid, tomato sauce, pimientos, parsley, coriander, cumin and pepper. Bring to a boil, lower heat and simmer 10 to 15 minutes. Preheat oven to 350 degrees. Cut chicken crosswise into thin strips. Add to skillet. Cook 5 minutes or until chicken is cooked. Crush taco shells into small pieces. Spray a 9 x 13-inch casserole with non-stick vegetable oil spray. Put ⅔ of the taco shells into casserole and spoon chicken mixture over shells. Sprinkle remaining shells over chicken and top with cheese. Bake in oven for 30 to 35 minutes or until bubbly.

Sweet Pepper Chicken
Serves: 4 to 6

3 pounds chicken breasts, skinned, boned and halved
3 tablespoons butter
3 tablespoons olive oil
Salt and pepper to taste
3 cloves garlic, minced
1/3 cup finely chopped onion
2 tablespoons chopped fresh parsley
2 red bell peppers, seeded and coarsely diced
2 green bell peppers, seeded and coarsely diced

In a skillet, melt 2 tablespoons butter and 2 tablespoons olive oil over medium-high heat. Sauté chicken breasts 4 to 5 minutes on each side until browned. Sprinkle with salt and pepper, remove from pan and set aside. In same pan, melt remaining butter and oil. Add garlic and onion, sauté over medium heat until onion is tender and translucent. Add parsley, peppers and chicken. Cover and simmer for 5 minutes until chicken is tender.

Special Chicken and Wild Rice
Serves: 4 to 5

6 boneless, skinless chicken
  breast halves
1 cup wild rice
4 cups water
4 chicken bouillon cubes
1/2 teaspoon salt
1 (10¾-ounce) can cream of
  chicken soup
1 cup plain yogurt
1/3 cup water
1/2 teaspoon lemon peel
1/2 teaspoon Italian seasoning
1/2 teaspoon beau monde
  seasoning
4 to 5 dashes white pepper
1/2 to 1 clove garlic, minced
3/4 cup shredded medium cheddar
  cheese

Rinse and drain wild rice. Add to 4 cups boiling water and stir in 4 cubes of chicken bouillon and salt. Simmer for 45 minutes until soft and tender. Drain. Butter a 9-inch square baking pan and add rice. Place chicken breasts on wild rice. Mix cream of chicken soup, yogurt, water, lemon peel, Italian seasoning, beau monde seasoning, white pepper and garlic. Pour over chicken and sprinkle with cheese. Bake at 350 degrees for 30 minutes.

NOTE: This can be prepared the day before. Refrigerate and bake later.

Oriental Chicken
Serves: 5 to 6

1½ pounds chicken breasts,
  skinned, boned and cut in bite-
  size pieces
1/2 cup white wine
3 tablespoons soy sauce
1 teaspoon sugar
1/2 cup cornstarch
1 egg, well beaten
1 cube margarine
1 cup filberts or almonds,
  halved or quartered
1/4 teaspoon ginger
1/2 teaspoon garlic powder
1/2 cup hot water
1/2 pound bamboo shoots
1 cup uncooked rice

Combine wine, soy sauce and sugar; pour over chicken in glass baking dish. Marinate overnight or at least 1 hour. Remove chicken (reserving marinade), dredge in cornstarch and dip in egg. Place chicken on a cake rack covered with waxed paper, and let dry for 30 minutes. Melt margarine in a large skillet and sauté nuts for 5 minutes. Remove with a slotted spoon. Add chicken, ginger and garlic to the skillet; sauté until golden brown. Add reserved marinade and hot water; cover and simmer for 10 minutes. Add nuts and bamboo shoots. Cook just until warm, then serve immediately over rice.

🍃

Spicy Chicken with Cashews and Mushrooms
Serves: 8

3 chicken breasts
6 shitake mushrooms
1 ounce piece fresh ginger root
4 cloves garlic
1 large carrot
2 bunches green onions
2 celery stalks
1 can bamboo shoots
1 can water chestnuts
1 medium red bell pepper
1 medium green bell pepper
6 ounces cashews
2 tablespoons peanut oil
2 tablespoons sesame oil

Sauce:
2 teaspoons chili paste
2 tablespoons fish sauce
2 tablespoons plum sauce
2 tablespoons seasoned rice
    vinegar
1 tablespoon soy sauce
2 tablespoons fermented black
    beans
6 tablespoons cold water
3 teaspoons cornstarch

If you are using dried mushrooms, soak for 20 minutes in hot water; remove stems and cut caps in thin strips about ¼-inch wide. Remove chicken from bone, cut into thin slices (2 x ¼ x ¼-inches). Finely chop ginger and garlic. Cut the carrot into matchsticks (2 x ¼ x ¼-inches). Cut the green onions into pieces about 1 inch to 2 inches long. Cut the remaining vegetables in bite-size pieces, about 1 inch square (you can put the celery and carrots in one bowl, and all the other vegetables in another bowl). Mix all the ingredients for the sauce except cold water and cornstarch in a glass or measuring cup and set aside. Combine the water and cornstarch in a second glass and set aside.

Stir-fry chicken in a wok with the oil, garlic and ginger until it is three-quarters cooked. It is best to get the oil very hot, and cook small amounts of chicken at a time, removing the cooked chicken into a mixing bowl. Don't overcook the chicken or it will be too tough and dry. Drain the oil from the chicken in the mixing bowl back into the wok. Add another tablespoons or two if needed. Heat the oil in the wok, then add the celery and carrot pieces. Stir to coat with oil, then cover wok and steam for 2 minutes. Next, add the sauce, and stir-fry until the sauce is hot. Add the remaining vegetables, and stir-fry for 2 or 3 minutes, until combination is hot. Add the chicken, mix together until chicken is coated with sauce. Push the mixture to the sides of the wok, so the sauce collects at the bottom. Stir the water and cornstarch to mix, and pour into sauce in bottom of wok. When it starts to bubble, add the cashews, and mix all the ingredients again. When the sauce thickens (about 30 seconds) remove from heat to serving bowl. Serve over white rice.

Curried Chicken
Serves: 4 to 6

2 pounds cubed chicken, un-cooked
2 tablespoons butter
1 medium onion, chopped
1/2 teaspoon salt
2 bay leaves, crushed
1 clove garlic, crushed
1 teaspoon thyme
2 tablespoons curry powder
1 quart chicken stock
2 tablespoons catsup
2 tablespoons shredded coconut
1 green apple, chopped
3 tablespoons chopped chutney
2 tablespoons cornstarch
2 tablespoons water
1/2 cup whipping cream

Brown chicken in butter and remove from pan. Brown onion in same butter and add salt, bay leaves, garlic, thyme, curry, chicken stock, catsup and chicken. Simmer 20 minutes and remove chicken. To sauce, add coconut, apple, and chutney. Mix cornstarch and water. Slowly add this to sauce, stirring gently to blend. Simmer and stir until slightly thickened. Stir in cream and cooked chicken. Heat thoroughly. Serve immediately over hot rice.

NOTE: Serve with condiments like raisins, cashews, sunflower seeds and coconut.

Hoisin Chicken Sandwich
Serves: 2 to 4

2 whole chicken breasts, boned, skinned and cut in strips

Sauce:
1/4 cup honey
1/4 cup soy sauce
1/2 cup hoisin sauce
1 clove garlic, crushed
1/4 teaspoon ginger
1/4 teaspoon dry mustard
4 onion hamburger buns, grilled

Toppings (optional)
Shredded cabbage, sliced green onions, mayonnaise, hoisin sauce.

Cut chicken breasts into strips and set aside. Mix together all sauce ingredients thoroughly and marinate chicken for at least 2 hours. Drain chicken, reserving marinade. Grill for 10 minutes basting with marinade. Grill hamburger buns at the same time chicken is grilling (during last 2 minutes). (If you choose to stir-fry the chicken, the cooking time will decrease significantly, and hamburger buns must be grilled separately). Put the chicken on the onion hamburger buns, add desired toppings and serve.

Hood River Turkey

Serves: 4 to 6

1 fresh turkey, (10 pounds)
4 apples
4 onions
1 cup water
1 cup soy sauce
1 cup white wine

Cut up apples and onions. Stuff turkey with apples and onions. Secure legs and wings. Put turkey in large pan. Mix water, soy sauce and wine. Cook on low setting of gas grill with lid closed. Baste the turkey with the soy mixture every 20 to 30 minutes. If the turkey becomes too brown, cover it with aluminum foil. The entire cooking time will be 1½ to 2 hours depending upon the exact size of the turkey.

NOTE: Serve with Cheddar Potato Bake and steamed broccoli.

Microwave Turkey Chili

Serves: 4

16 ounces ground turkey
2 cups chopped green and yellow
  bell peppers
1/2 cup chopped onion
2 garlic cloves, minced
1 cup tomato sauce
1/2 cup medium picante sauce
  or salsa
1 cup kidney beans
2 tablespoons chopped cilantro
  leaves
2 teaspoons chili powder
1/8 teaspoon ground cloves
1/4 teaspoon ground cumin
1/4 teaspoon oregano, crumbled

In a 3-quart covered microwave-safe casserole, combine peppers, onions and garlic. Cover and cook on high for 3 minutes. Crumble in turkey, stir to combine. Cover and cook on high for 6 minutes, stirring several times during cycle. Add remaining ingredients and mix well. Cook on high for 2 minutes.

NOTE: This is low-fat for the health conscience!

Spicy Stuffed Shells

Serves: 4 to 6

1 pound ground turkey
1 cup diced onion, divided
1/2 cup diced carrot
2 tablespoons all-purpose flour
1/4 teaspoon salt
1/4 teaspoon pepper
1/2 teaspoon dried basil
1/4 teaspoon red cayenne pepper
1/2 cup burgundy or red wine
1/4 cup freshly grated parmesan cheese, divided
Non-stick vegetable oil spray
1/2 teaspoon minced garlic
1 (14½-ounce) can chopped tomatoes
1/4 teaspoon salt
16 cooked jumbo macaroni shells (1 manicotti shell can be substituted for 2 shells)

Coat skillet with non-stick vegetable oil spray; place over medium heat until hot. Add ½ cup onion and carrot; cook for 5 minutes. Add turkey and cook for 5 minutes, or until turkey is browned. Drain off fat. Add flour, salt, pepper, basil, red pepper and wine. Cook for 4 minutes or until thickened. Add 2 tablespoons grated cheese; stir well and place mixture in a bowl to cool. Coat pan with non-stick vegetable oil spray and add remaining ½ cup onion and garlic. Cook over medium heat for 3 minutes. Add tomatoes and salt; cook for 7 minutes, stirring occasionally. Cook macaroni or manicotti shells according to package directions, rinse and drain well. Stuff each shell with the turkey mixture. Pour ½ of the sauce over the bottom of an 8-inch baking dish. Put shells on top of sauce and spoon remaining sauce over the shells. Cover and bake at 350 degrees for 30 minutes. Sprinkle with the remaining parmesan cheese.

Savor
the
Flavor
of
BREADS

❧ ❧ ❧

Best Ever French Bread
Yield: 3 loaves

1½ tablespoons active dry yeast
1/2 cup warm water
1 tablespoon salt
1 tablespoon sugar
1 tablespoon vegetable oil
1¾ cup very hot tap water
5 to 5½ cups flour

Soften yeast in bowl with ½ cup warm water. Add salt, sugar and oil to hot water; stir and add in dissolved yeast. Add flour and knead for 5 minutes, until smooth and elastic. Cover and let rise in warm place for 1 to 2 hours until doubled in size.

Divide dough into 3 portions and knead on floured board. Make into a thin long roll about 12-inches long. Place on a greased cookie sheet. Let rise in warm place. Before baking, slash top of loaf at an angle with a sharp knife. Bake at 375 degrees for 20 to 30 minutes until golden brown. Brush top of bread with butter while warm.

Oatmeal Bread
Yield: 2 loaves

1 cup quick cooking rolled oats
2 cups milk, scalded
1 package active dry yeast
   or
1 tablespoon yeast
1/2 cup water (105 to 115 degrees)
1/2 cup molasses, dark
1 teaspoon salt
1/4 teaspoon ginger powder
4½ cups unsifted flour

Put oats in a large bowl and cover with milk. Stir and let stand until luke warm. Sprinkle yeast into water and stir until dissolved; let stand. Add yeast mixture, molasses, salt and ginger to oat mixture. Stir in flour. Cover and let rise in a warm place until doubled (about 1 hour). Knead down on a well-floured board until "elastic" and put into 2 greased loaf pans (9 x 5 x 3). Let rise until almost doubled (45 minutes). Bake at 350 degrees for 45 to 50 minutes, or until loaf sounds hollow when tapped on top.

Grandmother Kroener's Refrigerator Rolls

Yield: 2 dozen rolls

1 teaspoon salt
1/4 cup sugar
1½ tablespoons butter, softened
1 cup hot milk
1 package active dry yeast
1/8 cup warm water
1/2 teaspoon sugar
1 egg, beaten
3½ to 4 cups white flour

Put salt, sugar and butter in a large bowl; add milk and let mixture cool to lukewarm. Dissolve yeast in ⅛ cup warm water and add ½ teaspoon sugar. Stir yeast mixture and egg into the milk mixture. Add 2 cups flour and beat until smooth. Add an additional 1½ cups flour and gather dough into a round ball. Put dough into a lightly greased bowl and cover. Let dough rise for about 1½ hours until doubled in size. Roll dough out on a lightly floured board until ½-inch thick, cut into rounds with a biscuit cutter and fold in half. (Dough may be refrigerated or frozen at this point. Return dough to room temperature before continuing). Let folded biscuits rise on a cookie sheet for 2 hours. Brush with melted butter and bake at 425 degrees for 12 to 15 minutes.

French Peasant Bread
Serves: 8

2 cups warm water
1 package active dry yeast
   or
1 tablespoon yeast
1 tablespoon sugar
2 teaspoons salt
4 cups flour
Oil
Cornmeal
Melted butter

Into warm bowl, place water, yeast, sugar and salt; stir until dissolved. Add flour and stir until blended. Do not knead. Cover and let rise 45 minutes or until doubled in size. Flour hands, remove dough from the bowl and place in 2 rounds on a greased and cornmealed cookie sheet. Do not knead. Let rise an additional 45 minutes. Brush the top with melted butter if desired. Bake at 425 degrees for 10 minutes. Reduce oven temperature to 375 degrees and cook an additional 20 minutes. Remove from oven and brush with butter. Serve warm.

NOTE: This is an easy no-knead French bread.

Mixer Batter Buns
Yield: 2 dozen

1¼ cups warm water
   (110 to 115 degrees)
2 packages active dry yeast
1/4 cup sugar
1 teaspoon salt
1/2 cup shortening
2 eggs
2 cups flour, sifted
1¼ cups flour

In mixing bowl, combine water and yeast. Stir until dissolved. Add sugar, salt, shortening, eggs and 2 cups flour; mix on low speed. Beat 2 minutes on medium speed. Add remaining flour and beat with spatula until smooth. Spoon into greased muffin cups ½ full. Let rise in a warm place (85 degrees), until the batter reaches the top of the muffin cups (30 to 40 minutes). Bake at 375 degrees for 18 to 20 minutes until golden brown. Serve warm.

Garlic Cheese Bread

Serves: 8 to 10

1 package active dry yeast
  or
1 tablespoon yeast
1 cup warm water
1 teaspoon sugar
2¼ cups flour
1 cup cake flour
1½ teaspoons salt
2 tablespoons butter or margarine
1 egg

  Filling:
1/2 cup grated parmesan cheese
1½ cups shredded mozzarella
  cheese
2 tablespoons fresh minced
  parsley
1 clove garlic
1 egg

Mix yeast, water and sugar; set aside for 5 minutes. Put flours, salt and butter into food processor bowl. Add ½ of the yeast mixture and process with chopper blade pulsing on and off. Add other ½ of yeast and process on and off. Add egg and process for 40 seconds. Place dough mixture into a lightly oiled bowl, cover and let rise until doubled in size.

For filling: In food processor, shred cheeses, parsley and garlic. After the dough has risen, roll into a 8 x 16-inch rectangle and spread with cheese filling. Roll up jelly roll style and pinch seam. Place on oiled cookie sheet and make 3 slits in the top. Let rise again until doubled in size. Beat remaining egg with fork and brush on the loaf. Bake at 375 degrees for 30 minutes.

Earth Bread
Yield: 2 to 3 loaves   12 to 15 rolls

3 tablespoons sugar
2/3 cup warm water
2 packages active dry yeast
2 cups milk
4 teaspoons salt
1/3 cup sugar
4 tablespoons butter or oil
4 cups unbleached bread flour
2½ cups whole wheat flour
2 cups quick oatmeal, uncooked
2 cups cooked cracked wheat
   (1 cup raw)
1/2 cup sesame seeds

In a small bowl, combine 3 tablesoon sugar, warm water and yeast; let stand 10 minutes. Scald milk and add salt, ⅓ cup sugar and butter or oil; let cool and place in a large bowl. Add unbleached bread flour, whole wheat flour, uncooked oatmeal, cooked cracked wheat and sesame seeds. Pour in yeast and mix to a stiff dough. Turn onto a lightly floured board and knead for 10 minutes. Place in a greased bowl and let rise until doubled in size. Place on a floured board and divide into 2 or 3 portions (depending on the size desired), and shape into round flat loaves. Place in well-oiled 10 or 12-inch round pans. Brush tops of loaves with oil or butter. Let rise in a warm place until doubled in size. Bake at 375 degrees until golden and loaves start pulling away from the sides of the pan.

NOTE: For 2 loaves, bake at 350 degrees for 50 minutes. For rolls, bake at 375 degrees for 20 minutes. For flat loaf, bake at 350 degrees for 30 minutes.

Tomato Basil Bread
Yield: 2 loaves

2 cups tomato juice
2 tablespoons butter or margarine
1 package active dry yeast
2 teaspoons salt
4 teaspoons fresh basil, chopped
  or
2 teaspoons dried basil
2 tablespoons sugar
2 to 6 cups unbleached white flour
1 egg
1 tablespoon water
Basil for topping

Heat tomato juice and butter until warm to the touch (120 to 130 degrees). Stir until butter melts. Pour into a large bowl and add yeast, salt, basil, sugar and 2 cups flour. Beat with wooden spoon until perfectly smooth. Add additional flour until dough is stiff enough to knead. Knead 5 minutes until smooth and springy. Put into a greased bowl, turning dough to coat. Cover and let rise until doubled. Punch down and knead for 1 or 2 minutes. Cut in half with a knife. Form each piece of dough into a loaf and place in an 8 x 4-inch greased loaf pan. Cover pans and let rise until doubled. Brush with an egg and water glaze. Sprinkle with extra basil. Bake at 375 degrees for 30 minutes or until tops are very brown and loaves are hollow when tapped on bottom. Remove from pans and cool.

Fresh Pear Breakfast Bread

Serves: 10 to 12

2 fresh bartlett pears
   (about 2 cups)
1½ cups flour
2 teaspoons baking powder
1/2 teaspoon salt
1/4 teaspoon baking soda
3/4 cup wheat germ
1 egg
1/4 cup milk
1/4 cup vegetable oil
1/3 cup honey

   Streusel Topping:
4 tablespoons brown sugar
4 tablespoons flour
2 teaspoons cinnamon
2 tablespoons butter, melted
(Combine all and mix until
   crumbly)

Core and finely dice pears, but do not peel. Sift together flour, baking powder, salt and soda. Stir in wheat germ. Beat egg slightly and blend with milk, oil, and honey. Add to dry ingredients along with pears. Stir until mixed.

For coffee cake: Pour batter into a greased 9-inch round cake pan. Sprinkle with streusel topping. Garnish with additional pear slices, if desired. Bake at 400 degrees for 25 to 30 minutes.

For muffins: Fill cups ⅔ full. Sprinkle with streusel topping. Bake at 400 degrees for 15 minutes.

Overnight Hobo Bread

Yield: 3 loaves

2 cups raisins
4 teaspoons baking soda
2½ cups boiling water
3/4 cup brown sugar
1 cup sugar
4 tablespoons vegetable oil
1 teaspoon salt
4 cups flour

Put raisins, baking soda and boiling water in a large bowl and soak overnight. The next day, combine brown sugar, sugar, oil, salt and flour. Add to raisin mixture and mix well. Pour into 3 greased and floured 9 x 5 loaf pans. Bake at 350 degrees for 50 minutes to 1 hour.

Fresh Apple Whole-Wheat Muffins
Yield: 1 dozen

1/4 cup butter or margarine
1/2 cup brown sugar
2 eggs
1¾ cup whole wheat flour
1/2 teaspoon salt
2 teaspoons baking powder
1 teaspoon cinnamon
1/2 teaspoon nutmeg
1 cup milk
1 cup peeled and chopped apple
1/2 cup raisins
1/2 cup chopped walnuts

Grease muffin pans or line them with paper baking cups. Cream butter and sugar together, add eggs and beat until creamy. In another bowl, combine whole-wheat flour, salt, baking powder, cinnamon and nutmeg; mix well. Add the dry ingredients, milk, apples, raisins and walnuts to the creamed mixture and beat until ingredients are mixed. Spoon the batter into the muffin pans, filling each cup ¾ full. Bake at 425 degrees for 15 minutes. Serve warm.

NOTE: For a healthier muffin, substitute ½ cup oatmeal for 1 cup whole wheat flour.

Cranberry Almond Swirl Bread
Serves: 8

2 cups flour
1 teaspoon baking soda
1/2 teaspoon salt
1/4 cup butter
1 cup sugar
2 eggs
1 teaspoon almond extract
1 cup yogurt
1 (8-ounce) can whole
  cranberry sauce
1/2 cup chopped almonds

Sift together flour, baking soda and salt. In a second bowl, cream butter, sugar and eggs. Add almond extract to creamed mixture. Add flour mixture and yogurt alternately to creamed mixture, stirring well. Pour ½ of the batter into a greased and floured 9 x 5-inch bread pan. Add ½ of the cranberry sauce and nuts to batter and swirl, lightly. Pour rest of batter into the pan and repeat with remaining cranberry sauce and nuts. Bake at 350 degrees for 1 hour or until done. Cool 15 minutes.

Coconut Lemon Muffins
Yield: 1 dozen

Coconut Crust:
1/2 cup coconut, flaked
1/2 cup brown sugar
2 tablespoons flour
3 tablespoons butter or
 margarine, melted
1/8 teaspoon nutmeg

Muffins:
2 cups flour
1/4 cup sugar
1 tablespoon baking powder
1/2 teaspoon salt
1/4 teaspoon nutmeg
1 egg
1 cup milk
3 tablespoons vegetable oil
1 tablespoon grated lemon
 peel
1 tablespoon lemon juice

For crust: Combine ingredients in a small bowl. Divide into well greased muffin tins, pressing against bottoms and up the sides.

For muffins: Combine flour, sugar, baking powder, salt and nutmeg; blend thoroughly. In a small bowl, beat egg lightly with milk, oil, lemon peel and lemon juice. Stir milk mixture into dry ingredients until moistened. Fill prepared muffin cups about ¾ full. Bake at 400 degrees for 15 to 20 minutes until golden brown. Immediately remove muffins from pan and place on racks to cool. Serve warm.

Sesame Cheese Muffins
Yield: 1 dozen

2 tablespoons toasted sesame
 seeds
2 cups flour
3 tablespoons sugar
1 tablespoon baking powder
3/4 teaspoon salt
1½ cups shredded sharp cheddar
 cheese
1 egg
1 cup milk
1/3 cup vegetable oil
4 tablespoons minced onion
2 tablespoons butter or margarine,
 melted

Combine flour, sugar, baking powder and salt; blend thoroughly, and stir in 1 cup cheddar cheese. In a small bowl, beat egg lightly with milk and oil; add onion. Gradually stir milk and egg mixture into the flour and cheese mixture until moistened. Fill well-greased muffin cups ¾ full with batter. Sprinkle the tops with remaining ½ cup cheese and toasted sesame seeds. Drizzle melted butter over the tops. Bake at 400 degrees for 15 to 20 minutes or until golden brown.

Cheddar Cheese Crisps
Yield: 32

1¾ cups flour
1/2 cup cornmeal
1/2 teaspoon baking soda
1/2 teaspoon sugar
1/2 teaspoon salt
1 cube butter or margarine,
    softened
1½ cups shredded extra sharp
    cheddar cheese
1/2 cup cold water
2 tablespoons white vinegar
Coarsely ground pepper

In a large bowl, mix flour, cornmeal, baking soda, sugar and salt. With a pastry blender, cut in the butter or margarine until crumbly. With fork, stir in cheese, vinegar, and the cold water, until mixture forms a soft dough. Shape into a ball, wrap with plastic and refrigerate for 1 hour. On a lightly floured surface, roll out ¼ of the dough (paper thin) into a 13-inch diameter circle, keeping remainder of dough refrigerated, until ready to use. Cut circle into 8 wedges, place on greased cookie sheet and sprinkle with pepper. Press pepper firmly into dough. Bake at 375 degrees for about 10 minutes until brown and crisp. Remove to a rack and cool. Repeat with remaining dough. Store in tight containers.

Molasses Corn Bread
Serves: 8

1½ cups whole bran cereal
1 cup flour
1/2 cup yellow cornmeal
1 tablespoon baking powder
1/4 teaspoon salt
1/3 cup shortening
1/4 cup sugar
2 eggs
1 cup milk
1/3 cup molasses

Combine bran cereal, flour, cornmeal, baking powder and salt; set aside. In a small mixing bowl, beat shortening with an electric mixer on medium speed for 30 seconds. Add sugar and beat until fluffy. On medium speed, add the eggs one at a time, beating well after each addition. Stir in the milk and molasses. Add the flour mixture to beaten ingredients, stir until combined. Pour batter into a greased 9 x 9 x 2-inch baking pan. Bake at 375 degreees for 30 minutes until top is golden. Cut into squares and serve warm.

Orange-Oatey Muffins
Yield: 1 dozen

3/4 cup oat bran
3/4 cup whole wheat flour
1/4 cup flour
1 teaspoon ground nutmeg
1 teaspoon baking powder
1 teaspoon baking soda
1/4 teaspoon salt
1 large orange, unpeeled
1/2 cup sugar
1/4 cup vegetable oil
1 teaspoon vanilla
2 beaten egg whites

Topping:
2 tablespoons sugar
2 tablespoons flour
1 teaspooon cinnamon
1 tablespoon butter, melted
1/4 cup finely chopped nuts

Stir together oat bran, flours, nutmeg, baking powder, baking soda and salt. Cut orange into pieces and chop in a blender or food processor until fine. Remove to another bowl and stir in sugar, oil and vanilla. Gently fold in beaten egg whites. Stir dry ingredients into orange mixture until just moistened. Fill muffin cups ⅔ full. Sprinkle with nut topping mixture. Bake at 400 degrees for 20 to 25 minutes or until toothpick inserted in center comes out clean.

Blackberry Orange Bread
Yield: 1 loaf

1 cup blackberries (may use blueberries)
2 tablespoons butter
1/4 cup boiling water
1/2 cup orange juice
4 tablespoons grated orange rind
1 egg
1/2 cup sugar
2 cups flour
1 teaspoon baking powder
1/2 teaspoon salt
1/4 teaspoon baking soda

Melt butter in boiling water, add orange juice and rind. In another bowl, beat egg with sugar until fluffy, then mix in flour, baking powder, salt and baking soda. Add orange juice mixture and gently fold in berries. Place batter in a greased loaf pan. Bake at 325 degrees for 1 hour.

Carrot Date-Nut Muffins
Yield: 1 dozen

1½ cups flour
1/2 cup rolled oats
1/2 cup brown sugar
1 teaspoon cinnamon
1 tablespoon baking powder
1 teaspoon salt
1 cup shredded carrots
1/2 cup chopped walnuts or
   hazelnuts
1/2 cup chopped dates
2 eggs
4 tablespoons butter or
   margarine, melted
3/4 cup milk

In a large bowl, mix flour, oats, brown sugar, cinnamon, baking powder and salt. Stir in carrots, nuts and dates. Beat eggs in a small bowl. Blend butter and milk into eggs. Add to flour mixture and stir until blended. Fill greased or paper-lined muffin pans ⅔ full. Bake at 400 degreees for 15 to 20 minutes.

Cranberry Scones
Yield: 1 dozen

1 cup cranberries, fresh or frozen
3 cups flour
1/2 cup sugar
1 tablespoon baking powder
1/4 teaspoon salt
1/2 teaspoon baking soda
3/4 cup butter or margarine,
   softened
1/2 cup chopped pecans or
   walnuts
1½ teaspoons grated orange rind
1 cup buttermilk
1 tablespoon milk
1 tablespoon sugar
1/4 teaspoon cinnamon
1/8 teaspoon nutmeg

In a large bowl, blend flour, sugar, baking powder, salt and baking soda. Cut butter into flour mixture until it becomes a coarse crumb texture. Stir in cranberries, nuts and orange rind. Add buttermilk and mix with a fork until moistened. Gather dough into a ball and place on a floured board. Roll or pat into a circle ¾-inch thick. Cut into 12 pie shaped pieces. Place on a greased baking sheet 1½-inches apart. Brush tops of scones with milk and sprinkle with sugar, cinnamon and nutmeg mixture. Bake at 400 degreees for 12 to 15 minutes, until lightly browned.

Lemony Blueberry Muffins

Yield: 1 dozen

1 cup blueberries, fresh or frozen
2 eggs
1/2 cup margarine, melted and
  cooled
1 cup sugar
1 cup plain yogurt
2 cups flour
1 teaspoon baking powder
1/2 teaspoon baking soda
1 teaspoon grated lemon rind

Beat together eggs, melted margarine and sugar. Stir in yogurt. Add dry ingredients until just blended, then fold in blueberries. Spoon batter into greased or paper-lined muffin tins. Bake at 375 degrees for 25 minutes.

Banana Muffins

Yield: 12 to 16 muffins

1 cup mashed bananas (2 large)
1/2 cup butter
1 cup sugar
1 egg
1 teaspoon baking soda, dissolved
  in 1 tablespoon cold water
1½ cups flour
1 teaspoon nutmeg
1 teaspoon vanilla

Cream butter and sugar, then beat in eggs. Add baking soda, flour, nutmeg and vanilla until combined, then add well mashed bananas. Put batter into greased or paper lined muffin tins. Bake at 350 degrees for 20 minutes.

Hot Herb Bread

Yield: 10 slices

1 loaf french bread
1/2 cup soft butter
1 teaspoon parsley flakes
1/2 teaspoon dried oregano
1/2 teaspoon dried dill weed
1 to 2 cloves garlic, minced
Grated parmesan cheese
Foil

Slice loaf in half lengthwise or into 1-inch slices. Blend butter, parsley, oregano, dill weed and garlic. Spread butter mixture on sliced bread and top liberally with parmesan cheese. Wrap in foil and bake at 400 degrees for 15 to 20 minutes.

Yogurt Raisin Bran Muffins
Yield: 3 dozen

1 cup 100% bran cereal
1 cup boiling water
1¼ cups sugar
1/2 cup salad oil
2 eggs
2 cups plain yogurt
2½ cups flour
2½ teaspoons baking soda
1/2 teaspoon salt
2 cups bran flakes
2 cups raisins

Pour boiling water over bran cereal and let stand. Mix sugar with oil, then add eggs and mix well. Add yogurt to mixture. In a separate bowl, mix flour, baking soda and salt together. Combine flour mixture with sugar, oil and eggs. Then mix in bran cereal, followed by the bran flakes and raisins. Spoon into well-greased muffin tins or into paper cups. Bake at 350 degrees for 20 to 25 minutes, or until done.

Pumpkin Raisin Bread
Yield: 1 loaf or 16 muffins

2 cups flour
2 teaspoons baking powder
1/2 teaspoon baking soda
1 teaspoon salt
1 teaspoon cinnamon
1 teaspoon nutmeg
1/4 teaspoon cloves
1/2 teaspoon ginger
1 cup cooked pumpkin
1 cup brown sugar
1/2 cup evaporated milk
2 eggs, slightly beaten
1/4 cup butter or margarine,
    softened
1 cup raisins
1 cup chopped nuts (optional)

Grease and flour a 9 x 5 loaf pan, 2 mini-loaf pans, or 16 muffin cups. Sift together: flour, baking powder, baking soda, salt, cinnamon, nutmeg, cloves and ginger; set aside. In a bowl, mix pumpkin, sugar, milk, eggs and margarine. Pour pumpkin mixture into flour and mix until blended. Add raisins (and nuts if desired); stir to distribute evenly through batter. Pour batter into prepared baking pan(s) or muffin cups. Bake at 350 degrees for one hour (9 x 5 pan); 30 to 40 minutes (2 mini-pans) or 25 to 30 minutes (muffins). Bread or muffins are done when toothpick inserted into center comes out clean.

Cheese Filled French Bread

Serves: 8

1 loaf french bread, uncut
1/2 cup melted margarine
5 cloves garlic, crushed
2 cups shredded Monterey Jack cheese
1/2 cup grated parmesan cheese
1 pint sour cream
2 teaspoons minced parsley
1 teaspoon lemon pepper

Topping:
1/2 cup shredded Monterey Jack cheese
1/2 cup shredded cheddar cheese

Cut bread in half lengthwise. Scoop out center of bread leaving a ½ to 3/4-inch shell all around. Cube cut out bread. Add garlic to melted butter, stir and pour into a bowl. Mix in bread cubes and toss lightly. Blend Monterey Jack, parmesan, sour cream, parsley and lemon pepper. Add to bread mixture and mix well. Fill bread shells with this mixture. Mix the topping ingredients and sprinkle evenly over the two shells. Wrap each half in foil, covering the sides, but not the top. Bake at 350 degrees for 20 minutes until cheese is thoroughly melted.

Cream Biscuits

Serves: 6 to 8

2 cups flour
2 tablespoons sugar
4 teaspoons baking powder
1/2 teaspoon cream of tartar
1/2 cup unsalted butter, cut in pieces
2/3 cup whipping cream

Sift dry ingredients together into a large mixing bowl. Cut in butter, until mixture resembles coarse meal. Add cream and stir just until combined. Knead dough for 15 seconds on a lightly floured board. Pat or roll dough to a ½-inch thickness. Using cookie cutter or inverted glass, cut into 2½-inch rounds. Arrange on large baking sheet 1-inch apart. Bake at 425 degrees for 15 minutes, until biscuits have risen and tops are golden brown. Serve hot or at room temperature.

Almond Poppy Seed Bread
Yield: 2 loaves

3 eggs, slightly beaten
2¼ cups granulated sugar
1⅓ cups vegetable oil
1½ cups milk
3 cups flour
1½ teaspoons baking powder
1½ teaspoons salt
2 tablespoons poppy seeds
2 teaspoons almond extract

Glaze:
1/4 cup orange juice concentrate
3/4 cup powdered sugar
1/2 teaspoon vanilla
1 teaspoon almond extract

Grease and flour two 8½ x 4½ x 2½-inch loaf pans. Beat together eggs, sugar, oil and milk. Combine flour, baking powder and salt, beat into egg mixture. Stir poppy seeds and almond extract into batter. Pour into loaf pans and bake at 350 degrees for 50 to 60 minutes.

For glaze: combine glaze ingredients to a spreading consistency. Cool breads in pan for 10 minutes. Remove from pans and spread glaze over the top while bread is still warm.

Pecan Breakfast Rolls
Yield: 6 to 8 rolls

2 cans Pillsbury Crescent Rolls
2 tablespoons butter or margarine, softened
1/2 cup sugar
1 to 2 teaspoons cinnamon
1/4 cup chopped pecans

Topping:
2 tablespoons honey
1/4 cup powdered sugar
2 tablespoons butter or margarine
1 teaspoon vanilla
1/4 cup pecan halves

Unroll crescent rolls and separate into 16 triangles. Spread each triangle with butter. Combine sugar, cinnamon and chopped pecans. Sprinkle on each triangle. Roll up each triangle starting at widest end and roll to opposite point. Place rolls point side down in a greased 9 x 5 loaf pan, forming 2 layers of 8 rolls each. Bake at 375 degrees for 40 to 45 minutes. If rolls start to brown, cover pan with foil during the last 10 minutes of baking. Remove from pan at once, placing right side up.

Topping: In sauce pan, add all topping ingredients except pecan halves. Bring to a boil, stirring constantly. Drizzle over warm rolls, then top with pecan halves.

Lemon-Cream Cheese Croissants
Yield: 2 dozen

1 cube butter, softened
1 cup small curd cottage cheese
1 cup flour
1/4 pound cream cheese, softened
1/4 cup granulated sugar
1 tablespoon grated lemon zest
　Powdered sugar

In a large bowl, beat together butter and cottage cheese until blended. Beat in the flour until blended. Shape the dough into a 6-inch circle and wrap in floured waxed paper. Refrigerate for 1 hour. Beat together the cream cheese, granulated sugar and lemon zest until blended. Divide the dough into thirds. Roll each third out on a floured pastry cloth until the circle measures 9-inches. Spread ⅓ of the filling over each circle of dough and cut each circle into 8 pie-shaped wedges. Roll each wedge from the wide end toward the center and curve slightly into a crescent. Place croissants on a lightly greased cookie sheet and bake at 350 degrees for 25 minutes, or until golden brown. Remove to rack and cool. Sprinkle with powdered sugar, as desired.

French Breakfast Muffins
Yield: 10 to 12 muffins

1/2 cup shortening
1/2 cup sugar
1 egg
3/4 cup whole wheat flour, sifted
3/4 cup white flour, sifted
1½ teaspoons baking powder
1/2 teaspoon nutmeg
1/2 cup milk

Topping:
1/2 cup butter or margarine
1/2 cup sugar
1 teaspoon cinnamon

Grease muffin tins and dust with flour. Mix ingredients in order listed. You may use a food processor. Fill muffin tins ½ full and bake at 350 degrees for 20 to 25 minutes. While muffins are baking, melt butter. Place sugar and cinnamon in a bowl large enough to roll muffins in. When muffins are done, remove from pans and immediately dip tops in butter or margarine and then in the sugar and cinnamon mixture. Serve warm.

Blueberry Streusel Coffee Cake

Serves: 16

Cake:
2¾ cups flour
1½ teaspoons baking powder
1½ teaspoons baking soda
1/2 teaspoon salt
3/4 cup butter or margarine,
    softened
1 cup sugar
3 eggs
1 pint sour cream
    (may use plain yogurt)
2 teaspoons vanilla extract

Streusel:
3/4 cup brown sugar
3/4 cup chopped walnuts
1 teaspoon cinnamon

2 to 2½ cups blueberries
    (if frozen, drain before using)

Grease and flour a 10-inch tube pan. Combine flour, baking powder, baking soda and salt. Set aside. In a large bowl, cream butter or margarine and sugar until light and fluffy. Add eggs one at a time, beating well after each addition. Add flour mixture alternately with sour cream and vanilla, to batter.

Combine ingredients for streusel. Set aside ½ cup for topping. Toss remaining streusel with berries.
Spread ⅓ of the batter in prepared pan, sprinkle with ½ of the berry mixture. Spread ⅓ of the batter over that and sprinkle with remaining berry mixture. Top with remaining batter and reserved streusel. Bake at 375 degrees for 60 to 65 minutes or until toothpick inserted in center comes out clean. Cool in pan on wire rack for 10 minutes. Remove from pan and serve.

Banana-Sour Cream Coffee Cake

Serves: 12 to 16

Cake:
1 cup butter or margarine, softened
2 cups sugar
2 eggs
1 cup sour cream
1/2 teaspoon vanilla
2 to 3 ripe bananas, mashed
1 teaspoon baking powder
1/4 teaspoon salt
2 cups flour

Nut Mixture:
3 tablespoons sugar
1 teaspoon cinnamon
1 cup chopped pecans or walnuts

Glaze:
1½ cups powdered sugar
3/4 teaspoons vanilla
3 tablespoons milk
1/4 cup chopped pecans or walnuts (optional)

Grease and flour a bundt or 9-inch tube pan. For cake: Cream butter and sugar; beat until light and fluffy. Add eggs one at a time, beating well after each addition. Stir in sour cream, vanilla and bananas. Sift baking powder, salt and flour together. Add this mixture to the banana mixture and mix well.

For nut mixture: Combine sugar, cinnamon and nuts in a small bowl; set aside. Pour ⅓ of the cake batter into the prepared baking pan. Sprinkle with ¾ cup of the nut mixture. Spoon remaining batter over the nut mixture, then sprinkle with remaining nut mixture. Bake at 350 degrees for 1 hour, or until toothpick inserted in center comes out clean. Cool on a rack for 10 minutes, then remove from pan and continue to cool.

For glaze: Mix powdered sugar, vanilla and milk until smooth, (adding more milk if necessary). Drizzle over cooled coffee cake and garnish with additional nuts if desired.

Raspberry Cream Cheese Pastry

Serves: 10 to 12

1 (3-ounce) package cream cheese, softened
1/4 cup margarine or butter, softened
2 cups packaged biscuit mix
1/4 cup milk
1/2 cup raspberry preserves

Frosting:
1 cup sifted powdered sugar
1 to 2 tablespoons milk
1/2 teaspoon vanilla

In a medium mixing bowl, beat the cream cheese and margarine or butter into the biscuit mix until crumbly. Stir in the milk and turn onto a lightly floured surface. Knead dough 8 to 10 strokes. On waxed paper, roll dough into a 12 x 8-inch rectangle. Invert dough onto greased baking sheet; remove paper. Spread preserves down center of dough. Along the long sides, make 2½-inch cuts into center of dough at 1-inch intervals. Fold these strips over the filling. Bake at 375 degrees for 20 minutes or until golden brown. Let cool 5 minutes before frosting.

For frosting: In a small mixing bowl stir together powdered sugar, 1 to 2 tablespoons milk and vanilla. Drizzle over pastry. Serve warm.

Savor
the
Flavor
of
DESSERTS

What's In These Cookies?

Yield: 5 dozen

12 ounces chocolate chips
1½ pounds chocolate
  flavored almond bark
1 pound butter crackers,
  (Ritz, Hi Ho, etc)
2 cups peanut butter,
  crunchy or creamy

Melt chips and almond bark in a double boiler. While chocolate is melting, prepare approximately 60 peanut butter cracker sandwiches (spread peanut butter between 2 butter crackers). When chocolate is smooth, dip each cracker sandwich into mixture (using tongs), then place each on wax papered cookie sheet. Refrigerate 15 minutes to set chocolate and store in an airtight container.

NOTE: With left over dipping chocolate, add nuts and spoon out nut clusters. You can buy the almond bark at Christmas and freeze for use later.

Sugar Cookies

Yield: 2 dozen

1½ cups powdered sugar
1 cup butter
1 egg
1 teaspoon vanilla
1/2 teaspoon almond extract
2½ cups flour
1 teaspoon baking soda
1 teaspoon cream of tartar
Granulated sugar

Cream together powdered sugar, butter, egg, vanilla and almond extract. Add flour, baking soda and cream of tartar. Chill dough until firm. Roll dough to ³⁄₁₆-inch thickness and cut into shapes with your favorite cookie cutters. Sprinkle with granulated sugar and place on a lightly greased cookie sheet. Bake at 375 degrees for 7 to 8 minutes until slightly brown around the edges.

Gammy's Peanut Cookies
Yield: 8½ dozen

1 cup margarine
1 cup granulated sugar
1 cup brown sugar
2 eggs, beaten
2½ cups flour
1 teaspoon baking soda
1 teaspoon baking powder
1/2 teaspoon salt
1 cup old fashioned oats
1 cup crumbled corn flakes
1/2 pound Spanish peanuts

Mix together margarine and sugars. Add eggs and mix well. In a separate bowl, mix together remaining ingredients. Gradually add dry ingredients to the creamed mixture; mix well. Roll cookie dough into 2-inch diameter tubes. Wrap with foil then place into freezer until frozen, 2 hours or more. Preheat oven to 350 degrees. With a sharp knife, cut into paper thin slices about ⅛-inch thick. Place on a greased cookie sheet. Bake at 350 degrees for 8 minutes. The cookies should be crispy-crunchy.

Cracked Sugar Cookie
Yield: 4 dozen

1 cup margarine, softened
1 cup brown sugar
1 cup granulated sugar
2 eggs
1 teaspoon vanilla
2 teaspoons cream of tartar
2 teaspoons baking soda
1/2 teaspoon salt
3 cups flour
Granulated sugar

Cream together margarine and sugars. Beat in eggs and vanilla. Stir in cream of tartar, baking soda, salt and flour; mix well. Shape into walnut size balls, roll in granulated sugar and place on an ungreased cookie sheet. Bake at 375 degrees for 8 to 10 minutes. The cookies should be chewy when done, not crunchy.

Butter Pecan Turtle Cookies
Yield: 4 dozen

Crust:
2 cups flour
1 cup brown sugar
1/2 cup butter, softened
1 cup finely chopped pecans

Caramel layer:
2/3 cup butter
1/2 cup packed brown sugar

1 cup milk chocolate chips

In a large bowl, combine flour, brown sugar and butter; mix until fine. Pat firmly into an ungreased 9 x 13-inch pan. Sprinkle pecans evenly over unbaked crust. For caramel layer: In a heavy 1-quart pan, combine butter and brown sugar, cook over medium heat, stirring constantly until entire surface of mixture begins to boil. Boil 30 seconds to 1 minute, stirring constantly. Pour caramel mixture evenly over pecans and unbaked crust. Bake at 350 degrees for 18 to 22 minutes until the entire caramel layer is bubbly and crust is light golden. Remove from oven and sprinkle chips over all. Allow to melt 2 to 3 minutes. Swirl slightly as they melt, do not spread evenly. Cool and cut into small squares.

Lemonade Cookies
Yield: 4 to 5 dozen

1 cup butter or margarine,
  softened
1 cup sugar
2 eggs
3 cups sifted flour
1 teaspoon baking soda
1 (6-ounce) can frozen
  lemonade concentrate, thawed
Powdered sugar

Cream butter and sugar. Add eggs and beat until light and fluffy. Sift flour and soda. Add flour alternately with ½ cup lemonade concentrate to butter mixture. Drop dough by tablespoonfuls 2-inches apart onto an ungreased cookie sheet. Bake at 400 degrees for 8 minutes. Brush warm cookies with remaining lemonade concentrate and dust with powdered sugar.

Ginger Cookies
Yield: 3 dozen

2 cups sugar
1⅓ cups cooking oil
1/2 cup molasses
2 eggs
4 cups flour
4 teaspoons baking soda
1 teaspoon salt
2 teaspoons cinnamon
2 teaspoons ginger
Granulated sugar

Cream together first 4 ingredients. Add flour, baking soda, salt, cinnamon and ginger. Chill in refrigerator. Form into balls and roll in granulated sugar. Bake on ungreased cookie sheet at 350 degrees for 8 minutes.

Snickerdoodles
Yield: 3 dozen

1/2 cup shortening
1/2 cup butter, softened
1½ cups sugar
2 eggs
2 teaspoons cream of tartar
1 teaspoon soda
1/2 teaspoon salt
2½ cups flour

Topping:
2 teaspoons cinnamon
2 tablespoons sugar

Cream shortening, butter and sugar. Add eggs. Mix dry ingredients together and add to shortening mixture. Chill dough. Roll dough into walnut size balls. For topping: Mix cinnamon and sugar together in a small bowl. Roll balls in topping mixture and place 2-inches apart on an ungreased cookie sheet. Bake at 375 degrees for 12 to 15 minutes.

Lemon Coconut Balls

Yield: 4 dozen

Cookies:
3/4 cup margarine, softened
1/2 cup granulated sugar
1 egg
1/2 teaspoon vanilla
1 teaspoon lemon extract
1 cup flaked coconut
2 cups flour
1/2 teaspoon cream of tartar

Frosting:
1/4 cup butter or margarine,
  softened
1 teaspoon grated lemon peel
Salt to taste
2 cups powdered sugar
2 tablespoons lemon juice
Dash of yellow food coloring

Cream margarine and sugar until fluffy. Add egg, vanilla and lemon extract. Blend in coconut, flour and cream of tartar. Roll into small balls (1-inch) and place on an ungreased cookie sheet. Bake at 350 degrees for 8 to 10 minutes until lightly browned. Cool.

For frosting: Blend all ingredients with wooden spoon or electric mixer and frost cookies.

Double Chocolate Chip Cookies

Yield: 3 dozen

1 cup butter
1½ cups brown sugar
2 eggs
1½ teaspoons vanilla
2¼ cups flour
2 tablespoons cocoa
1 teaspoon salt
1 teaspoon baking soda
12 ounces semi-sweet chocolate
  chips
1/2 cup chopped walnuts

In a food processor or mixer, cream butter, sugar, eggs and vanilla. Combine flour, cocoa, salt and baking soda. Add to creamed mixture and blend well. Stir in chocolate chips and nuts by hand. Drop by tablespoonfuls onto ungreased cookie sheets and bake at 325 degrees for 10 to 12 minutes.

Chocolate Monster Cookies

Yield: 5 to 6 dozen

1 pound margarine, softened
2 cups granulated sugar
2 cups brown sugar
4 eggs, beaten
2 teaspoons vanilla
2 cup oats
2 cups corn flakes
4 cups flour
3 teaspoons baking powder
2 teaspoons baking soda
1 (12-ounce) package chocolate
   chips
1 teaspoon salt
1 cup chopped nuts (optional)
7 to 8 ounces coconut (optional)

In a very large bowl, cream together margarine and sugars. Add eggs and vanilla, beat until fluffy. Stir in oats, corn flakes, flour, baking powder and baking soda. When well mixed, add remaining ingredients. Roll into 3 to 4 logs. Refrigerate overnight. Cut ½-inch slices from logs. Bake on ungreased cookie sheet at 350 degrees for 13 to 15 minutes.

Almond Crescents

Yield: 4 dozen

1 cup butter, softened
2/3 cup finely ground almonds
1/3 cup sugar
1⅔ cups flour

Topping:
1/4 cup sugar
1/4 teaspoon cinnamon

Combine butter, almonds and sugar in a large bowl. Beat until light and fluffy. Add flour and beat until well blended. Refrigerate dough about two hours. For topping: Stir together sugar and cinnamon and set aside. Divide dough into eighths. Work with one section at a time leaving remaining dough refrigerated. Divide each eighth into 6 equal parts. With floured hands, roll each piece into a 2½ x ½-inch cylinder and form into crescent shapes. Place on ungreased cookie sheet and bake at 325 degrees for 12 to 14 minutes. Dip tips in cinnamon-sugar topping mixture while cookies are still slightly warm.

Cream Cheese Cookies
Yield: 4 to 5 dozen

1 cup butter or margarine,
   softened
1 cup sugar
6 ounces cream cheese, softened
1 egg yolk
1/2 teaspoon vanilla
2½ cups flour

Cream together the butter, sugar and cream cheese. Beat in the egg yolk, vanilla and flour. Form dough into a roll about 2-inches in diameter. Wrap in waxed paper and chill until hard (about 2 hours), turning roll occasionally to keep round. Slice dough into thin ⅛-inch circles. Put slices on greased cookie sheets. Bake at 375 degrees for 8 to 10 minutes until edges turn a light brown. Cool cookies on racks and store in air-tight containers.

White Chocolate Macadamia Cookies
Yield: 2½ dozen

1¼ cups flour
1/2 cup butter or margarine,
   softened
1/2 cup brown sugar
1/4 cup granulated sugar
1 teaspoon vanilla
1/2 teaspoon baking soda
1/2 teaspoon salt
1 egg
1 tablespoon water
6 ounces white chocolate,
   coarsely chopped
1 (7-ounce) jar macadamia nuts,
   coarsely chopped

In a large bowl, combine flour, butter, brown and white sugar, vanilla, baking soda, salt, egg and water. Beat with mixer at low speed until blended. Stir in white chocolate and macadamia nuts. Drop mixture by tablespoonfuls, about 2-inches apart, onto ungreased cookie sheets and flatten slightly. Bake at 375 degrees for 10 to 15 minutes until lightly browned. Remove from baking sheets and cool on wire racks.

Italian Anise Cookies
Yield: 2 dozen

4 eggs
1⅓ cups sugar
2 teaspoons anise seed or
extract equivalent
2 cups sifted flour

Beat eggs and sugar well. Add anise seeds or extract. Gradually blend in flour. Spread in a very lightly greased 9 x 13-inch pan. Bake at 375 degrees for 20 minutes. Remove and slice on the diagonal. Put pieces on a greased cookie sheet and bake at 375 degrees for an additional 5 minutes on each side to get a golden color. Store in a covered container.

Peanut Butter Balls
Yield: 4 dozen

6 ounces semi-sweet chocolate
chips
6 ounces butterscotch chips
1 tablespoon shortening
(approximate)

Mixture #1
1 cup creamy peanut butter
1 cup powdered sugar
1 cup chopped walnuts
1 cup chopped dates
2 tablespoons butter, melted

Mixture #2
2/3 cup peanut butter
2½ cups powdered sugar
15 chopped maraschino cherries
1 cup finely shredded coconut
3 tablespoons butter, melted
1/2 cup chopped walnuts

Combine ingredients of mixture #1 or mixture #2 and chill on cookie sheet for about 1 hour. In top of double boiler, melt chips and a small amount of shortening as needed to keep chocolate smooth. Roll chilled cookie mixture into balls. Quickly drop one ball at a time into the melted chocolate, rotate with a toothpick and lift out. Place on waxed paper lined cookie sheet and freeze. When frozen transfer to an air-tight container and keep in freezer.

Best Ever Hazelnut Cookies

Yield: 3 dozen

1/2 cup shortening
1/2 cup granulated sugar
1/2 cup brown sugar
1 egg
1 teaspoon vanilla
1 cup flour
1/2 teaspoon salt
1/2 teaspoon baking soda
1/2 teaspoon baking powder
3/4 cup oats
1/2 cup coconut
1 cup chopped hazelnuts

Cream shortening, sugars, egg and vanilla. Add flour, salt, baking soda, and baking powder. Blend in oats, coconut and hazelnuts. Roll into small balls. Place on a greased cookie sheet. Flatten. Bake at 350 degrees for 7 to 10 minutes.

Angel Cookies

Yield: 36 Cookies

1/2 cup butter, softened
1/2 cup shortening
1/2 cup brown sugar
1/2 cup granulated sugar
1 egg
1 teaspoon vanilla
2 cups flour
1 teaspoon baking soda
1 teaspoon cream of tartar
1/2 cup chopped nuts
1 cup finely shredded coconut
Cold water
Granulated sugar

In a large bowl, cream butter, shortening and sugars. Add egg and blend in vanilla, flour, baking soda, cream of tartar, nuts and coconut. Roll into small balls. Dip balls in cold water, then into granulated sugar. Place on an ungreased cookie sheet, 2-inches apart and bake at 425 degrees for 6 to 8 minutes.

Not Mrs. Fields Chocolate Chip Cookies

Yield: 40 Cookies

1 cup unsalted butter, softened
1 cup sugar
1 cup brown sugar
2 eggs
1 teaspoon vanilla
2½ cups oatmeal, powdered in blender or food processor
1/2 teaspoon salt
1 teaspoon baking powder
1 teaspoon baking soda
2 cups flour
12 ounces semi-sweet chocolate chips
1 (8-ounce) milk chocolate bar, finely grated
1½ cups chopped nuts

In a large bowl, cream butter and sugars. Blend in eggs and vanilla. Add powdered oatmeal and mix. Sift together salt, baking powder, baking soda and flour. Add in batches to creamed ingredients. Batter will be very stiff, mix with a spoon. Mix in the chips, grated chocolate and nuts. Place golf ball size pieces of dough 2-inches apart on ungreased cookie sheets. Lightly flatten. Bake at 400 degrees for 8 minutes. Do not overbake. Cookies will not look done, but over baking ruins them. This is a soft cookie.

Butter Cookie Sandwiches

Yield: 4 dozen

Cookies:
1 cup butter, softened
1/3 cup whipping cream
2 cups sifted flour
1/2 cup granulated sugar

Filling:
1/4 cup butter, softened
3/4 cup powdered sugar, sifted after measuring
1 egg yolk
1 teaspoon vanilla

Mix 1 cup butter, whipping cream and flour. Chill well. On a lightly floured board, roll dough to ⅛-inch thick. Cut with a small cookie or doughnut hole cutter. Dip cookies in sugar, place on ungreased cookie sheets and prick with a fork. Bake at 375 degrees for 7 to 9 minutes.

For filling: Whip butter, powdered sugar, egg yolk and vanilla in an electric mixer. Use mixture as filling between two cookies. Store in air-tight containers.

262

Ice Cream Cookies
Yield: 2 dozen

1/2 cup sugar
1/2 cup shortening
1 egg
1 teaspoon vanilla
1 cup sifted flour
1/2 cup chopped nuts (optional)

Cream together sugar and shortening, add egg and vanilla; mix thoroughly. Stir in flour, then nuts. Drop by small rounded teaspoonfuls on a lightly greased cookie sheet. Bake at 350 degrees for 6 to 8 minutes, or until lightly browned on the bottom. Serve with your favorite ice cream.

Chewy Coconut Macaroons
Yield: 3½ dozen

14 to 16 ounces shredded coconut
1 (14-ounce) can sweetened
   condensed milk
2 teaspoons vanilla

Mix ingredients. Drop by spoonfuls on a well-greased cookie sheet. Bake at 350 degrees for 10 to 12 minutes. Cool slightly before removing from cookie sheet.

Amaretto Balls
Yield: 5-5½ dozen

2 cups (24) Oreos or Hydrox
   cookies
2 cups powdered sugar
2 cups almonds
2/3 cup Amaretto
6 ounces fine shredded coconut
   flakes

Put first four ingredients into food processor. Process with steel blade until smooth. Refrigerate for 10 to 15 minutes. Shape into balls and roll in coconut flakes. Store in covered container in refrigerator.

Hazelnut Dessert Squares
Serves: 8 to 10

Crust:
1 cup flour
1/2 cup sugar
1 teaspoon baking powder
3 tablespoons cocoa
1/2 cup butter, softened
1 egg, separated
**1/2 cup finely ground, roasted
  hazelnuts**
1 teaspoon vanilla

Filling:
**1 (8-ounce) package cream
  cheese, softened**
1/3 cup sugar
1/2 cup sour cream
1 tablespoon flour
**2 tablespoons hazelnut liqueur
  (optional)**
Grated rind of 1 small orange
1/2 teaspoon orange flavoring
1 egg
1 egg white
Chocolate curls (garnish)
Hazelnuts (garnish)

For crust: Combine flour, sugar, baking powder and cocoa; mix in butter until crumbly. Add egg yolk (saving egg white for filling), hazelnuts and vanilla. Press firmly into a 9 x 9-inch baking pan. Bake at 325 degrees for 15 minutes.

For filling: Beat all filling ingredients until well blended. Add filling to cooked crust, and bake an additional 25 to 30 minutes or until set. Cool and garnish with chocolate curls and hazelnuts. Cut into squares.

Texas Chews
Yield: 3 dozen

2 cups flour
2 teaspoons baking powder
1/4 teaspoon salt
2 cubes butter
1 box brown sugar
2 eggs, beaten
1 teaspoon vanilla
1½ cups chopped pecans

Sift flour, baking powder and salt. Melt butter and brown sugar in a large saucepan. Remove from heat, add eggs and vanilla. Add in 1 cup of the dry ingredients and mix well. Dust pecans with the remaining cup of dry ingredients and combine with other mixture. Spread in a 13 x 9½ x 2-inch pan. Bake at 350 degrees for 30 minutes. Do not over bake. Cool and cut into bars.

Chocolate Mint Squares
Yield: 4 dozen

Cake:
1 cup sugar
1/2 cup butter, softened
4 eggs, beaten
1 cup flour
1/2 teaspoon salt
1 tablespoon vanilla
1 (16-ounce) can chocolate
   syrup

Mint Layer:
2 cups powdered sugar
2 tablespoons green Creme de
   Menthe
1/2 cup butter, softened

Glaze:
1 (6-ounce) package semi-sweet
   chocolate chips
6 tablespoons butter

For cake: Mix all ingredients together and pour into a 9 x 13-inch pan. Bake at 350 degrees for 30 minutes. Cool completely.

For mint layer: Beat all ingredients together and spread on the cooled cake. Let set.

For glaze: Melt all ingredients in a double boiler and spread on top of the mint layer. (The top layer will not break up as badly if the sections are scored after top layer is completely set.) Chill 1½ to 2 hours, then cut into small squares. Store, covered, in the refrigerator.

Peanut Butter Taffy Bars
Yield: 3 dozen

2/3 cup butter or margarine
1 cup brown sugar
1/2 cup light corn syrup
4 cups quick oatmeal
1/2 cup wheat germ
1 cup peanut butter
1 (6-ounce) package chocolate
   chips

Melt butter, sugar and corn syrup in a large saucepan over medium heat. Remove from heat and stir in oatmeal and wheat germ. Put mixture into a well-greased 12 x 16-inch cookie sheet. Bake at 350 degrees for 10 minutes. Frost with peanut butter and sprinkle chocolate chips on top. Return to warm oven for several minutes to melt. Spread melted chocolate evenly over peanut butter. Cool and cut into bars.

Caramelitas
Yield: 2 dozen

36 caramels
1/4 cup milk
1 cup oatmeal
3/4 cup brown sugar
1 cup flour
3/4 cup melted margarine
1/2 teaspoon baking soda
1/4 teaspoon salt
1 cup semi-sweet chocolate chips
1/2 to ¾ cup chopped nuts

In a double boiler or microwave oven, melt caramels in milk, stir until blended; cool slightly. Combine all other ingredients except chocolate chips and nuts. Press ½ of the crumb mixture into the bottom of a greased 11 x 7-inch or 9-inch square pan. Bake at 350 degrees for 10 minutes. Sprinkle with chocolate chips and nuts and spread melted caramel mixture over the top (do not go over edges). Crumble remaining topping mixture over all. Bake at 350 degrees for an additional 15 to 20 minutes until top is brown. Cool slightly, then refrigerate for 1 to 2 hours before cutting into small bars or squares.

Lemon Bar Cookies

Yield: 3 dozen

Crust:
1 cup butter, softened
2 cups flour
1/2 cup powdered sugar
Salt to taste

Filling:
2 cups granulated sugar
1/4 cup flour
4 eggs, beaten
6 tablespoons fresh lemon juice
Powdered sugar

Mix crust ingredients well. Press into at 9 x 13-inch lightly greased baking dish. Bake crust at 350 degrees for 15 minutes or until lightly browned.

For filling: Combine granulated sugar and flour. Mix in eggs and lemon juice. Pour into cooled crust. Bake at 350 degrees for an additional 25 minutes or until set. Cool. Sprinkle with powdered sugar. Cut into squares. Keep in air-tight containers. Chill in warm weather.

NOTE: For a "zestier bar" add ½ to 1 teaspoon grated lemon rind to filling mixture.

Toffee Bars

Yield: 2 dozen

1 cup butter, softened
1 cup brown sugar
1 egg yolk
1 teaspoon vanilla
1/4 teaspoon salt
2 cups flour
1 (½ pound) milk chocolate bar
Chopped nuts

Cream together butter, sugar, egg yolk, vanilla and salt. Add flour. Spread dough on a 10 x 13-inch cookie sheet or shallow pan. Bake at 350 degrees for 15 minutes. While bars are still warm, break up chocolate bar on top. Once melted, spread chocolate over top and sprinkle with nuts. Cut while warm.

Cherry Custard Bars
Yield: 24 Bars

1 cup flour
1/2 cup butter or margarine
3 tablespoons powdered sugar
2 eggs
1 cup sugar
1/4 cup flour
1/2 teaspoon baking powder
1/4 teaspoon salt
1 teaspoon vanilla
3/4 cup chopped nuts
1 cup chopped maraschino
   cherries

Blend together flour, butter and powdered sugar. Press into a 9-inch square pan and bake at 350 degrees for 25 minutes. Beat eggs, sugar, flour, baking powder, salt, vanilla, nuts and cherries. Pour on top of baked crust. Bake at 350 degrees for an additional 25 minutes. Cool before cutting into bars.

Oatmeal and Apple-Butter Bars
Yield: 16 Bars

2 cups old-fashioned oats
1 cup flour
3/4 cup sugar
1/4 teaspoon salt
1/2 teaspoon ground cinnamon
3/4 cup butter or margarine
1 cup apple butter

Lightly grease a 9-inch square baking pan. In a large bowl, combine oats, flour, sugar, salt and cinnamon. Cut in the butter or margarine with a pastry cutter or 2 butter knives, until mixture is crumbly. Pat ½ of the mixture (2 cups) into the prepared pan. Spread apple butter evenly over crumb layer. Sprinkle remaining crumbs over apple butter and press down gently. Bake at 350 degrees for 30 to 35 minutes until golden brown. Let cool in pan on a wire rack. Cut into bars.

NOTE: You may substitute any other type of jam or jelly and dust with powdered sugar.

Raspberry Truffle Brownies

Yield: 3 dozen

Brownies:
1 cup semi-sweet chocolate chips
1/2 cup margarine
3/4 cup brown sugar
2 large eggs
2 tablespoons water
  or
2 tablespoons coffee liqueur
3/4 cup flour
1/2 teaspoon baking powder

Filling:
1 cup semi-sweet chocolate chips
1 (8-ounce) package cream cheese,
  softened
1/4 cup powdered sugar
1/3 cup seedless raspberry
  preserves

Glaze:
1/4 cup semi-sweet chocolate
  chips
1 teaspoon vegetable shortening

For brownies: In a heavy saucepan, melt chocolate chips and margarine over low heat; cool slightly. In a large bowl, beat sugar and eggs together. Add chocolate mixture, water or coffee liqueur; mix well. Stir in flour and baking powder; blend well. Spread batter into a greased 9 x 9-inch pan. Bake at 350 degrees for 30 to 35 minutes, until toothpick inserted in center comes out clean. Cool on wire rack.

For filling: In a heavy saucepan, melt chocolate chips over low heat; set aside. In a small bowl, beat cream cheese until fluffy. Add powdered sugar and raspberry preserves, beat until fluffy. Beat in melted chocolate until well blended. Spread over top of cooled brownies.

For glaze: Melt chocolate chips and shortening; drizzle over filling layer. Chill at least 1 to 2 hours. Bring to room temperature and cut into small squares or bars.

Chocolate Peanut Butter Bars
Yield: 4 dozen

1½ cups chunky peanut butter
1½ cups powdered sugar
3/4 cup margarine, melted
1 package graham
crackers (11 double graham
crackers), crushed
6 ounces chocolate chips

Mix together first 4 ingredients. Press into a 9 x 13-inch, ungreased pan. In top of double boiler, melt chocolate chips, stirring constantly. Spread over top. Chill for 1 to 2 hours and cut into bars. Store in an air-tight container in the freezer.

Rocky Road Brownies
Yield: 3½ dozen

1 cup margarine
4 ounces unsweetened chocolate
2 cups sugar
4 eggs
1 tablespoon vanilla
1 cup flour
1/4 teaspoon salt
2 cups semi-sweet chocolate
chips
1½ cups chopped walnuts,
divided
4 cups mini-marshmallows

Butter a 9 x 13 inch baking dish. In top of double boiler, melt margarine and unsweetened chocolate, stirring constantly; set aside to cool. In a large mixing bowl, beat sugar and eggs for 3 minutes. Beat in chocolate mixture and vanilla. Beat in flour and salt until just combined. Stir in chocolate chips and 1 cup nuts. Scrape batter into prepared pan. Bake at 350 degrees for 30 to 35 minutes. Top with marshmallows and ½ cup nuts and bake for an additional 2 minutes or until marshmallows have melted. Cool and cut into squares with a serrated knife dipped in hot water. Store in air-tight containers.

Danish Shortbread
Serves: 8

1½ cups flour
3/4 cup powdered sugar
1/4 teaspoon salt
1/2 pound butter
Powdered sugar

Mix all ingredients together until consistency is doughy. (A food processor dough blade works well.) Press firmly into a 9-inch pie plate greased with butter. Bake at 325 degrees for 40 minutes or until shortbread is pale in color, not brown. Let cool a few minutes before unmolding. Sprinkle with powdered sugar and cut into pie shape pieces while warm.

Wonderful Brownies
Yield: 2 dozen

8 ounces unsweetened chocolate
½ cup butter
5 large eggs
1 tablespoon vanilla
1½ teaspoons almond extract
1/4 teaspoon salt
3 tablespoons expresso (instant dry)
3¾ cups sugar
1⅓ cups flour
1½ cups chopped walnuts

Generously butter a 9 x 13 inch baking dish. In top of double boiler, melt chocolate and butter together, stirring constantly; set aside. In a large bowl, beat eggs, vanilla, almond extract, salt, expresso and sugar at high speed for about 10 to 12 minutes. On low speed, add chocolate mixture and beat until just blended. Add flour and beat until just mixed. Stir in nuts. Turn into prepared dish and smooth. Bake at 425 degrees for 30 minutes. (The inside will be very moist). Watch edges for browning. Cool at least 6 hours before cutting.

NOTE: It is a good idea to make this a day ahead.

Brandy Alexander Brownies
Yield: 2 dozen

8 ounces unsweetened chocolate
2/3 cup margarine
3 cups sugar
4 eggs
1½ teaspoons vanilla
1/4 teaspoon salt
2 cups flour
1/4 cup brandy
1/4 cup Creme de Cacao
2 teaspoons brandy
2 teaspoons Creme de Cacao

Topping:
1 pint whipping cream
1 teaspoon brandy
1 teaspoon Creme de Cacao
2 tablespoons powdered sugar

Grease a 9 x 13-inch baking dish. Melt chocolate and margarine; set aside to cool. In a large bowl, beat sugar and eggs for 5 minutes. Beat in chocolate mixture and vanilla. Beat in salt and flour until just combined. Beat in brandy and Creme de Cacao. Scrape into prepared dish. Bake at 350 degrees for 25 to 30 minutes or until toothpick inserted in center comes out clean. Let cool for 30 minutes. Combine 2 teaspoons brandy and 2 teaspoons Creme de Cacao and brush over brownies. Cover with plastic wrap and cool completely.

For topping: Lightly whip cream. Add brandy, Creme de Cacao and powdered sugar, whip until stiff peaks form. Spread over cooled brownies, cut into squares and serve.

Double Fudge Brownies
Yield: 16

2 ounces unsweetened chocolate
1/2 cup butter or margarine
2 cups sugar
4 eggs, beaten
1 cup sifted flour
1 teaspoon vanilla
1 cup chopped walnuts
1 (6-ounce) package chocolate chips

In the top of double boiler, melt the unsweetened chocolate and butter, stirring constantly; set aside. Gradually add sugar to eggs, beating well. Pour in chocolate mixture. Add flour, vanilla, ½ of the nuts and ½ of the chocolate chips. Spread in a greased 9-inch pan. Sprinkle remaining chocolate chips and nuts over batter and bake at 325 degrees for 30 minutes or until done. Do not overbake or they will be dry.

Raisin Spice Bars
Yield: 2 to 2½ dozen

Spice bars:
- **1 cup raisins**
- **2 cups water**
- **1/2 cup margarine**
- **1 cup granulated sugar**
- **1¾ cups flour**
- **1 teaspoon baking soda**
- **1 teaspoon ground cloves**
- **1 teaspoon cinnamon**
- **1 teaspoon nutmeg**
- **1/2 cup chopped nuts**

Lemon frosting:
- **3 ounces cream cheese, softened**
- **1/3 cup margarine, softened**
- **3 to 3½ cups powdered sugar**
- **1/2 teaspoon vanilla**
- **2 teaspoons grated lemon peel**
- **2 to 3 tablespoons fresh lemon juice**

Grease and flour a 9 x 13-inch baking dish. Boil raisins in water for 10 minutes. Remove from heat (reserve liquid). Add margarine and stir to melt. Cool. Sift together sugar, flour, baking soda, cloves, cinnamon and nutmeg. Add this mixture to the raisins, water and butter mixture. Stir in nuts. Spread batter into prepared baking dish. Bake at 350 degrees for 35 minutes. Cool for 3 hours.

For frosting: Blend cream cheese and margarine. Slowly add powdered sugar, vanilla, lemon peel and lemon juice. Beat until frosting is smooth and easily spreadable. Thin with milk or lemon juice, if necessary, adding 1 teaspoon at a time. Frost and cut into bars.

Rhubarb Bars
Yield: 18

3 cups cut-up rhubarb
1½ cups granulated sugar
2 tablespoons cornstarch
1/4 cup water
1/2 teaspoon vanilla

1½ cups oats
1½ cups flour
1/4 cup wheat germ
1 cup brown sugar
1/2 teaspoon baking soda
1/2 teaspoon salt
1 cup shortening
1/2 cup chopped nuts (optional)

In a large saucepan, cook rhubarb, sugar, and cornstarch (dissolved in ¼ cup water) until ingredients are thick. Add vanilla and cool. In a large bowl, mix oats, flour, wheat germ, sugar, baking soda, salt, shortening and nuts. (Reserve 1½ cups for topping). Press crumb mixture into a greased 9 x 13-inch pan. Pour rhubarb mixture over the top and sprinkle with reserved 1½ cups crumbs. Bake at 350 degrees for 35 minutes.

NOTE: You may wish to mix ½ rhubarb and ½ strawberries for a different taste.

Mimi's Date Bars
Yield: 40 Bars

2 cups chopped dates
1/2 cup boiling water
1/2 cup butter or margarine, softened
1 cup sugar
2 eggs
1 cup flour
1/2 teaspoon salt
1/4 teaspoon baking soda
1 teaspoon cinnamon
1/4 teaspoon nutmeg
1 to 1½ cups chopped nuts
Powdered sugar

Place dates and boiling water in a bowl and let cool. Cream butter, sugar and eggs; set aside. Sift flour, salt, baking soda, cinnamon and nutmeg. Stir into creamed mixture. Stir in date mixture and add nuts; mix well. Pour into greased 9 x 13-inch pan. Bake at 325 degrees for 40 minutes. Let cool. Cut into bars and sprinkle with powdered sugar, if desired.

Raisin Bars
Yield: 2 dozen

2 cups raisins
2 cups water
1 cup oil
1 cup granulated sugar
1 cup brown sugar
3½ cups flour
1 teaspoon salt
2 teaspoons cinnamon
2 teaspoons baking soda
2 teaspoons vanilla

  Glaze:
4 tablespoons butter
4 tablespoons water
3 cups powdered sugar, sifted
2 teaspoons vanilla

In a saucepan, bring raisins and water to a boil. Lower heat and simmer for 10 minutes. Remove from heat. Add oil and sugars. Stir until all ingredients are blended. Let mixture cool completely (about 2 hours). Add dry ingredients and vanilla. Pour into 2 greased 9 x 13-inch pans. Bake at 375 degrees for 15 minutes.

For glaze: In a large saucepan, heat butter and water until butter melts. Add powdered sugar and vanilla; stir thoroughly until smooth. Let glaze cool. Glaze the raisin mixture 15 minutes after it is removed from the oven. Cut into bars and serve.

Caramel Bars
Yield: 2 dozen

3/4 cup brown sugar
1 cup quick oats
1 cup flour
1 teaspoon baking soda
1/4 teaspoon salt
3/4 cup margarine, melted
1 cup semi-sweet chocolate chips
1/2 cup chopped nuts
3/4 cup caramel ice cream
  topping

Mix first six ingredients (reserving ⅓ cup for topping). Pat remaining mixture into an ungreased 9 x 13-inch pan. Bake at 350 degrees for 10 minutes. Remove from oven and sprinkle with chocolate chips and nuts. Add caramel ice cream topping. Sprinkle reserved crumb mixture over top. Bake at 350 degrees for an additional 15 to 20 minutes. Cool and cut into small bars.

Chocolate Peppermint Brownies

Yield: 2 dozen

Cookie:
**2 squares unsweetened baking
  chocolate**
1/2 cup butter
2 eggs
1 cup granulated sugar
1/4 teaspoon peppermint extract
1/2 cup flour
Pinch of salt
1/2 cup chopped nuts

Frosting:
1 cup powdered sugar, sifted
1 tablespoons butter
**1 tablespoon evaporated milk or
  half and half**
1/2 teaspoon peppermint extract
Drop green food coloring

Glaze:
**2 squares unsweetened baking
  chocolate**
2 tablespoons butter

For cookie: Grease bottom and sides of a 9-inch square baking pan with butter or margarine. Melt chocolate and butter together over a double boiler or in microwave. In a large bowl, cream eggs and sugar. Add chocolate mixture and stir in peppermint extract, flour, salt and nuts. Pour batter into prepared pan and bake at 350 degrees for 15 to 20 minutes. Cool.

For frosting: Mix all ingredients for frosting in a small bowl. Spread over baked cookie layer and chill.

For glaze: Melt butter and chocolate together over a double boiler or in microwave and spread over frosting, score lightly. Chill. Cut into small squares and serve.

Caramel Brownies
Yield: 5 dozen

Brownies:
2 ounces unsweetened chocolate
1/2 cup unsalted butter
2 large eggs, beaten
1 cup sugar
1/2 cup all-purpose flour
1 teaspoon vanilla
1 cup chopped walnuts

Caramel Topping:
5 tablespoons unsalted butter
1 cup powdered sugar
1/2 cup whipping cream
1 tablespoon light corn syrup

Glaze:
1 tablespoon unsalted butter
2 ounces semi-sweet chocolate

For brownies: Line an 8-inch square baking pan with aluminum foil. Butter foil lightly. In a heavy pan, melt chocolate and butter over low heat. When melted, remove from heat and stir until smooth. Slowly add eggs to chocolate mixture, stirring constantly. When blended, add sugar, flour, vanilla and walnuts; mix well after each addition. Pour batter into prepared pan; spread evenly for a smooth surface. Bake at 350 degrees for 20 to 25 minutes. Remove from oven and cool in pan on a wire rack. While brownies cool, prepare topping.

Topping: In a heavy saucepan over medium heat, bring butter, powdered sugar, cream and corn syrup to a boil. Do not stir once mixture has come to a boil. Continue to boil until topping reaches 220 to 225 degrees. Remove from heat and cool until topping is set and not tacky. Spread over cooled brownies.

For glaze: Melt butter and semi-sweet chocolate in double boiler or microwave. Remove from heat, stir until smooth and spread over caramel topping layer. Chill until firm. To serve, invert the pan over a large plate; remove pan and peel off foil. Invert brownies again (should now be right side up) and cut into squares. Store in tightly covered container or wrap in foil and freeze.

Strawberry Meringue Cake
Serves: 10 to 12

Cake:
**1/2 cup shortening
1/2 cup sugar
4 eggs, separated, (whites
  reserved for topping)
1 cup sifted flour
2 teaspoons baking powder
1/8 teaspoon salt
1 teaspoon vanilla
5 tablespoons milk**

Meringue topping:
**4 egg whites
1 cup granulated sugar
1 teaspoon vanilla
3/4 cup chopped pecans**

Strawberry filling:
**1/2 pint whipping cream
1 pint fresh strawberries,
  stemmed and sliced
Sugar to sweeten berries**

Grease and flour two 8-inch round cake pans. For cake: Cream shortening and sugar. Add egg yolks and mix thoroughly. Add flour with baking powder and salt; alternating with vanilla and milk; mix well. Pour into cake pans.

For meringue: Beat egg whites until stiff. While beating, add sugar and vanilla. Spread the meringue on each unbaked cake layer and sprinkle with pecans. Bake at 350 degrees for 30 minutes. Cool. Remove cake layers from pans onto a rack.

For strawberry filling: Beat whipping cream until peaks form. Place 1 layer of cake on plate with the meringue side down. Cover cake layer with ⅓ of the whipped cream and top with ½ of the strawberries. Place next layer over top with the meringue layer up. Frost sides of cake with remaining whipped cream, mounding it up over the edges of the cake top. Pile the remaining strawberries in the center of the cake top.

Classic Chocolate Cake
Serves: 15

Cake:
2 cups flour
2 cups sugar
2/3 cup cocoa
1/2 teaspoon baking powder
1 teaspoon baking soda
3/4 cup butter, softened
1 cup cold water
1 teaspoon vanilla
2 eggs
2/3 cup buttermilk

Icing:
**6 tablespoons butter or margarine,
  softened**
**Cocoa, (⅓ cup for light flavor, ½
  cup for medium flavor, or ¾ cup
  for dark flavor)**
2⅔ cups powdered sugar
1/3 cup milk
1 teaspoon vanilla

For cake: Mix dry ingredients. Add butter and water; beat for 2 minutes. Add vanilla, eggs and buttermilk; beat an additional 2 minutes. Pour into a lightly greased 9 x 13-inch cake pan. Bake at 350 degrees for 40 minutes. Cool.

For icing: Cream butter. Add cocoa and sugar alternately with milk. Beat to a smooth consistency (an additional tablespoon of milk may be needed). Blend in vanilla. Frost cake and serve.

Cranberry Loaf Cake
Yield: 1 loaf

Loaf:
2 cups flour
1 cup sugar
2 teaspoons baking powder
1/2 teaspoon salt
2/3 cup evaporated milk
1/3 cup water
1 tablespoon melted butter
2 cups whole fresh cranberries

Sauce:
1/2 cup butter
1 cup sugar
2/3 cup evaporated milk
1 teaspoon vanilla

In a medium bowl, combine flour, sugar, baking powder and salt. Add evaporated milk, water and butter. Stir until thoroughly blended. Mix in cranberries. Spoon into a buttered 8½ x 4½ x 3-inch loaf pan. Bake at 350 degrees for 50 to 60 minutes, or until toothpick inserted in center comes out clean. Cool for 10 minutes on wire rack before removing from pan.

For sauce: In a small saucepan, melt butter, add sugar and evaporated milk. Heat to a rolling boil. Boil for 1 minute, stirring constantly. Remove from heat; stir in vanilla. Serve warm over cranberry loaf.

Pumpkin Roll

Serves: 10

3 eggs
1 cup sugar
2/3 cup cooked, mashed pumpkin
1 teaspoon lemon juice
3/4 cup flour
1 teaspoon baking powder
1/2 teaspoon salt
2 teaspoons cinnamon
1 teaspoon ginger
1 teaspoon nutmeg
1/4 cup powdered sugar

Filling:
1 cup sifted powdered sugar
1 (8-ounce) package cream cheese, softened
1/4 cup butter, softened
1/2 teaspoon vanilla

With electric mixer on high speed, beat eggs for 5 minutes, gradually adding sugar. Stir in pumpkin and lemon juice. Combine flour, baking powder, salt, cinnamon, ginger and nutmeg. Add to pumpkin mixture and blend well. Spoon into a greased and floured 15 x 10 x 1-inch jelly-roll pan, spreading evenly to corners. Bake at 375 degrees for 15 minutes. Turn cake out onto a towel sprinkled with powdered sugar. Beginning at the narrow end, roll up cake and towel together in a jelly-roll fashion and cool.

For filling: Combine powdered sugar, cream cheese, butter and vanilla. Beat until smooth and creamy. Unroll cake and spread with filling. Roll cake up again and chill, seam-side down.

Hazelnut Chocolate Chip Cheesecake

Serves: 16 to 20

Crust:
1/3 cup semi-sweet chocolate
  chips, finely ground
1½ cups ground vanilla wafers
3/4 cup toasted chopped hazelnuts
2 tablespoons sugar
3 tablespoons butter, softened

Filling:
3 (8-ounce) packages cream
  cheese, softened
1 cup sugar
3 eggs
3 tablespoons hazelnut liqueur
1 cup chocolate chips, coarsely
  chopped

Glaze:
2/3 cup chocolate chips
10-15 whole hazelnuts, toasted and
  skinned
4 tablespoons sour cream
1 tablespoon hazelnut liqueur

For crust: Mix together chocolate chips, vanilla wafers, hazelnuts, sugar and butter; mix well. Press into bottom and up sides of a greased 9-inch spring form pan. Bake at 300 degrees for 15 minutes.

For filling: With electric mixer, blend cream cheese, sugar, eggs, liqueur and chocolate chips; mix well. Pour into crust. Bake at 350 degrees for 1 hour. Cool.

For glaze: Melt chocolate chips in bottom of double boiler. Dip hazelnuts, covering ½ the nut. Blend sour cream and liqueur into the melted chocolate. Spread on top of cooled cheesecake. Decorate with dipped hazelnuts, around outside edge with one in the center, chocolate side up.

Hazelnut Chocolate Chip Cheesecake

Chocolate Cheesecake

Serves: 10

Crust:
1/2 cup butter
2 cups finely ground chocolate wafer crumbs
1/4 cup sugar

Filling: (All ingredients should be at room temperature)
4 (8-ounce) packages cream cheese, softened
1¼ cups sugar
1 tablespoon rum
1½ teaspoons vanilla
3½ ounces sweet chocolate, melted
1/4 cup milk
1/8 teaspoon salt
4 eggs
1/4 cup chopped chocolate

Topping:
2 cups sour cream
1/4 cup sugar
1 teaspoon almond extract

For crust: Melt butter over low heat, add chocolate wafer crumbs and sugar; blend well. Press mixture over bottom and up sides of an ungreased 10-inch spring form pan. Coat entire pan.

For filling: With electric mixer on low speed, beat cream cheese and sugar for 2 minutes. Add rum, vanilla, melted chocolate, milk and salt. Blend thoroughly. Add eggs one at a time, slowly mixing at lowest speed (to avoid beating in too much air). Stir in chocolate bits and pour filling into crust. Bake at 350 degrees for 40 minutes. Remove from oven and let stand for 10 minutes.

For topping: Combine sour cream, sugar and almond extract; spread evenly over cheesecake. Bake at 350 degrees for an additional 10 minutes. Refrigerate immediately.

Oatmeal Cake
Serves: 12

1¼ cups hot water
1 cup oatmeal
1 cube margarine
2 eggs, beaten
1 cup granulated sugar
1 cup brown sugar
1 teaspoon vanilla
1½ cups flour
1 teaspoon cinnamon
1 teaspoon baking soda
1 teaspoon baking powder
1/8 teaspoon salt

Topping:
1 cup brown sugar
1/2 cup evaporated milk
4 tablespoons butter
1 cup coconut or oatmeal

Combine hot water, oatmeal and margarine; cool slightly. Add eggs, sugars and vanilla; mix well. Sift together remaining ingredients and add to other mixture; mix well. Pour into a greased 2 x 9 x 12-inch pan. Bake at 350 degrees for 30 to 35 minutes, until toothpick inserted in center comes out clean.

For topping: Blend ingredients and pour over warm cake. Place under broiler for 3 to 5 minutes or until browned.

Meringue Cake
Serves: 6

1/2 cup butter
1/2 cup sugar
4 egg yolks, beaten
4 tablespoons milk
1½ teaspoons vanilla
3/4 cup sifted flour
1/2 teaspoon baking powder
4 egg whites
1 cup sugar
6 to 8 ounces whipping cream
Sliced fruit (strawberries,
   kiwi, bananas, or pineapple)
Chopped almonds

In a large mixing bowl, cream together butter and sugar. Add egg yolks and blend in milk and vanilla. Add flour and baking powder. Put into 2 greased and floured metal layer cake pans or wax paper lined glass pans. With electric mixer, beat egg whites until stiff. Gradually add 1 cup sugar. Spoon lightly over cake batter, being sure it touches pan all around. Bake at 350 degrees for 25 to 30 minutes. Cool. Whip cream.

To assemble: Place 1 layer, meringue side down on a plate. Spread with ½ of whipped cream. Add sliced fruit and nuts. Put other layer on top, meringue side up. Top with small amount of whipped cream and decorate with additional fruit. Chill until ready to serve.

Apple Cheesecake
Serves: 12

2 cups graham cracker crumbs
1/3 cup packed light brown
   sugar
1/2 cup melted butter, divided
4 teaspoons cinnamon
3 medium size cooking apples,
   peeled and cored
4 eggs
3/4 cup sugar
8 ounces ricotta cheese
8 ounces cream cheese
2 teaspoons vanilla
8 ounces whipping cream
Cinnamon (garnish)

Mix graham cracker crumbs, brown sugar, 4 tablespoons melted butter and cinnamon. Press on bottom and up sides of a 9-inch spring form pan. Slice apples into 12 rings and sauté on both sides in remaining 4 tablespoons of butter. Arrange 6 apple rings on crust. Beat eggs, sugar, ricotta cheese, cream cheese and vanilla until smooth, scraping bottom of bowl several times. Add whipping cream and blend. Place spring form pan on foil-lined cookie sheet to catch drips. Pour cheese mixture into pan. Arrange remaining 6 apple rings on top. Press apples lightly under mixture. Sprinkle heavily with cinnamon. Bake at 450 degrees for 10 minutes, reduce heat to 300 degrees and bake for an additional 55 minutes. Cool for 30 minutes and refrigerate overnight.

Coconut Pecan Cream Cake
Serves: 12 to 16

1 cup shortening
2 cups granulated sugar
5 eggs, separated
2 cups flour
1/2 teaspoon salt
1 teaspoon baking soda
1 cup buttermilk
1 teaspoon vanilla
2 cups shredded coconut
1 cup chopped pecans

  Frosting:
12 ounces cream cheese, softened
3/4 cup butter, softened
1½ boxes powdered sugar
2 teaspoons vanilla
1½ cups chopped pecans

Cream shortening and sugar. Add egg yolks (reserving egg whites), and beat well. Sift flour, salt and baking soda together. Add ½ of the dry ingredients to sugar mixture, then add ½ cup buttermilk; repeat. Fold in vanilla, coconut and pecans. Beat egg whites until stiff, fold into cake batter. Pour batter into three 9-inch greased and floured cake pans, dividing batter evenly between pans. Bake at 350 degrees for 25 to 30 minutes, until toothpick inserted in center comes out clean. Cool cake for 5 minutes in pans, then turn out and cool on wire racks.

For frosting: Cream together cream cheese and butter. Gradually beat in sugar and vanilla. Fold in pecans. Frost cake between layers, on sides and on top.

English Lemon Cake
Serves: 10

1 cup unsalted butter
1 cup sugar
2 eggs
1¼ cups flour
1 teaspoon baking powder
1/2 teaspoon salt
1/2 cup milk

  Glaze:
1/4 cup lemon juice
1/3 cup sugar
2 teaspoons grated lemon
  peel

Cream butter and sugar in mixer. Add eggs and mix well. Add dry ingredients and milk; mix until smooth. Pour into a 9 x 5 x 3 greased loaf pan. Bake at 350 degrees for 45 minutes to 1 hour.

For glaze: Combine all ingredients in a saucepan and heat to boiling. Pour glaze over cake immediately after removing from oven. Cool completely in pan. Slice and serve.

Chocolate Refrigerator Cupcakes
Yield: 2 dozen

1/2 cup butter or margarine
1½ ounces unsweetened
   chocolate (1½ squares)
1 cup granulated sugar
2/3 cup all-purpose flour
1 teaspoon vanilla
2 eggs, well beaten
1 cup coarsely chopped nuts

Icing:
2 tablespoons butter or
   margarine
1 ounce unsweetened chocolate
3/4 pound powdered sugar
Cold coffee

Line muffin tins with 24 cupcake papers. Melt butter and chocolate together in double boiler; set aside. In a large bowl, mix sugar, flour, vanilla and eggs. Stir in nuts and add the chocolate mixture. Fill cupcake papers ½ full. Bake at 350 degrees for 12 minutes. (They may not look done, but do not overcook.)

For icing: While cupcakes are baking, melt butter and chocolate together. Add powdered sugar gradually. Add enough coffee to make a smooth, fluffy frosting. Ice cakes while hot, filling to the top of the paper liners. Refrigerate, then serve.

Zucchini Chocolate Chip Cake
Serves: 12

1/2 cup soft margarine
1/2 cup oil
1¾ cups sugar
2 eggs
1/2 cup buttermilk
2½ cups flour
1/2 teaspoon baking powder
1 teaspoon baking soda
1/2 teaspoon cinnamon
1/2 teaspoon cloves
2 tablespoons vanilla
2 cups shredded zucchini
1 cup chocolate chips
1/2 cup chopped walnuts

Cream together margarine, oil and sugar. Add eggs and buttermilk; mix well. Sift together flour, baking powder, baking soda, cinnamon and cloves; add to the creamed mixture. Stir in vanilla and shredded zucchini; mix well. Pour into a greased and floured 9 x 13-inch pan. Sprinkle chocolate chips and walnuts over top. Bake at 325 degrees for 40 to 45 minutes.

Chocolate Sigh
Serves: 10 to 12

4 ounces unsweetened chocolate
1/4 cup butter or margarine
1 cup milk
4 eggs, separated
2 cups sugar
1 cup sifted cake flour
1½ teaspoons baking powder

Chocolate topping:
2 ounces unsweetened chocolate
1 tablespoon butter or margarine
1 tablespoon cornstarch
1/2 cup sugar
2/3 cup milk

In the top of a double boiler melt chocolate and butter. Stir in milk and set aside. In a large mixing bowl, stir together egg yolks and sugar. Blend in chocolate mixture. Add flour and baking powder, mixing until smooth. In large chilled bowl, beat egg whites, until stiff, moist peaks form. Add to chocolate mixture and gently fold in until blended. Pour into a greased and floured 9-inch round spring form pan. Bake at 350 degrees for 45 to 55 minutes until cake moves when shaken. Remove pan sides after cake cools.

For topping: In the top of a double boiler melt chocolate and butter or margarine. In a bowl, stir together cornstarch and sugar; mix in milk. Add this to chocolate mixture. Cook over simmering water stirring often, until glossy and thick like pudding, about 20 minutes. Stir over ice water or chill until very thick. Spread on top and sides of cake. Cover with a large bowl and chill until ready to serve.

Hazelnut White Chocolate Cheesecake
Serves: 16

Crust:

1 (8-ounce) package hazelnut or shortbread cookies, crushed
1/4 cup finely chopped toasted hazelnuts
3 tablespoons butter, melted

Filling:

1 pound white baking bar with cocoa butter
4 (8-ounce) packages cream cheese, softened
1/2 cup butter
3 tablespoons hazelnut liqueur
1 tablespoon vanilla
Dash of ground nutmeg
4 eggs
1 egg yolk
2 (3-ounce) bars milk chocolate with hazelnuts, chopped
or
4 (1½-ounce) bars milk chocolate with almonds, chopped
Chocolate curls (garnish)
3 tablespoons chopped toasted hazelnuts (garnish)

Butter sides of a 10-inch spring form pan. Press crust evenly over bottom of pan. Place in a shallow baking pan. Melt baking bar over low heat. In mixer, beat melted baking bar with cream cheese, butter, liqueur, vanilla and nutmeg until well mixed. Add eggs and egg yolk, beat on low until mixed. Stir in chopped milk chocolate bars. Pour into crust. Bake at 350 degrees for 60 to 65 minutes, or until knife inserted midway between center and edge comes out clean. Cool, cover and chill thoroughly. Top with chocolate curls and chopped nuts.

Sour Cream Chocolate Surprise Cake

Serves: 8 to 10

1/2 cup butter or margarine
1½ cups sugar
3 eggs
1 teaspoon vanilla
2 cups all-purpose flour
1 teaspoon baking powder
1 teaspoon baking soda
1/4 teaspoon salt
1/2 cup cocoa powder
1 cup water
1 cup sauerkraut, drained
  rinsed and finely chopped

Sour cream frosting:
1 (6-ounce) package semi-sweet
  chocolate pieces
4 tablespoons butter
1/2 cup sour cream
1 teaspoon vanilla
1/4 teaspoon salt
2½ to 3½ cups sifted
  powdered sugar

Cream butter and sugar until light. Beat in eggs one at a time; add vanilla. Sift together flour, baking powder, baking soda, salt and cocoa. Add sifted ingredients to the creamed mixture alternately with water, beating after each addition. Stir in sauerkraut. Turn mixture into a greased 9 x 13 x 2-inch pan. Bake at 350 degrees for 35 to 40 minutes. Cool in pan.

For frosting: Melt chocolate and butter together over low heat. Remove from heat and blend in sour cream, vanilla and salt. Gradually add the powdered sugar and mix until smooth. Cover cake with frosting and serve.

Pumpkin Pecan Cheesecake

Serves: 8 to 10

1½ cups graham cracker crumbs
1 tablespoon sugar
1/4 cup butter, melted
1/3 cup finely chopped pecans
2 (8-ounce) packages cream
   cheese, softened
3/4 cup sugar
3 eggs
1/2 cup whipping cream
1 cup canned pumpkin
2 tablespoons maple syrup
1/2 teaspoon ground ginger
1/2 teaspoon ground cinnamon
1/4 teaspoon ground nutmeg

Topping:
1 cup sour cream
3 tablespoons sugar
1/4 teaspoon vanilla

1/3 cup pecan halves

In a small bowl, mix graham cracker crumbs, sugar, butter and pecans. Press mixture over bottom and about 1½-inches up sides of an ungreased 9-inch spring form pan. Refrigerate 4 hours or overnight. In a large bowl, beat cream cheese and sugar until light. Beat in eggs, one at a time, then whipping cream. Stir in pumpkin, syrup, ginger, cinnamon and nutmeg. Pour into chilled crust. Bake at 325 degrees for 55 to 60 minutes. Remove from oven.

For topping: Mix sour cream, sugar and vanilla. Spread over hot cheesecake. Arrange pecan halves on top. Bake at 325 degrees for an additional 10 minutes. Let stand until cool. Chill at least 4 hours before serving.

Rich Chocolate Cake

Serves: 8 to 10

1/4 pound butter
1 cup sugar
4 eggs
1 (16-ounce) can chocolate syrup
1 cup sifted self-rising flour
1 teaspoon vanilla
1 pint whipping cream
Grated chocolate (garnish)

Beat butter and sugar together until light and fluffy. Add eggs one at a time, mixing well after each addition. Pour in syrup and mix well. Fold in flour with spatula. Add vanilla. Pour evenly into 2 greased and floured cake pans. Bake at 350 degrees for 35 minutes. Cool cake layers. Whip cream until stiff peaks form. Spread between layers and over top and sides of cake. Garnish with grated chocolate, if desired.

Apple Cake
Serves: 12

3 cups chopped apples, peeled
2 cups sugar
2 teaspoons cinnamon
1 teaspoon nutmeg
1 teaspoon salt
3 cups flour
2 teaspoons baking soda
2 eggs
1 cup oil
2 teaspoons vanilla
1 cup raisins
Whipped cream

Mix apples, sugar, cinnamon, nutmeg and salt. Add flour and baking soda, mix and set aside. In another bowl, thoroughly beat eggs until creamy, then add oil and vanilla. Add egg mixture to apple-flour mixture; mix well. Fold in raisins. Pour into a greased and floured 9 x 13-inch pan. Bake at 350 degrees for 45 to 50 minutes. Serve warm or let cool. Top with a serving of whipped cream.

Autumn Pumpkin Cake
Serves: 6

1 cup sugar
1/2 cup brown sugar
2/3 cup flour
1/4 teaspoon baking powder
1 teaspoon baking soda
1/2 teaspoon salt
1/2 teaspoon nutmeg
1/2 teaspoon cinnamon
1/4 teaspoon cloves
1 cup pumpkin
2 eggs
1/3 cup oil
1/2 cup chopped walnuts

Mix dry ingredients. Add pumpkin, eggs, oil and nuts. Pour into a greased and floured 8-inch square pan. Bake at 300 degrees for 45 to 55 minutes, until toothpick inserted in center comes out clean.

Almond Cake
Yield: 2 cakes

1/2 cup butter
1/2 cup margarine
1½ cups sugar
2 eggs (1 egg separated)
1/2 teaspoon almond extract
2½ cups sifted flour
Sugar for topping
Sliced almonds for topping

Cream butter, margarine, sugar, whole egg, plus separated egg yolk and almond extract. Add flour and mix well. Press into two 8 to 9-inch lightly greased pie pans. Beat egg white until foamy and brush on top of cake batter. Sprinkle with sugar and almonds. Bake at 325 degrees for 30 to 40 minutes. Cool. Remove from pans. Cut each cake into 16 wedges.

Spicy Gingerbread
Serves: 12

1 cup sugar
1 cup molasses
1 cup melted butter
3 eggs
3 cups sifted flour
1 tablespoon baking soda
1 tablespoon ground ginger
2 teaspoons cinnamon
1 teaspoon ground cloves
1/2 teaspoon salt
1½ cups boiling water

Beat sugar, molasses, butter and eggs until smooth. Mix together flour, baking soda and spices. Alternating with boiling water, mix flour mixture into the creamed mixture. Pour into a greased and floured 9-inch tube pan. Bake at 350 degrees for 40 minutes. Cool in pan for 15 minutes.

NOTE: This is very good during the Holidays served warm with whipped cream.

Woahink Lake Cakes
Serves: 12

1 cup packed brown sugar
3 eggs, slightly beaten
3 tablespoons flour
1/2 teaspoon vanilla
1 cup chopped nuts
Powdered sugar

Mix first five ingredients and let stand for 15 minutes. Stir and pour into well greased small muffin tins or tart tins. Bake at 350 degrees for 15 minutes. Sprinkle with powdered sugar and serve.

Chocolate Mocha Magic
Serves: 8 to 10

12 ounces semi-sweet chocolate chips
2 tablespoons instant coffee powder or crystals
2 tablespoons sugar
1/8 teaspoon salt
2 tablespoons water
7 eggs, separated
1 teaspoon vanilla
1 (8½-ounce) package chocolate wafers, crushed
Whipped cream (optional)

In a double boiler, melt together the chocolate, coffee, sugar, salt and water. Cool mixture to room temperature. Blend in egg yolks and vanilla. Beat egg whites until stiff and fold into chocolate-egg yolk mixture. Butter an 8 x 8-inch baking pan. Divide crushed cookies into thirds. Put ⅓ into the bottom of the baking dish. Gently spread ½ of the chocolate mixture over the crumbs. Chill in freezer for 1 hour (chilling the remaining chocolate mixture until ready for use). Put another layer of crumbs over chilled filling and top with remainder of chocolate mixture. Sprinkle the last layer of crumbs over all. Let dessert stand in refrigerator for 3 to 4 hours or overnight. This may be served with whipped cream on top. Cut in small portions as this is very rich.

Oreo Cookie Cheesecake
Serves: 12

Crust:
1¼ cups chocolate cookie crumbs
3 to 4 tablespoons butter, melted

Filling:
1½ cups whipping cream
**3 (8-ounce) packages cream
cheese, softened**
1 cup sugar
24 Oreo cookies

Frosting:
4 ounces semi-sweet chocolate
1/2 teaspoon vanilla
1/2 cup whipping cream

For crust: Combine cookie crumbs and butter. Press into a 9 or 10-inch spring form pan. Place in freezer while preparing filling.

For filling: Whip cream until stiff peaks form. Place in refrigerator. Whip cream cheese until smooth. Add sugar and blend. Coarsely chop 24 Oreo cookies and fold into cream cheese mixture. Fold in whipped cream. Turn filling into crust and spread evenly. Cover and refrigerate at least 4 hours. Loosen cheesecake by running knife around edges. Release sides of pan.

For frosting: Melt chocolate over low heat, stirring constantly. Cool slightly. Whisk in whipping cream and vanilla. Glaze top and sides of cheesecake with frosting mixture. Place in refrigerator about 30 minutes, or until hardened.

Blueberry Cream Pie
Serves: 8

1 (9-inch) unbaked pie shell
2½ cups blueberries
1 cup sour cream
2 tablespoons flour
3/4 cup sugar
1 teaspoon vanilla
1/4 teaspoon salt
1 egg, beaten

Topping:
3 tablespoons flour
1½ tablespoons butter, softened
3 tablespoons chopped walnuts or
  pecans

Set aside pie shell and blueberries. Beat with electric mixer until smooth: sour cream, flour, sugar, vanilla, salt and egg. Fold in blueberries and pour filling into pie shell. Bake at 400 degrees for 25 minutes.

For topping: mix all ingredients together using a fork. After pie has cooked, remove from oven and sprinkle with topping. Bake at 400 degrees for an additional 5 to 10 minutes. Refrigerate.

Frozen Pecan Pie
Serves: 8

1 egg white, at room
  temperature
1/4 cup sugar
1½ cups finely chopped
  pecans
1 quart butter pecan ice cream

Caramel sauce:
3 tablespoons butter or
  margarine
1 cup light brown sugar
1/2 cup whipping cream
1½ teaspoons vanilla

With electric mixer on high speed, beat egg whites until very foamy, gradually adding sugar 1 tablespoon at a time. Beat until stiff peaks form. Fold in chopped pecans. Spread mixture into a buttered 9-inch pie plate. Bake at 400 degrees for 10 minutes or until lightly browned. Cool completely. Spread ice cream over crust, wrap and freeze until firm.

For caramel sauce: In a small pan, melt butter, add sugar and cream. Stir over low heat until sugar dissolves. Add vanilla and stir. Makes 1½ cups sauce. To serve, spoon caramel sauce over each piece of pie.

French Silk Pie

Serves: 6

1/2 cup butter
3/4 cup sugar
1 ounce unsweetened chocolate, melted and cooled
1 teaspoon vanilla
2 eggs
Baked pie shell (8-inch)
Whipped cream

Cream butter and sugar. Melt chocolate in double boiler, stirring until smooth; add in vanilla. Add melted chocolate to the creamed mixture. Add eggs, one at a time, beating 3 to 5 minutes after each addition. Pour into baked pie shell. Chill 1 to 2 hours. Top with whipped cream.

Kahlua Apple Pie

Serves: 8 to 10

Pastry for double crust 9-inch pie
6 large cooking apples, (about 6 cups when sliced)
1/2 cup apple juice
1/2 cup sugar
1/2 cup Kahlua
1 tablespoon butter
1 teaspoon lemon juice
1½ tablespoons cornstarch

For topping:
1 tablespoon butter, melted
1 teaspoon sugar

Prepare pastry. Peel, core and cut apples into small wedges. Heat apple juice and sugar in a 3-quart saucepan. Add apples and cook gently, covered, until apples are almost tender (do not overcook). Remove apples with slotted spoon and set aside. Pour cooking liquid into a 2 cup measuring cup and add Kahlua. Then add apple juice to make 1¼ cups liquid. Return liquid mixture to saucepan and add butter. Blend lemon juice and cornstarch and add to liquid mixture. Cook, stirring, until smooth and thickened. Return apples to sauce. Turn mixture into pastry shell. Cover with top crust, seal and flute edges. Prick top crust or cut small decorative pattern. Brush top lightly with melted butter and sprinkle with sugar. Bake below oven center at 425 degrees for 25 to 30 minutes or until golden brown.

Peach Melba Pie

Serves: 8

1 (10-ounce) package frozen
  raspberries
1 (10-ounce) can peach slices,
  drained
1/4 cup sugar
3 tablespoons cornstarch
1/4 teaspoon cinnamon
1 tablespoon lemon juice
1 (9-inch) unbaked pie shell

  Streusel topping:
1/4 cup butter
3/4 cup flour
1/2 cup firmly packed brown
  sugar

Thaw the raspberries and combine with peaches. Combine sugar, cornstarch and cinnamon; add to fruit. Sprinkle with lemon juice and mix well. Turn into pie shell. Bake at 375 degrees for 30 to 35 minutes.

For streusel topping: Cut butter into flour and brown sugar. Remove pie from oven, sprinkle with streusel topping and bake at 375 degrees for an additional 10 to 15 minutes until golden brown.

Peanut Butter Pie

Serves: 8 to 10

  Crust:
1½ cups graham cracker crumbs
1/4 cup granulated sugar
1/2 cup butter or margarine,
  melted

  Filling:
1 (8-ounce) package cream cheese
1 cup creamy peanut butter
1½ cups powdered sugar
1/2 cup milk
1/2 pint whipping cream, whipped
  stiff

Combine first three ingredients and press into a 9-inch pie plate, covering bottom and sides. Combine cream cheese, peanut butter and sugar; beat until creamy. Add milk and continue to mix until blended. Fold in whipped cream. Pour into crust and chill for several hours.

NOTE: Garnish with grated chocolate.

Oregon Raspberry Cloud Pie
Serves: 8

1 (9 or 10-inch) baked pie shell
   with high fluted edge
1 cup whipping cream, whipped
2 cups fresh raspberries
1 cup white sugar
2 egg whites, at room temperature
1 tablespoon fresh lemon juice
1/4 cup sliced toasted almonds

Prepare pie shell ahead of time. Whip the cream and refrigerate until ready to use. Combine raspberries, sugar, egg whites and lemon juice in large bowl of electric mixer. Mix at highest speed for 15 minutes, until stiff. Gently fold in the whipped cream and almonds (reserving a few almonds for garnish). Mound filling into pie shell. Freeze until ready to serve.

Sour Cream Lemon Pie
Serves: 8

1/4 cup cornstarch
3 tablespoons water
1 cup sugar
1¼ cups water
2 tablespoons butter
9 tablespoons lemon juice
3 egg yolks
2 tablespoons milk

1 (8-inch) baked pie shell
1 cup sour cream
1 pint whipping cream, whipped

Dissolve cornstarch in 3 tablespoons cold water. In a 2-quart saucepan, mix sugar, water and butter. Cook over low heat until sugar dissolves. Add cornstarch mixture and cook until clear (about 8 minutes), stirring occasionally. Add lemon juice and cook 2 minutes. Mix egg yolks with milk and add to saucepan. Cook over low heat until mixture boils, stirring occasionally. Cool. Pour ½ of this mixture into pie shell and refrigerate. Add sour cream to the other ½ of the mixture. When the refrigerated half is set, spread sour cream mixture over top. Refrigerate. Top with whipped cream before serving.

Cranberry-Apple Tart
Serves: 8 to 10

Cranberry filling:
1/4 cup water
3/4 cup sugar
1/2 cup red currant jelly
3 cups fresh cranberries
   or
1 (12-ounce) package frozen
   cranberries
1 cup peeled, chopped apple

Tart shell:
1/2 cup butter
1¼ cups flour
1/4 cup sugar
2/3 cup finely chopped or
   ground walnuts
1/2 teaspoon ground cinnamon
2 egg yolks

Meringue:
4 egg whites
1/8 teaspoon cream of tartar
1/2 cup sugar

For filling: Combine water, sugar and jelly in a medium size saucepan. Over medium heat, melt jelly and dissolve sugar, then bring to a boil and add cranberries and apple. Cook, uncovered, over medium heat until cranberries pop and mixture thickens slightly (about 10 to 15 minutes). Cool completely.

For shell: Cut butter into flour; mix in sugar, nuts and cinnamon. Add egg yolks and mix lightly with fork just until pastry holds together. Press dough over bottom and up sides of a 9-inch tart pan. Prick with fork and refrigerate for 30 minutes. Bake shell at 375 degrees for 12 to 15 minutes until golden. Cool completely. Spoon cooled cranberry filling into cooled pastry shell.

For meringue: Beat egg whites with cream of tartar in a medium-size bowl until soft peaks form. Gradually beat in the sugar until stiff peaks form. Spread ½ of the meringue over the top of the tart. Pipe remaining meringue in a lattice pattern. Bake at 400 degrees for 3 to 6 minutes or until golden.

Fruit Flan
Serves: 8 to 10

1/2 cup butter
3/4 cup sugar
1⅓ cups flour
1/2 teaspoon salt
1/2 teaspoon cinnamon
1/4 teaspoon baking powder
1 to 2 pounds canned, unpeeled
   apricots
1 cup whipping cream
1 egg

Mix together the butter, sugar, flour, salt, cinnamon and baking powder, until fine. (This can be mixed easily in a food processor.) Press mixture into a flan pan and up sides of pan (reserving ⅓ cup for topping). Drain the canned apricots, lay apricots on top of crust mixture. Sprinkle the reserved ⅓ cup topping over apricots. Bake at 375 degrees for 20 minutes. Mix cream with egg and pour over flan in oven. Bake at 375 degrees for an additonal 20 to 25 minutes.

NOTE: You may wish to substitute blueberries, peaches or pears for apricots. Use your imagination!

Frozen Pumpkin Squares
Serves: 12

2 cups canned pumpkin
1 cup sugar
1 teaspoon salt
1 teaspoon cinnamon
1 teaspoon nutmeg
1 cup chopped walnuts
1/2 gallon vanilla ice cream,
   softened
36 crushed gingersnaps
Whipped cream

Combine pumpkin, sugar, salt, cinnamon and nutmeg; mix well and stir in nuts. Put softened ice cream into a chilled bowl, gently fold pumpkin mixture into ice cream. Line bottom of a 13 x 9 x 2-inch glass or metal pan with ½ of the crushed gingersnaps. Cover with ½ of the ice cream-pumpkin mixture. Repeat with remaining crushed gingersnaps and ice cream-pumpkin mixture. Freeze overnight. Cut into squares, serve with whipped cream.

NOTE: You may substitute vanilla frozen yogurt for the ice cream.

Hazelnut Tarts

Serves: 12

2 cups sifted flour
1 teaspoon salt
3/4 cup shortening or margarine
1/4 cup water

   Filling:
1/2 cup butter or margarine
1 cup light brown sugar
2 eggs
2 teaspoons grated orange or
   lemon peel
1/2 cup half and half
1 cup chopped hazelnuts
1 cup chopped dried figs
   (8-ounces)
1/2 cup raisins
1 teaspoon vanilla

Combine flour and salt in a bowl. Cut in shortening until a coarse mixture is formed. Sprinkle with water and mix into dough. Divide into 12 parts. On a lightly floured surface, roll each part into a 5-inch circle. Fit circle into a 3½-inch tart pan and trim the edges. Repeat until 12 tart shells are made.

For filling: Cream butter and sugar. Add eggs, one at a time, mixing well after each addition. Stir in remaining ingredients. Fill tart shells ¾ of the way full. Bake at 425 degrees for 10 minutes, reduce heat to 350 degrees and bake for an additional 30 minutes, or until firm. Cool tarts on wire rack. Remove from pans and serve.

Apple Nut Whip

Serves: 8 to 10

2 cups plain yogurt
1 lemon rind, grated
Juice of ½ lemon
1/2 cup sugar
3 to 5 golden delicious apples,
   peeled, cored and grated
1 teaspoon vanilla
1/2 cup whipping cream, whipped
1/2 cup chopped walnuts
   or almonds

In a large bowl, mix yogurt, lemon rind, lemon juice and sugar. Add apples and vanilla. Fold in whipped cream and nuts. Chill for 2 hours.

Sour Cream Lime Tart
Serves: 6 to 8

Crust:
**1½ cups crushed graham crackers
(9 double crackers)
1/2 cup sugar
6 tablespoons butter or margarine,
melted**

Filling:
**1 cup sugar
3 tablespoons cornstarch
1 cup whipping cream
1/3 cup fresh lime juice
4 tablespoons butter
1 tablespoon grated lime peel
1 cup sour cream**

Topping:
**1/2 cup whipping cream
2 tablespoons powdered sugar
3/4 teaspoon vanilla**

For crust: Combine graham crackers with sugar and melted butter. Press into bottom and up sides of a 9-inch pie pan. Freeze for 15 minutes. Bake at 350 degrees for 12 to 15 minutes until lightly browned. Cool completely.

For filling: Bring first 6 ingredients to a boil in a large saucepan. Cool, then fold in sour cream. Pour into crust.

For topping: Whip cream until soft peaks form. Stir in sugar and vanilla. Spread over filling. Refrigerate at least 4 hours.

Amaretto Chocolate Mousse
Serves: 4

**3/4 cup milk
6 ounces semi-sweet chocolate
morsels
2 tablespoons sugar
1 tablespoon Amaretto
1 egg**

Scald milk (do not boil). Put milk and remaining ingredients into a blender. Blend for 1 minute. Pour into small serving cups and chill several hours.

Apricot Mousse
Serves: 8 to 10

2 cups small dried apricots
1/2 cup water
1/3 cup sugar
1/4 cup water
3 egg whites, beaten stiff
1 cup whipping cream
1/2 teaspoon vanilla
2 tablespoons sugar
1 teaspoon grated lemon peel

Simmer apricots in ½ cup water until very tender (about 45 minutes). (If apricots cook too quickly, add water as necessary). Continue cooking on low until water has evaporated. Purée cooked apricots; set aside. Combine sugar and ¼ cup water and cook over medium-high heat until syrup forms a thread when dripped from a spoon; remove from heat. In a large bowl, beat egg whites until stiff. Continue beating constantly while slowly adding sugar syrup. Fold puréed apricots carefully into egg white mixture. In another bowl, whip the cream with the vanilla and sugar, until soft peaks form. Add lemon peel to apricot mixture, and fold in whipped cream. Put mixture in a buttered 2-quart mold and freeze for 6 hours (or longer). Unmold by dipping mold in hot water for 2 minutes, and inverting on plate. Serve immediately or keep chilled in refrigerator until ready to serve.

Chocolate Mocha Mousse

Serves: 6 to 8

8 ounces bittersweet chocolate
1/4 cup coffee
6 tablespoons butter
3 eggs, separated
1/2 cup sugar
Whipped cream for topping

Melt chocolate in double boiler over hot (not boiling) water and remove from heat. Add coffee, butter and egg yolks; mix well. Beat egg whites until soft peaks form. Gradually add sugar, beating until very stiff. Fold egg whites into chocolate mixture. Refrigerate. Serve in individual ramekins or parfait glasses. Top with whipped cream.

Grand Marnier Mousse

Serves: 6 to 8

4 eggs, separated
1/2 cup sugar
1½ envelopes unflavored
   gelatin
1/3 cup cold water
1/3 cup Grand Marnier
1½ cups whipping cream
16 ladyfingers (optional)

Beat egg yolks with sugar until thick and creamy. In a small pan, sprinkle the gelatin on cold water and let set for 5 minutes; heat to dissolve the gelatin. Add Grand Marnier to gelatin. In a large bowl, whip the cream lightly; set aside. In a small bowl, beat the egg whites until they stand in soft peaks. Combine egg yolk and sugar mixture with whipped cream. Add gelatin and Grand Marnier mixture. Fold in the egg whites. Allow 4 hours for mousse to set in a mold or 2-quart soufflé dish (lined with ladyfingers, if desired).

Chocolate Rum Mousse

Serves: 6

1 (6-ounce) package chocolate
  chips
5 tablespoons boiling water
4 eggs, separated
2 tablespoons dark rum
1 pint whipping cream, whipped
Shaved chocolate (garnish)

Put chocolate in blender and turn on high for 6 seconds. Add boiling water and blend for 10 seconds on high. Add egg yolks and rum; blend 3 seconds. In a separate bowl, beat egg whites until very stiff; fold into chocolate mixture. Put in dessert cups and chill one hour. Top with whipped cream and shaved chocolate just before serving.

Frosty Strawberry Squares

Serves: 10 to 12

Crust:
1 cup sifted flour
1/4 cup brown sugar
1/2 cup chopped walnuts
1/2 cup butter or margarine,
  melted

Filling:
2 egg whites
1 cup sugar
  and
2 cups sliced fresh
  strawberries
  or
2/3 cup sugar
  and
1 (10-ounce) package frozen
  strawberries, partially thawed
2 tablespoons lemon juice
1 cup whipping cream, whipped
Strawberries (garnish)

For crust: Stir together all ingredients and spread evenly in a shallow baking pan. Bake at 350 degrees for 20 minutes; stirring occasionally. Cool and stir to break up into a crumb mixture. Sprinkle ⅔ of the crumb mixture into a 9 x 13 x 2-inch pan.

For filling: In a large bowl, combine egg whites, sugar, strawberries and lemon juice; beat with an electric mixer on high speed, until stiff peaks form. Fold in whipped cream. Spoon whipped cream mixture over crumbs. Top with remaining ⅓ of the crumb mixture. Freeze for 6 hours or overnight. Cut in 10 or 12 squares. Garnish with strawberries.

Caribbean Fruit Sherbert

Yield: 3½ cups

1/2 cup freshly squeezed
  orange juice
1/2 large fresh pineapple,
  peeled, cored and cut in
  chunks
2 teaspoons grated orange rind
2 tablespoons fresh lemon juice
1 medium banana
1/4 cup granulated sugar
1/4 cup light corn syrup
1 egg white
1/8 teaspoon salt
Strawberry or kiwi slices
  (garnish)

In a blender or food processor, combine orange juice, pineapple, orange rind, lemon juice and banana. Blend until fruit mixture is smooth. Pour fruit into a large bowl. Stir in sugar and corn syrup. Pour mixture into a shallow container and freeze until almost firm. Put semi-frozen mixture into a well-chilled bowl and beat with rotary beater or electric mixer until light and fluffy. In a small bowl, beat egg whites and salt together until stiff; fold into fruit mixture. Pour all into a 4 cup mold, refrigerator tray or pan; freeze for 3 to 4 hours, until firm.

Marshmallow Mocha

Serves: 4 to 6

1/2 cup hot black coffee (strong)
20 marshmallows
1/2 pint whipping cream, whipped

Melt marshmallows in coffee over low heat, and stir until mixture forms a syrup. Cool. Fold in whipped cream. Refrigerate several hours before serving.

NOTE: This can be served in individual parfait glasses garnished with chocolate curls or as a pie filling.

Lemon Souffle
Serves: 8

1 envelope unflavored gelatin
3/4 cup sugar, divided
1/4 cup cold water
4 egg yolks
1/2 cup lemon juice
2 tablespoons lemon peel
6 egg whites
1 cup whipping cream

Combine gelatin, ½ cup sugar and water in top of double boiler. Beat in egg yolks, lemon juice and lemon peel until well blended. Cook, stirring over boiling water until mixture coats a metal spoon evenly (15 to 20 minutes). Remove from heat, cool to room temperature. Beat egg whites to soft peaks. Gradually beat in remaining ¼ cup sugar. Continue beating until stiff peaks form. In a separate bowl, whip cream until soft peaks form. Fold whipped cream and lemon mixture into egg whites, just until blended. Spoon into individual dishes or a 4 to 6 cup souffle dish. Chill until firm (at least 4 hours).

NOTE: This can be served as a souffle or a filling for a pie or tart.

Frozen Lemon Cream
Yield: 1 pint

2 teaspoons lemon zest
4 tablespoons lemon juice
1 cup sugar
1 pint half and half
1/4 teaspoon salt

Beat together lemon zest, lemon juice and sugar. Slowly add half and half and salt. Place in a bowl in freezer. When it starts to freeze, take out and beat, then put back in freezer and freeze completely.

Ice Cream Balls with Fudge Sauce
Yield: 20

1/2 gallon vanilla ice cream
4 cups chopped pecans
1/2 cup butter
2¼ cups powdered sugar
2/3 cup evaporated milk
6 ounces unsweetened baking
  chocolate

Using an ice cream scoop form 20, 2½-inch balls. Place them into cupcake tins and freeze until firm. Remove from freezer, a few at a time, and roll in nuts to cover completely. Return to freezer as completed.

For sauce: In the top of a double boiler, cream butter and sugar. Add evaporated milk and unmelted chocolate squares. Do not stir mixture. Cook for 30 minutes. Remove from heat and beat by hand until sauce is smooth and creamy. When ready to serve, put the ice cream balls into cupcake papers and spoon warm sauce over them.

NOTE: Sauce may be stored in refrigerator and reheated as needed, thin (if necessary) with milk not water.

Raspberry Ice
Servings: 4

1 pint raspberries (fresh or frozen)
2/3 cup sugar
1/2 cup water
2 tablespoons orange juice
2 egg whites

In a saucepan, cook raspberries and sugar over medium heat for 5 minutes. When cool, strain to remove seeds. While stirring, slowly add water and orange juice. Cool mixture in refrigerator. Beat egg whites until foamy and fold into berry mixture. Freeze in ice cream maker.

Lemon Torte

Serves: 10

1 box lemon cookies
4 eggs, separated
1 cup sugar
1/2 cup lemon juice
2 tablespoons grated lemon rind
1½ cups whipping cream

Sauce:
1 pint raspberries (fresh or frozen)

Butter a spring form pan and line sides and bottom with lemon cookies. (You may want to cut the cookies in ½ to line the sides.) In a medium size bowl, beat egg whites until stiff. Add sugar gradually. In a separate bowl, beat egg yolks and add lemon juice and rind. In a third bowl, beat whipping cream until peaks form. Fold all ingredients together; pour into pan and freeze for 8 hours.

For sauce: Put the raspberries in a blender and mix well. Strain out the seeds. Spoon over frozen dessert before serving.

Chocolate Fondue

Serves: 6

1 cup sour cream
2 tablespoons half and half
1/4 cup sugar
1/2 teaspoon vanilla
1 ounce semi-sweet chocolate, grated
6 navel oranges, chilled, peeled and segmented

In a bowl, combine sour cream, half and half, sugar, vanilla and grated chocolate; stir well. Turn into a small serving bowl and chill. Arrange orange segments on serving platter with dip in the center.

NOTE: This dip is also good with fresh strawberries, apple or kiwi slices and grapes.

Raspberry Cream
Serves: 10 to 12

2 cups cottage cheese
3/4 cup brown sugar
1/2 teaspoon powdered ginger
2 cups whipping cream
4 cups fresh raspberries

Mix cottage cheese in food processor or blender until smooth and creamy. Add brown sugar and ginger; continue mixing until well blended. Whip cream until it peaks. Fold cheese mixture into whipped cream. Chill. Just before serving, gently fold in raspberries (reserving a few for garnish).

NOTE: This looks elegant served in tulip wine glasses.

Oregon Blueberry Crumble
Serves: 6

3 cups washed blueberries
1/2 cup sugar
Juice of 1 lemon
1/4 cup soft margarine
1/2 cup sugar
2/3 cup flour

Place blueberries in a 9 x 9-inch baking dish. Sprinkle with sugar and lemon juice. Blend together margarine, sugar and flour. Sprinkle mixture over berries. Bake at 350 degrees for 30 to 35 minutes. Serve with ice cream.

NOTE: For a different taste treat, try this with other berries or fresh peaches.

Oregon Blackberry Cobbler
Serves: 6

Topping:
1 cup flour
2 tablespoons sugar
1½ teaspoons baking powder
1/4 teaspoon salt
1/4 cup butter
1/4 cup milk
1 egg

Fruit filling:
4 cups fresh blackberries
  (may use frozen)
1/4 cup sugar
2 tablespoons cornstarch
1/4 teaspoon cinnamon
1/4 cup water
1 tablespoon butter

For topping: Sift together flour, sugar, baking powder and salt. Cut in butter until mixture resembles coarse crumbs. Combine milk and egg and add all at once to dry ingredients; stirring just until moist.

For filling: In a saucepan, combine blackberries, sugar, cornstarch, cinnamon and water; bring to a boil. Cook and stir until mixture is slightly thick and juice is clear.

Cooking time is 3 to 5 minutes. Stir in butter until melted. Pour into a 8¼ x 1¾-inch baking dish. Immediately spoon on topping in mounds over the filling. Bake at 400 degrees for 20 to 25 minutes.

NOTE: Freeze before baking for best results.

Vanilla Ice Cream
Yield: 2½ quarts

3¾ cups scalded milk
5 eggs, beaten
3¾ teaspoons vanilla extract
  Dash of salt
2 cups sugar
3¾ cups whipping cream

In top of double boiler, gradually stir milk into eggs. Place over hot water (not boiling), and cook until mixture just coats spoon. Add salt and sugar. Refrigerate overnight. Just before freezing, add vanilla and cream. Freeze in crank freezer until difficult to turn crank.

Swan Cream Puffs
Yield: 8

Cream puff pastry:
1 cup water
1/2 cup butter or margarine
1/4 teaspoon salt
1 cup all-purpose flour
4 eggs

Almond cream filling:
1 cup whipping cream
1 (3½ to 3¾-ounce) package vanilla flavor instant pudding and pie filling
1¼ cups milk
1/2 teaspoon almond extract

In a 2-quart saucepan over medium heat, heat water, butter or margarine and salt until butter melts and mixture boils. Remove saucepan from heat. Add flour all at once and vigorously stir with a wooden spoon until mixture leaves sides of pan and forms a ball. Add eggs, one at a time, beating well with wooden spoon after each addition. Spoon ½ cup of batter into a pastry bag with a large writing tube (tip about 1/2-inch in diameter). On greased cookie sheet, pipe eight, 3-inch long "question marks" for swan necks, making a small dollop at the beginning of each for head. Drop remaining batter, using a large spoon and pushing off with rubber spatula, onto cookie sheet into 8 large mounds, 3-inches apart. Gently smooth batter to round slightly. Bake at 375 degrees for 20 minutes or until necks are golden. Remove necks to wire rack and cool. Continue baking remaining cream puffs at 375 degrees for an additional 50 minutes, until golden. Remove to racks; cool. When cream puffs are cool, prepare the filling.

Filling: In a small bowl with mixer at medium speed, beat 1 cup whipping cream until soft peaks form; set aside. Prepare pudding as label directs using only 1¼ cups milk. With rubber spatula, gently fold whipped cream and almond extract into pudding. Cut off top ⅓ of cream puffs (swans bodies); set aside. Spoon some cream mixture into each swan's body. Cut reserved top pieces of swans' bodies in ½; set into cream for wings. Place swans' necks into cream. Refrigerate. Makes 8 cream puffs.

Fruit and Rum Ambrosia

Serves: 8 to 10

1 cantaloupe or pineapple
1 honeydew melon
1/4 watermelon
1 cup blueberries
2/3 cup sugar
1/3 cup water
1 teaspoon grated lime rind
6 tablespoons lime juice
1/2 cup light rum

Cut melons into cubes or balls. Add blueberries; cover and chill. In a saucepan, bring sugar and water to a boil and simmer for 5 minutes. Stir in grated lime rind and cool to room temperture. Stir in lime juice and rum; pour over fruit. Chill several hours or overnight.

NOTE: This makes a wonderful summer dessert served with light cookies.

Peaches with Sherry Cream

Serves: 6 to 8

3 to 4 fresh peaches
3/4 cup sugar
2 cups water
1 teaspoon vanilla

Sauce:
2 egg yolks
1/4 teaspoon salt
3/4 cup sifted powdered sugar
1/3 cup sherry (not cooking)
1/2 pint whipping cream
Nutmeg (garnish)

Peel, halve and pit peaches. In a saucepan, bring sugar and water to a boil, then add peaches. Simmer until tender (5 to 10 minutes). Add vanilla. Chill all until ready to serve. In a medium bowl, beat egg yolks with salt until thick. Add sugar gradually and continue beating until very thick and lemon colored. Add sherry. In a separate bowl, whip cream until stiff and fold into egg mixture. To serve, put ½ peach in an individual dish. Spoon sauce over peaches. Sprinkle with nutmeg.

Blueberry Filled Cantaloupes
Serves: 6

3 cantaloupes, chilled
4 cups fresh or dry pack
   frozen blueberries, rinsed
   and drained
1/2 cup grenadine
2 tablespoons lime juice
6 tablespoons sifted powdered
   sugar
Fresh mint leaves (garnish)

Cut melons into halves and remove seeds. Gently combine blueberries, grenadine, lime juice and sugar. Pile mixture lightly in cantaloupe cavities. Chill at least 1 hour before serving. Garnish with fresh mint leaves and serve.

NOTE: This is great served for brunch.

Caramel Popcorn
Serves: 6

2 cups brown sugar
1/2 cup light corn syrup
2 cups butter, softened
1 teaspoon salt
1 teaspoon baking soda
1 teaspoon butter flavoring (found
   in extract flavoring section
   of store)
8 quarts popped popcorn

In a large saucepan, combine sugar, corn syrup, butter and salt; bring to a boil. Boil for 5 minutes, stirring constantly. Remove from heat and add baking soda and butter flavoring. (This will make ingredients foam up.) Pour over popped popcorn and stir. Spread on cookie sheet. Bake at 200 degrees for 1 hour, turning after 30 minutes. Store into sealed containers.

Flower Pops
Yield: 2 dozen

3/4 cup M & M plain candies
1¼ cups sugar
1 cup butter or margarine
3 tablespoons water

On an ungreased cookie sheet, about 3-inches apart, arrange small clusters of 7 candies each to form a flower shape (1 in center, 6 around sides; set aside). Combine sugar, butter and water in a 3-quart heavy saucepan. Bring mixture to a boil, stirring frequently. Continue boiling over medium-high heat, stirring frequently, until mixture cooks to 280 degrees ("crack" stage). With a tablespoon, drizzle mixture over each candy cluster to coat and cover candies. Immediately place flat wooden stick into soft candy mixture to form pop. Let harden; cool thoroughly. Carefully remove from cookie sheet.

NOTE: Candy mixture is very hot; work carefully but quickly. If spoon becomes coated with too much syrup when covering candies, use another clean spoon.

Chocolate Sauce
Serves: 4

2 ounces milk chocolate or
   dark chocolate
1/2 cup sugar
1/2 cup whipping cream
1 teaspoon vanilla

Melt chocolate over top of double boiler. Remove from heated water and add sugar; stir well. Slowly add whipping cream; stir well. Return to double boiler and cook for 20 minutes, stirring occasionally. Remove from heated water. Let cool. Add vanilla. Store in refrigerator. To serve, warm in microwave or double boiler.

Microwave Caramel Corn

Serves: 6 to 10

12 quarts popped corn (popped in hot air or microwave popper)
1/2 teaspoon salt
1 cube margarine
1 cup brown sugar
1/4 cup light corn syrup
1/2 teaspoon baking soda

Put popcorn in a large brown grocery bag. Combine salt, margarine, brown sugar and corn syrup in a 1½-quart glass casserole. Put in microwave at highest setting for 2 to 2½ minutes, until it boils. Remove mixture from microwave and stir in ½ teaspoon baking soda (it will foam). Pour sauce over popcorn in the paper bag, stir and shake well until coated. Roll down top of bag ½ way and place in the microwave on its side with the top open. Microwave on high for 1½ minutes; remove and shake. Return for another 1½ minutes. Remove and cool.

NOTE: This is a great dessert that requires very little cleanup! You can serve it right out of the bag. Not recommended for use in recycled paper bags.

Triple Chocolate Peanut Clusters

Yield: 7 dozen

2 pounds white chocolate
1 (12-ounce) package semi-sweet chocolate chips
1 (12-ounce) package milk chocolate chips
1 (24-ounce) jar unsalted dry roasted peanuts

In top half of double boiler, melt chocolates, stirring constantly. Cool 5 minutes. Stir in peanuts. Drop by teaspoonfuls onto waxed paper. Let cool completely. Store in air tight containers.

NOTE: These make a great gift for Christmas or Valentine's Day. They are quick and easy.

Acknowledgments and Contributors:

The following businesses and individuals
have assisted
in making this project a success.

Baden & Company

Rachel Bard

Mark Bloom

Valerie Bloom

Muriel Byers

Karl Jr. Byers

Claytrade

Dwight Collins

Jean Crocker

John Crocker

Tina Daggett

Emerald Fruit and Produce Co., Inc.

Willard and Rena Gowing

Walt Johnson

Koke Printing

David Loveall

Darlene K. Mancuso

The Marketplace Gourmet

Beth Moloney

Mary Jo Moloney

Napoli Restaurant & Bakery

One If By Land

Petersen's Antiques

Elaine Phillips

The Quilt Patch

Skeie's Jewelers

Delbert and Ethyl Smith

Sally Swing

Ray Rocha

Libby Tower

Joyce Troup

Weyerhaeuser Company

Julie and Doug Wilkinson

Bette Williams

Rhea Wingard

Photo Credits:

Photographer: David Loveall
Food Stylist: Valerie Bloom
Art Direction: John Crocker
Studio: WHL Photographics
Project Coordination: Baden & Company

Acknowledgements:

FRONT COVER
Antique Peddlers I & II
Newman's Fish Co.

PASTA SPINACH SALAD
Antique Peddlers I & II
Down To Earth Home Store
Metropol Bakery
Reed & Cross

BARBECUED SKEWERED CHICKEN
Cook's Nook
Down To Earth Home Store
Old Glory Antiques

HALIBUT WITH ORANGE GLAZE
Harvey and Price Co.
Newman's Fish Co.
Reed & Cross

SHRIMP STUFFED MUSHROOMS
CRAB IN AVOCADO BOATS
Antique Peddlers I & II
Bloom's Flowers & Gifts
Old Glory Antiques
Wingard Antiques

STEAMED VEGETABLE MEDLEY
Antique Peddlers I & II
Fifthpearl Antiques
Kitchen Korner
Long's Meats
Old Glory Antiques
Reed & Cross

HAZELNUT CHOCOLATE CHIP CHEESECAKE
Coburg Inn Antique Shops
Euphoria Chocolate Company
Old Glory Antiques
Reed & Cross

BACK COVER
Johnson Farms
Newman's Fish Co.
Old Glory Antiques

Cookbook Contributors

Sandra Adams	Carole Chenkin	Melissa Finch	Carla Hoffman
Donna Addison	Heidi Christian	Jo Fisher	Ferne Hoffman
Barb Alberty	Kathy Clark	Sandra Franklin	Nancy Holland
Chris Allen	Pam Clifton	Joyce Freeman	D. Howard
Dorothy Amundson	Ev Close	Kinny Ann Friedrich	Katherine Howard
Linda Anderson	Nonnie Cole	Jan Gallagher	Peggy Hoyt
Susan Anderson	Susan Conlan	Karen Gallas	Lorna Hudson
Ruth Asbury	Cindy Conley	Monica Gardner	Liz Huenink
Chris Baird	Stephanie Connor	Sue Gardner	Jackie Hughes
Marie Baker	Catherine Cook	Julie Geier	Bonnie Huntsberger
Chris Bales	Cindy Cooley	Jo Gietter	Donna Intermill
Margaret Barlow	Lenice Cooper	Kathy Gillespie	Marlene Iverson
Margaret Barnard	Francis Creech	Kendra Gillian	Lisa James
Flossie Barnhart	Suzi Creech	Ann Gillian	Susan Janko
Cheryl Barnum	Lorraine Cross	Adriana Giustina	John Janzen
Bruce Becker	Fran Curtis	Carolyn Giustina	Kathy Janzen
Carol Becker	Jennifer Curtis	Mary Glass	Debbie Jeffries
Cathy Becker	Mike Curtis	Judy Godfrey	Carolyn Jennings
Curt Becker	Nancy Cutler	Jodi Goff	Karen Jewett
Mary Bennett	Joan David	Marjorie Gonzalez	Donna Johnson
Cynthia Biboux	Joan Davis	Kirsten Gram	Leslie Johnson
Dorothy Bick	Gillian De Wein	Sharon Greig	Pat Johnson
Nancy Billington	Diane Dearborn	Anne Gross	Dorothy Jones
Carol Black	Marilyn Deaton	Teresa Grube	Peggy Jorgenson
Cleve Boehi	Liz Deck	Sheila Gunthorp	Patti Kalal
Terri Boehm	Lesli Degge	Judy Hall	Bonnye Keller
Linda Bolton	Liz Degner	Diane Hallstrom	Slyvia Keller
Katharine Boness	Liz Diehl	Allyson Hamby	Andy Kessinger
Ann Booth	DeLyn Dunham	Pat Hamilton	Laura Kessinger
Jim Borovicka	Emily Eagle	Wanda Hamilton	Pat Kessinger
Vicki Bourdage	Debbi Eberle	Alice Hammond	Martha Kierstead
Chris Braatz	Roger Eberle	Rich Hammond	Judy Kilian
Karen Brandt	Teri Ehlers	Carol Hammons	Linda Kirk
Jennifer Brink	Peg Emery	Gail Hansen	Elsita Klohs
Jane Brody	Janice Empens	Gail Harris	Brenda Knight
Georgene Brooke	Maureen Emrick	Leslie Hartwig	Nancy Knudsen
Jacque Brown	Emily Engle	Cathy Hedberg	Betty Korfhage
Susan Brownings	Bert Erickson	Diane Hellekson	Billie Kay Krewson
Lisa Brus	Cathy Erickson	Mary H. Hemphill	Joyce Krueger
Julie Budge	Linda Erickson	Carol Henninger	Martha Lackie
Janet Buerstatte	Peggy Erickson	Sara Heywood	Cyndy Lane
Susan Burgott	Pam Farkas	Patti Hickson	Pat Le Brun
Donna Carlson	Lona Feldman	Francee Hillyer	Holly Leach
Lynn Carlson	Maureen Fender	Jean Hinman	Alicia Lee
Penny Carpenter	Kris Fergusson	Dr. Larry Hirons	Kathy Lee
Faris Cassell	Becky Fickas	Patti Hixon	Pam Lee

Cookbook Contributors continued

Judith Lidstrom
Nancy Lochner
Peg Lofsvold-Schill
Gina Lyle
Luanne Lynn
Tiffany Lynn
Jan Lyon
Teri Lyons
Suzette Malkasian
Ann Malos
Janet Martin
Kathy Martin
Penny Matsler
Meridith Maurer
Lora McCann
Debi McCarty
Judy McConnell
Carol McCornack
Joan McCornack
Lilla McDonald
Ruth McGlassen
Evelyn McKinley
Edie McKinnon
Mary McMillan
Martha McMillen
Leslie McNaught
Mary Ellen McNutt
Kathy Merrick
Marilyn Merrill
Kitty Meyer
Nancy Meyers
Kathy Miller
Anne Moffett
Linda Mohr
Vicky Money
Thelma Montgomery
Dolly Moore
Kendra Morberg-West
Karen Morray
Donald Moyer
Willie Moyer
Nancy Muhlheim
Marion Mullen
Judy Muller
Dee Dee Murray
Kathleen Nahorney

Lyn Neel
Jeni Nelson
Joni Nelson
Esther Newman
Mike Newman
Gail O'Donnell
Cathy O'Kelley
Barbara O'Neil
Jan Oberlink
Debbie Ogburn
Barbara Olson
Jackie Onstad
Leanne Orlich
Susie Osterud
Joyce Owens
Sue Paiement
Becky Palmer
Debbie Papé
Patty Papé
Susie Papé
Lezlie Pearce-Hopper
Claire Peel
Sandi Percell
Doreen Peterson
Jan Petrie
Barbara Pierce
Jesslyn Podley
Linda Pompel
Leslie Poole
Linda Post
Linda Potter
Marilyn Powers
Cindy Prewitt
Linda Rangus
Martha Raschio
Nancy Read
Connie Redhead
Paula Reents
Marni Reinmuth
Deena Reinwald
Donna Richards
Sandra Richmond
Carole Rintalin
Pat Rintalin
Mary Jayne Robert
Susan Roberts

Linda Roehl
Georgine Rohde
Lori Romania
Larry Roof
Karen Rose
Bonnie Rosen
Carolyn Rubenstein
Rosemary Rubenstein
Jill Rusch
Molly Salazar
Paula Salerno
Dee Sauder
L. Saul
Pat Scarlett
Kathy Schor
Valerie Schuelke
Sheila Schwartz
Tresa Schwary
Jackie Scott
Ann Seals
Emily Semple
Margaret Senn
Jan Shaver
Sharyn Shaw
Mary Sheffer
Martha Shepard
Steven Shepard
Linda Sheppard
Katy Sherman
Barbara Shevitz
Anne Siebel
Georgiana Singer
Ann Skeie
Rick Skeie
Sharon Skipworth
Brenda Smith
Lois Smith
Mary Smith
Mary Lou Smith
Jeanie Snyder
Linda Solin
Judy Sproul
Adrienne St. Clair
Janet Starr
Jane Sterett
Vicki Stewart

Sharon Stirtz
Jody Stokes
Debra Stoll
Marsha Strooband
Anne Stroud
Judy Sullivan
Kendra Sullivan
Shermaine Swearingen
Cara Takamori
Martha Taylor
Bobbie Teague
Mary Terzenbach
Marion Thielke
Liz Thwing
S. Thwing
Joyce Tierney
Kathie Turner
Mike Turner
Stan Turner
Gloria Tyree
Judy Van Scholten
Jeannie Verkest
Cleo Vik
Ann Voas
Judi Vos
Fran Warren
Kay Weigand
Sharon Wendell
Gretchen Weza
Alison Wheeler
Cindy Wheeler
Chris White
Julie Whitmore
Cathy Wierman
Amy Williams
Kitty Williams
Ellen Williamson
Kay Wilson
Cindy Wiser
Rosemary Wold
Gordon Wright
Shari Wright
Carolyn Yaegar
Emilie York
Leslie Zoref

Index

A

Acapulco apple punch, 36
ACORN SQUASH
  glazed rings, 127
Addiction, 29
Alcoholic beverages
  See Beverages
Almond poppy seed bread, 246
Almond cake, 295
Almond crescents, 258
Amaretto balls, 263
Amaretto chocolate
  mousse, 305
Angel cookies, 261
Antipasto salad, 89
APPETIZERS, 7-29
  addiction, 29
  artichoke dip, 10
  artichoke dip, hot and
    spicy, 20
  artichoke dip with bread
    sticks, 20
  asparagus ham roll-ups, 21
  avocado boats, crab, 18
  avocado crab dip, 14
  bean dip, Mexican hot, 15
  bean dip, nacho, 11
  bean dip, olé, 11
  bean roll-up, pickled, 25
  Bermuda onion dip, 16
  Boursin cheese spread,
    mock, 14
  caviar pie, 28
  cheese ball, old English, 9
  cheese ball, spicy, 10
  cheese spread, mock
    Boursin, 14
  cheesey bacon broils, 24
  chicken nuggets, herbs, 21
  chicken wings, Oriental, 22
  chile fondue dip, quick, 16
  chutney, 15
  crab dip, avocado, 14
  crab dip, hot, 13
  crab mousse, 24
  crab spread, layered, 17
  crab-avocado boats, 18
  dill dip, 9
  dilled shrimp dip, 12
  fondue dip, quick chile, 16
  fresh tomato salsa, 12
  Greek appetizer, 26

APPETIZERS CONTINUED
  hot crab dip, 13
  Mexican hot bean dip, 15
  mock Boursin cheese
    spread, 14
  mushrooms, filbert
    stuffed, 25
  mushrooms, savory
    stuffed, 18
  mushrooms, shrimp
    stuffed, 29
  mushrooms, stuffed, 23
  mustard vegetable dip, 14
  nacho bean dip, 11
  old English cheese ball, 9
  olé bean dip, 11
  onion dip, Bermuda, 16
  Pacific seafood spread, 10
  salmon mousse, smoked, 27
  salmon spread, 13
  salsa, fresh tomato, 12
  sausage appetizers, grilled
    shrimp and, 23
  seafood dip, 20
  seafood spread, Pacific, 10
  shrimp dip, dilled, 12
  shrimp puffs, 26
  shrimp and sausage
    appetizers, grilled, 23
  shrimp spread, tangy, 16
  shrimp stuffed
    mushrooms, 29
  shrimp-cheese spread, 17
  spicy cheese ball, 10
  sticky wings, 24
  tiropetes, 22
  tomato salsa, fresh, 12
  tortilla roll-ups, 28
  tortilla wedgies, 27
  vegetable dip, mustard, 14
Apple-butter bars, oatmeal
  and, 268
Apple cake, 294
Apple cheesecake, 287
Apple nut whip, 304
Apple pie, Kahlua, 299
Apple whole-wheat muffins,
  fresh, 238
Apricot mousse, 306
Armenian pilaf, 157
ARTICHOKE(S)
  croissants, crab and, 185
  dip, 10

ARTICHOKE(S) CONTINUED
  dip, hot and spicy, 20
  dip with bread sticks, 20
  Italian chicken and, 213
  pasta, seafood and, 184
  rice, 158
  salad, wild rice, 89
ASPARAGUS
  chicken asparagus, 213
  ham roll-ups, 21
  marinated, 88
  salad, sesame seed, 73
  salad, spear, 74
Aspen Village salad, 90
Astoria seafood soup, 66
Autumn pumpkin cake, 294
AVOCADO
  crab, boats, 18
  crab dip, 14

B

Bacon broils, cheesey, 24
Bacon salad, broccoli, 76
Bacon salad, spinach, 75
Baked omelet, 111
Baked sesame fish, 175
Baked Sicilian frittata, 112
BANANA(S)
  muffins, 243
  sour cream coffee cake, 249
BARBECUE(D)
  chicken, Java, 210
  chicken, skewered, 210
  chuck steak, black tie, 193
  potatoes, Mike's, 135
  salmon, 165
Barber's chili, the, 192
BARLEY
  casserole, 156
  mushroom pilaf, 156
BEAN DIPS
  Mexican hot, 15
  nacho, 11
  olé, 11
BEAN SOUPS
  market day, 47
  rainy day, 52
BEANS, BAKED
  calico, 127
BEANS, BLACK
  spicy salad, 82
BEANS, GREEN
  pickled bean roll-up, 25

Index

Index

Index

Index

Index

Index

Index

Index

Index

Index

Index

SAVOR THE FLAVOR OF OREGON

To order additional copies please send $19.95 per copy plus $3.00* per copy to cover postage and handling. Make checks payable to "SAVOR THE FLAVOR OF OREGON."

Send to: "SAVOR THE FLAVOR OF OREGON"
Junior League of Eugene
2839 Willamette Street
Eugene, Oregon 97405

If paying by Visa or MasterCard, please include card number and expiration date.

For more information please call (503) 345-7370.

On orders of one hundred or more copies, postage and handling will be paid by the Junior League of Eugene.
*Outside USA, Europe & Canada, $4.00 postage & handling.